Cold War 2.0

Dawn of the Asian Millennium

by Andranik Aghazarian

First Edition (1)

Edits and Book Design by Tamar Hela
Proofreading by Pamela Alvarez
Cover Design by Kim Moro

Font: Garamond

Summary:

In a post-Covid-19 world, a new millennium has dawned: The Asian Millennium. With the collapse of western hegemony and a new Cold War looming in the near future, it's inevitable that "business as usual" is a distant memory. The world as we once knew it has forever changed, ushering in a power vacuum for a new world order. In Cold War 2.0, examine all the factors contributing to the deterioration of the economy in the West and learn why we should look to the East for our future.

[Non-Fiction-Business, Non-Fiction-Economics, Non-Fiction-Asian]

ISBN-13: 9798560854294

TABLE OF CONTENTS

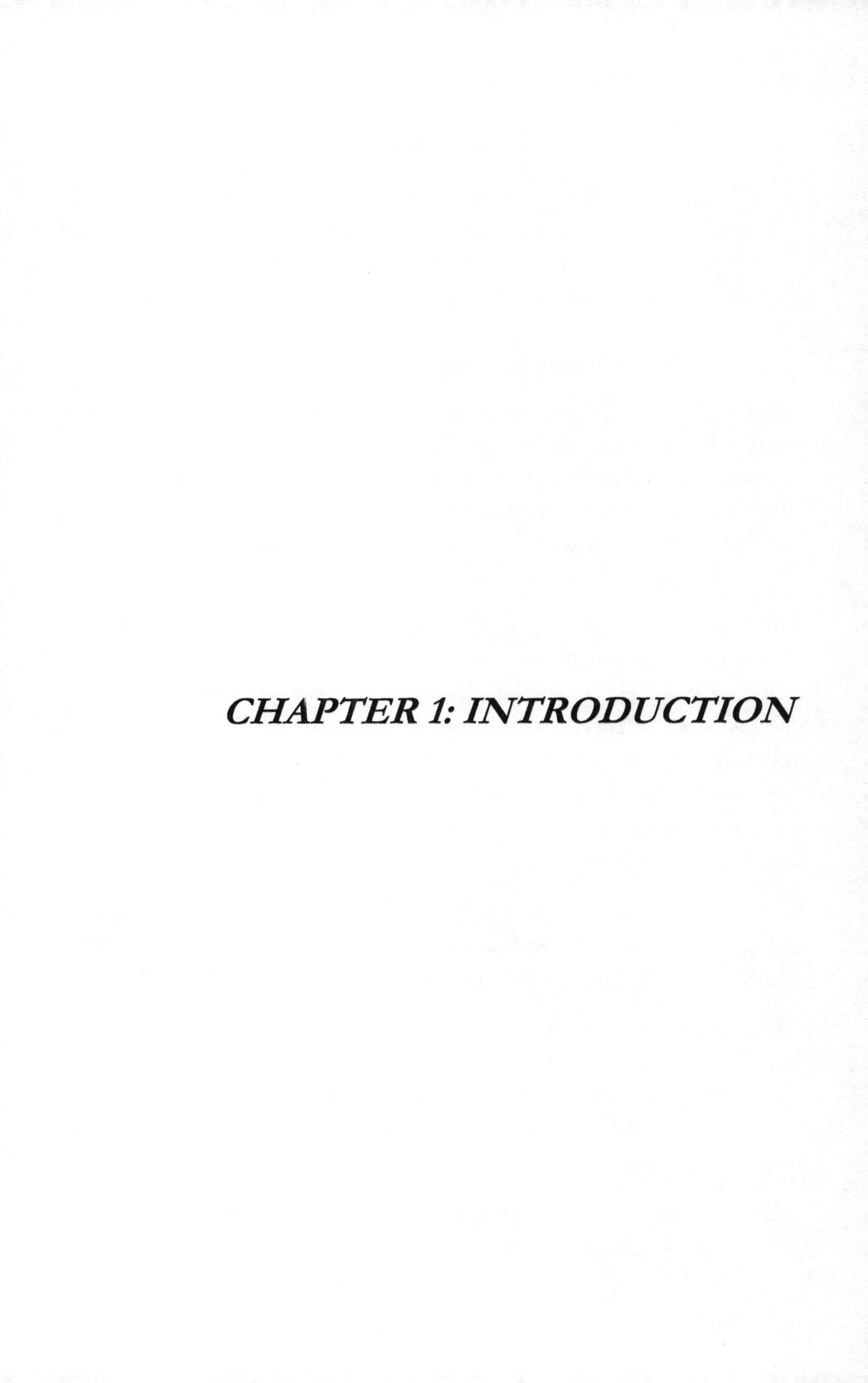

CHAPTER 1: INTRODUCTION

INTRODUCTION

"In his essay, 'Perpetual Peace,' the philosopher, Immanuel Kant, argued that perpetual peace would eventually come to the world in one of two ways, by human insight or by conflicts and catastrophes of a magnitude that left humanity no other choice. We are at such a juncture."
Henry Kissinger, American politician and diplomat

With each passing day, the world around us is becoming more chaotic, making it harder to find and understand global events. To the casual observer, the news is more confusing than ever and is being shunned at rates never before seen. Fake news and media narratives have taken an emotional toll upon countless individuals. The COVID-19 crisis is one of many unusual events in a string of events plaguing us in the early 21st century.

2020 has changed numerous people's lives, and as of the writing of this book, it is just halfway through. No matter who you are or where you live, it seems we have more questions than answers. The seemingly unrelated unfolding events around us are connected, and their outcomes have profound effects on everyone alive today. We left the world we knew behind in ushering this new year. While the hopes of many are for a return to normal, I firmly believe that it is impossible. Instead, we are creating a new normal—a normal that is unrecognizable and unwanted.

In this book, I seek to explain the background of the issues we are facing today while showing their relationships and projecting their outcomes. How did we get here? What is happening? Where are we going?

While you may not agree with all my analyses, it is essential to be informed so we can make better decisions. I have always been a macro analyst type of person, and this ability has served me well throughout life. The times when we can still ignore global events, thinking they have no relationship to our daily lives, are finished.

Since the primary audience of this book is a Western audience, it is from a Western perspective and has a Western focus. However, I plan to follow this up with a second book from a distinct Eastern perspective. Whether we wish to admit it or not, the Western world is still the dominant force in shaping global affairs and their issues are, thus, global. Thanks to globalization and technology, we are living in a world that is tightly integrated and reliant upon one another. However, we often see these relationships strained and, in some cases, broken down completely. There are no more regional issues; there are only global issues requiring global solutions.

This story begins with the role of oil and its relationship to the world's reserve currency, the petrodollar. Global economies have been lubricated by oil and petrodollars for decades, but we see this finally break down. Since the Great Recession of 2008, Western economies have artificially inflated their economies to delay the inevitable economic crash. While these measures were able to prolong the effects, they only made the outcome much worse.

Last time, China was able to come to the aid. But this time, China is focused on saving itself and its regional projects. The media would have you believe that since the U.S. stock market was in the longest bull rally on record, the economy would be better than ever. However, the developed world has been slowly decaying, which is led by the most significant factor: U.S. unemployment is at historic levels, and income inequality has never been worse, much to the chagrin of those entering the workforce.

Over the past decade, the U.S. auto market failed to regain its former economic state before the Great Recession of 2008. Retail store closings increased over the last 4 years to such historical levels that it was dubbed as the "retail-apocalypse." The big-box stores which used to drive traffic to malls have closed for good, leaving the small mom and pop businesses out to the wind. Brick and mortar stores are also going extinct as the trends shift to online shopping more and more.

Similarly, the service sector is being crushed by regulations. The housing market has become overinflated as easy access to credit saturated the market. These days, owning a home or renting one is becoming a luxury. The airline industry, which was barely profitable at the best of times, is facing lackluster demand, travel restrictions, and calls for social distancing, making it economically unviable.

These effects are not only felt in the U.S. but across the economies of the globe. These are unfairly being attributed to the black swan event of COVID-19. However, these effects have building up for years and are part of the natural cycle—something that governments should have been dealt with during the last crash, instead of making the situation more fragile.

Global financial markets have become disassociated from the health of the economy and even more so from the general populations' economic well-being. Government bailouts and stimulus packages have managed to delay the coming wave of delinquencies and bankruptcies, but not in avoiding them. Since the Great Recession of 2008, companies that were too big to fail and had no business in the market were propped up, leading to the continued zombification of the economy we see today.

In what is a sure sign of madness, bankrupt companies are being allowed to sell shares of stocks to investors. Free market capitalism died a long time ago despite what the media and pundits would have you believe. An over-bloated government and the Federal Reserve (FED) balance sheet has created a financial system that is oversaturated with bad debt and falsely labeled credit scores. As the dollar runs the risk of either a massive deflationary or inflationary event, central banks and governments have become wise to stacking gold. Over the past decade, gold buying has risen to historical levels as confidence in fiat currencies fade away.

One by one, nation by nation, we see collapses occur as results of failed policies and greed. What will come next will be the single most significant wealth transfer in human history. Throughout the ages, we have witnessed the same course of events take place, and the hegemony of the U.S. will be no different.

As governments become desperate to try to explain their incompetence, nations are being driven closer to conflicts. Contrary to popular belief, the Cold War never really ended. The actors only shifted, with China and its allies taking the place of the Soviet-allied bloc. This time, it will become clear that in this battle, the West will lose.

For years, the U.S. has been in an asymmetric war against all those who oppose its global influence, which has taken the form of economic sanctions as acts of war, and been used for decades as a precursor to traditional warfare. Also, cyberwarfare is being used to influence global populations' hearts and minds while seeking military advantage. Trade wars, sanctions, and cyberwarfare are all just steps along the road to traditional warfare. In the modern age, it is important not to think of warfare being conducted on the terms of the last war, but in the ways of the future. Where do we stand today? We are firmly in the midst of Cold War 2.0, the newly improved and modernized version of warfare.

While often overlooked or minimalized, it is essential to consider that as we seek new ways to kill ourselves, our planet is too. Climate change has led to conditions that contribute to water and food scarcity in areas of the world experiencing the highest population growth. These tragedies have led to radicalization and conflicts as access to resources come under threat. Water resources and viable agricultural land are becoming national and geopolitical interests. As climate change has and is expected to continue to wreak havoc on developing countries, the developed countries have been scooping up the best agricultural lands and water sources for pennies on the dollar.

With no hope for the future and facing conflicts at home, these actions have caused the most significant mass migration the world has ever experienced. As the developing world pours into the developed one, shifting demographics have caused xenophobic tensions. The issues faced by the global community require comprehensive solutions and cooperation that are unlikely to occur on the global stage due to competing interests and institutional structures.

Instead of going after the source of the numerous crises globally, nations are taking the easy route towards hostilities and protectionism. We are indeed facing the culmination of such a wide range of factors at home and abroad that it is impossible, given our current democratic political systems, and ineffective United Nations (UN), to truly address any of them in a meaningful way. Across the globe, people are angry, with symptoms arising from the crises described in this book. Social unrest is sweeping across the world and the economic and financial crises are finally beginning to be felt by the general population, but this is just the beginning. The worst is yet to come.

As a cheap and unscrupulous way to distract people away from the real causes, governments are using the media to portray themselves as innocent victims to foreign actors. Across the U.S., the streets are swarming with fury from the people, increasing the threat of a possible civil war. The developed world has come to the end of its cycle and it is time for Asia to regain its rightful place in the world's leadership, just as history dictated.

As Western nations become fractured and seek failed socialist and protectionist measures, China has been laying the foundation of a new world order. A new community is forming from Europe to Asia and from Africa to Oceana. Nations usually allied with the U.S. are slowly siding with the economic forces emerging in Asia. U.S. hegemony has been in retreat across the globe and will only accelerate as domestic issues continue to rise. All this will lead to Asia rightfully taking its place as the central hub for global economic activities and developments. Spearheaded by China, through the Belt and Road Initiative and other policies, Asian policymakers have shown farsighted planning absent from their Western counterparts.

For the first time, the global economy is being rebuilt from the ground up in a genuinely democratizing way and giving voice to those formerly oppressed by Western domination. Technology has allowed for more connectivity, flow of ideas, and trade. In the past, globalization was designed for the developing world to create goods for the developed world; but in the future, the roles will reverse. When the U.S. again retreats to its island fortress, we will begin not just the "Asian Century" but the "Asian Millennium."

The mighty economic powers of the Western world were built upon a strong manufacturing base in the past. But this has already eroded away and been replaced by the fragility of financial markets. These corrupted markets have allowed a select few to extract the wealth of the world through a new form of colonization called globalization. Not unlike in the past, debt has become the new chains of bondage as class divisions arise between the haves and the have-nots. The corrosion of wealth and opportunity begins on the individual level and goes all the way up to the state level for some. How did it come to this? It all began with oil.

CHAPTER 2: OIL WARS

SECTION 1: INTRODUCTION

In 280 BC, Rome was just a small state, one of the many small states inhabiting the Italian Peninsula and arguably there were more Greeks there than Romans. Which was why when the small Greek city-state of Tarentines requested aid from King Pyrrhus of Epirus against the encroaching Romans, he was happy to oblige. Pyrrhus arrived on the shores with an army of 20,000 infantry, 3,000 cavalries, 2,000 archers, 500 slingers, and 20 war elephants.

Estimates vary, but in his first battle with the Romans, it's been said he lost about 25% of his army, including some of his best men. But luck would have it that other Greek city-states would join him. Reinforced and confident in victory, he decided to attempt the takeover of several small cities but failed before marching on Rome, only to find out it was too well-defended.

After resting and regrouping, King Pyrrhus set out again in 279 BC to try to finish his campaign. However, this time, the Roman soldiers met him near the city of Asculum. Until this point, the Roman Legions were apprehensive about facing the Greeks after their crushing defeat. But now, they were left with no choice as King Pyrrhus was threatening their critical cities along the Aegean Sea. The Romans faced off with about 40,000 legionaries, 5,000 cavalries, and 300 chariots designed to face the war elephants against the Greek king's 38,000 infantry, 5,000 cavalries, and 19 war elephants.

When the 2 armies finally confronted one another, neither side could get a decisive edge over the other. The Romans sent soldiers behind the Greek lines to burn and loot their encampment. When the Greeks and their allies saw their camps looted and destroyed behind them, the Romans gained an edge, and the Greeks began to break rank. With his line in danger of collapse, King Pyrrhus rushed to plug the gap with his elite cavalry. Next, his war elephants finally managed to break the stalemate with the chariots and charged the flanks of the Romans. After facing another crushing defeat, the Romans were left with no choice but to retreat.

However, after this battle, King Pyrrhus surveyed the losses and said, "If we are victorious in one more battle with the Romans, we shall be utterly ruined." After several more years campaigning in southern Italy and losing more and more of his best men, finally, King Pyrrhus was faced with a much larger and reorganized Roman Legion. In the end, after all his victories, he was obligated to retreat once and for all back to Epirus in Greece, leaving the Greek city-states to their own devices.

We remember this battle courtesy of the annals of Plutarch titled *The Life of Pyrrhus*. This famous battle is where we got the term "Pyrrhic victory" from, which refers to a success that incurs such staggering losses to all sides that it cannot be considered a victory at all. A Pyrrhic war is a war that drains both sides with a battle of attrition that no sane person would call worthwhile; yet time after time, this option is chosen.

Today, we are witnessing Russia and Saudi Arabia, 2,300 years later, embark on a Pyrrhic war against the American energy sector. These countries have decided to flood the oil markets with record levels of supply in a time when demand is diminishing. To capture more significant market share and bankrupt the American shale industry, the Russians and Saudis have been forced to dig deep within their cash reserves to balance their budgets.

Meanwhile, the already unprofitable shale oil sector in the U.S. is forced to shut down wells and go into bankruptcy, because around the world, we are running out of places to store crude. This has sent oil prices tumbling to record lows, even trading in negative figures, destroying the profitability of an already increasingly tricky market.

While the costs of storage are skyrocketing to historic highs, the oil war cannot go on forever as both nations' economies are heavily reliant on the energy sector, respectively. But as the shipments of oil keep coming, we are left wondering: What we are going to do with all this crude oil?

SECTION 2: COLLAPSE OF THE OIL INDUSTRY

"Across the country, people are willing to tighten their belts and sacrifice. The president should ask the oil industry to do the same."

John Salazar, former United States congressman

On March 10, 2020, Russia and Saudi Arabia went to war with the American energy sector. To crush the competition, they flooded the market with cheap oil, causing prices to plummet to all-time lows. According to a post from *The Guardian*, on April 20, 2020, U.S. benchmark West Texas Intermediate (WTI) closed oil as low as -$37.63 USD, leading to the first time in history that suppliers (theoretically) need to pay consumers to take their oil. The U.S. oil revolution was crushed, along with prices, leading to a lack of storage. Producers were forced to shut down their wells, which could lead to a decrease in production in the future.

While many producers are faced with a mountain of debt and bad loans, many are and will be forced into bankruptcy and government bailouts. With oil consumption at record lows due to mass quarantines and restrictions, it seems this could not have come at a worse time for U.S. energy producers. American energy consumption is at levels not seen since the 1970s[1]. Economists have often used oil consumption as an indication of a nation's state in terms of the Gross Domestic Product (GDP). As global oil consumption rapidly declines, the effects of the economy will be profound.

Trading Economics estimated that Russia had amassed foreign exchange (FX) reserves totaling $570 billion USD, including a National Wealth Fund at $150 billion USD which they can use to offset low oil prices. Financially, the Russian economy relies on energy sales and would needs a crude price of $40 USD to balance its 2020 budget. In recent years, Saudi Arabia has been investing heavily in future megaprojects to shift their dependence away from their energy sector. However, as reported by *Reuters* on March 20, 2020 in an article titled *Russia vs.*

---

[1] https://www.economist.com/briefing/2020/04/08/an-unprecedented-plunge-in-oil-demand-will-turn-the-industry-upside-down

Saudi, how much pain can they take in oil price war?, Saudi Arabia needed closer to $80 USD to balance its 2020 budget.

As oil producers increase production in an environment with limited demand, it is quickly turning out to be a race to the bottom, which is terrible for any business model. It is even worse when you think that nation-states rely on these energy revenues for their budgets. According to the Organization of the Petroleum Exporting Countries' (OPEC) official data from 2018, OPEC nations possessed 79.4% of the world's proven reserves. OPEC+ is the meeting of OPEC nations, with the addition of 10 new exporting countries, including Russia, one of the most influential oil producers.

The Russians, by making a deal with the devil, were betting that they could outlast both the Saudis and the American energy sectors as they are in a well-established supplier position in Eurasia and can use their FX reserves to budget their economy. Regardless of whether they can cut a deal or not, it will take time, and lower oil prices will continue for the near term.

The Real Investment Advice article written by Lance Roberts on April 24, 2020, revealed the revolutions in fracking technology that led to a transformation of the industry and the American energy sectors. When oil prices hit all-time highs in 2008, in some cases near $150 USD a barrel[2], unviable technology such as fracking, and previously unprofitable energy developments, suddenly became profitable.

In a rush from Wall Street to find new forms of investment, the industry was flooded with wave after wave of investment capital over the following years. These were the golden days of the fracking industry where everyone and their grandmother were making a fortune. With interest rates at record lows, any debt was seemingly good debt. However, oil prices began to decline in 2014 and the profitability of these start-ups came into question. Instead of cutting production, OPEC+ increased production to increase market share and push out North American and Iranian oil producers. Pippa Stevens of CNBC

---

[2] https://www.macrotrends.net/1369/crude-oil-price-history-chart

reported on March 8, 2020 that as a result of this action, Brent crude prices fell dramatically from $112 USD a barrel to $32 USD a barrel in January of 2016.

But as CNN's Matt Egan reported on September 12, 2018, recent data showed that American crude oil producers were still able to overtake their Russian and Saudi counterparts in February 2018. But now, hundreds of billions of dollars in bad debt has come up for renewal, with no way to pay it.

For the first time, according to an Oil Price report on April 3, 2020 titled *Has Russia Reached Its Limit In the Oil Price War?*, we saw seemingly wealthy nations like Saudi Arabia increasing their taxes, and lowering the benefits and services for their citizens. Furthermore, the Americans would be forced to bail out their failing energy sector in one form or another.

The outbreak of COVID-19 came with many geopolitical implications. Not only were its effects medical, but it had also created issues in the political and economic spheres. The coronavirus pandemic has given rise to new threats of poverty and brought political instability throughout the world. The oil price in the past often declined in the crude markets but this time, it was different. Currently, the oil price fell due to oversupply and a rapid decline in the demand, both domestically and internationally. This plummeting demand came in the wake of the response to COVID-19, which shuttered significant components of the economy, a slowdown in all sorts of commercial enterprises, and supply chains. Notably, there was a sharp decrease in commuting through automobile.

In a report from The Guardian on April 20, 2020 titled *COVID-19 Crisis Will Wipe Out Demand for Fossil Fuels, Says IEA*, several analysts estimated that fossil fuel demand had plummeted by 80% in the past few months, mostly because of the COVID-19 pandemic. As spreads inverted and inventories started to pinnacle across the fuel distribution and retail community, refinery closures could be required for the export markets.

One silver lining was the diesel market, which was experiencing notably much less-severe demand declines (nearer to 20%). Organizations and supply chains in that region remained open for critical offerings, in addition to industrial and retail groups, which were less exposed to the financial outcomes of the COVID-19 pandemic.

Lockdown estimates set up to contain the spread of COVID-19 spoke to an exceptional stun to worldwide oil demand. According to The International Energy Agency (IEA) in their April 2020 report, the drop in global interest in April 2020 was as much as 29 million barrels a day, year-on-year (around 30% of market share). This drop was trailed by another critical year-on-year fall of 26 million barrels/day in May. The world had returned to oil levels not seen in decades. Because of this remarkable fall, oil storage facilities in the U.S. had topped off rapidly at a rate of 16 million barrels for each week during April 2020.

According to Noah Browning of the Financial Post, on April 27, 2020, the excess of oil was additionally apparent in Cushing, Oklahoma, a significant logistical exchanging hub for U.S. raw petroleum and where U.S. oil is delivered. With an absolute oil stockpiling limit of 80 million barrels, Cushing presently had just 20 million barrels of the free stockpiling left which was currently wholly reserved and liable to be used before the end of May 2020. For the first time in history, crude oil values were trading in negative figures. These negative figures came about because of a progression of events directly targeting the U.S. oil industry, leaving room for economic instability in the future.

While the WTI for May contract sank to -$37 USD a barrel[3], the July WTI kept on exchanging at about $20 USD, and the October WTI exchanged at about $30 USD. Be that as it may, a circumstance like April 20 may be rehashed in the near term (this agreement is as of now under extreme tension in the market), and significantly after if oil request does not recoup. What oil markets are encountering is a physical pressure emerging from unprecedented low interest rates, increasing debt, and constrained stockpiling limit. This will continue to worsen the situation for energy markets, unless there are drastic measures taken.

The unexpected spread of COVID-19 had plunged a significant number of the world's oil production sites in limbo, with terminations and vulnerability in

---

[3] https://www.macrotrends.net/2516/wti-crude-oil-prices-10-year-daily-chart

China driving the way. As indicated in a report by Carbon Brief on February 19, 2020 titled *Analysis: Coronavirus temporarily reduced China's CO2 emissions by a quarter*, the level of petroleum processing plants active in the Shandong region tumbled from 71.4% in December 2019 to 38.9%, 2 months after the fact. This reduction was a breakdown of a substantial portion representing a more extensive, abrupt mechanical blackout. Thus, government figures indicated a 3.3% decrease in unrefined petroleum handling in the initial 2 months of the year, contrasted with a similar period in 2019, and a 6.6% fall in the creation of refined oil.

The spread of COVID-19 represented a critical danger to the worldwide oil and gas industry. The actions taken to decrease the spread of the infection hampered a significant number of the division's key procedures: specialists needed to adjust in keeping up social separation while at the same time confined in living and working spaces; travel bans and isolation hindered organizations' capacity to travel and lead gatherings, and the vulnerability experienced through the pandemic did nothing to console a truly unpredictable industry.

The IEA, in a February 2020 report, highlighted the 2003 SARS pandemic as an equivalent to the current situation, yet the part played by China had changed drastically over the past 2 decades. The report detailed that since 2013, China had taken a central role in global supply chains and contributed enormously to global travel. With how much easier this virus spread than SARS, travel restrictions became the key focus. Furthermore, in 2019, China represented three-quarters of the global oil demand growth, a figure which had been on the rise over the last decade.

This issue goes past the U.S. and concerns the entire world. Free worldwide stockpiling limits are presently evaluated at 500-600 million barrels, which could be used up by June. As reported by The Wallstreet Journal on March 4, 2020 by Joe Wallace and Benoit Faucon, we saw cruise liners being converted into makeshift tankers due to the surging record-high costs of transporting and storing crude oil. This was the motivation behind why, after the WTI drop, Brent (the primary worldwide oil value benchmark, covering 66% of internationally exchanged raw petroleum) saw a boost from President Trump's tweet on April 22, 2020, compromising of military action against Iranian gunboats in the Persian Gulf.

To forestall such a situation, as reported by CNBC's Natasha Turak on April 15, 2020, the world's top oil producers, the OPEC+ coalition, on April 12 pulled off a notable arrangement to cut worldwide oil production by almost 10%. Beginning May 1, this ended an oil war that was activated only a month before by Saudi Arabia. Still, it included Russia's refusal to mutually reduce oil production and adjust the pandemic's impact on demand. Nonetheless, the latest improvements unmistakably indicated that the degree of the unbalance in the oil markets was well past flexibility to cut an understanding.

The Trump Administration was putting pressure on its Middle Eastern allies, Saudi Arabia, and the United Arab Emirates, to decrease oil production since it could lead to an increase and stabilization in prices. They had even gone so far as to threaten the security agreement between the Arab countries and America. According to a report published on Bruegel by Simone Tagliapietra, on April 23, 2020, domestic organizations such as ConocoPhillips and Continental Resources said they will close 25%-30% of their oil production, and all US producers were compelled to take similar measures. U.S. oil creation remained at 13 million barrels a day in February 2020, according to IHS Markit, a research firm with over 5,000 analysts and specialists in a May 21, 2020 article, and to drop by 2.9 million barrels a day before the year's past, due to the decrease in demand.

Be that as it may, sudden shutdowns can cause catastrophic harm to oil fields, and restarting them once they request returns will take a long time and hamper their future capabilities. When an oil well is shut down, there is no guarantee it can ever open again.

To forestall harm to the U.S. oil industry, President Trump may need to seek different measures. For example, they can rescue American oil producers by presenting taxes on foreign oil imports, opening capacity limit, or, in any event, purchasing oil that makers leave on the ground until costs recuperate.

In the meantime, the OPEC+ union has been forced to scale-down production and cut an understanding in an urgent endeavor to add to a rebalancing of the market. But the progress of cuts will have little effect upon oil prices and revenues until the significant glut in oil consumption is cleared. In short, people are consuming far less than the producers could viably reduce.

According to the U.S. Energy and Information Administration (EIA), the GDP of a nation is proportional to oil consumption[4]. Every part of the economy consumes fossil fuels and there is a cost associated with its production, transportation, and use. Goods and services would not arrive at your doorstep via Amazon if it were not for the massive amounts of fossil fuels consumed each day. Therefore, we see supply chains break down when there are mobility restrictions put in place. The effect the oil industry has and will have upon the economy is profound.

According to Sunny Oh of MarketWatch, on April 21, 2020, the American energy industry accounted for 12% of the overall American junk bond market. These companies suffered from an already abysmal credit score which could be worsened by lower oil prices, as well as the structural inefficiency and inabilities to pay back the debt. Many of these companies had not been economically viable in a long time, if ever.

Instead of letting the free market take its course and allowing these inefficient businesses to go bankrupt, we see politics dictate the market. The oil industry has become a highly politicized sphere of influence, which is setting itself up for a major failure. A failure in one primary American industry will inevitably influence other major American industries, leading to a chain of developments. Major banking and financial institutions bailouts mean the American public will ultimately be left holding the bag when the American energy industry collapses.

Every one of the current measures to mitigate the harm to the U.S. and worldwide oil makers will affect the market. However, it is not sensible to expect that this oil emergency will, at last, be tackled by pent up demand in worldwide oil when lockdowns are lifted, and the economy is restarted. That is, COVID-19 is prompting a breakdown of oil markets and they will have

---

[4] See the figures of the U.S. Energy and Information Administration (EIA) Oil & Gas General/GDP VS OIL CONSUMPTION 2017

fewer options for profitability in the near term. Government bailouts and taxpayer-funded loans may be the only way to save these sinking ships that never should have sailed in the first place.

The option to go back to a "new normal", since harm may be enduring, when the infection is vanquished is fading with each passing day. Lockdowns and restrictions are being given extensions on top of extensions with no glimmer of hope upon the horizon. The everyday citizens are left to shoulder the burden of an uncertain future. While the government continues to push a narrative that there is "pent-up demand" and "green shoots" are ready to sprout in the economy, they are characteristically ignoring the truth which is staring at us in the face: there is no going back to normal. We have only begun to feel the effects of what has and will come.

SECTION 3: THE PETRODOLLAR

"My grandfather rode a camel, my father rode a camel, I drive a Mercedes, my son drives a Land Rover, his son will drive a Land Rover, but his son will ride a camel."

Rashid bin Saeed Al Maktoum, the Emir of Dubai

Following World War II (WWII), the Bretton Woods Agreement solidified the U.S. dollar as the world's reserve currency. But the recent collapse in oil prices, coupled with foreign policy choices, has put this into question.

In 1944, nearing the end of WWII, the Bretton Woods Agreement was set up as a new system of regulations and procedures for the major economies of the world. The goal was to promote economic stability, the crucial factor in peace, prosperity, and growth. The International Monetary Fund and the World Bank were created to promote peace and prosperity, as the U.S. was the only major nation that was not reeling from WWII. And the country held most of the world's gold supply; the world had been on a gold/silver monetary standard before the war, so the U.S. economy was the most stable.

When countries decided to peg their new currencies to the dollar, due to the gold standard, their currencies would be redeemable via the U.S. dollar in gold. Most oil-exporting nations had nationalized oil industries, leaving their economies vulnerable to price fluctuations. Therefore, the U.S. dollar peg created better stability for them.

The petrodollar refers to any U.S. dollar paid to oil-exporting countries in exchange for oil. The American agreement with Arab counties stipulated that all fuel sold must be priced in dollars, solidifying the U.S. dollar as the world's reserve currency. Once these nations receive dollars for their oil, they reinvest their dollars into American goods and services. If the price of the dollar's value fall, so does their domestic services and products. This is a way to avoid large swings in deflation or inflation. However, this type of monetary policy, while very fiscally responsible, do not allow for rapid debt creation or increase in the money supply without increasing gold reserves. Currently, we are witnessing the gradual replacement of the petrodollar as the world's reserve currency, as nations step up against American hegemony.

On February 14, 1945, President Franklin D. Roosevelt entered an alliance with Saudi Arabia. At the time, most of the Arab nations were reeling from Ottoman, British and French occupation in the early 20th century and were relatively undeveloped. At the time, the U.S. was both the most significant oil consumer and producer in the world, with the oil market being dominated by a group of multinational companies known as the "Seven Sisters." This economic and military agreement with the Americans allowed for the creation of the oil-rich Gulf states today, along with their rapid development. This was when the petrodollar was born. Each nation required oil at this stage, and this made the U.S. dollar the best choice.

In September of 1960, several vital oil-producing countries sat down and, thus, the OPEC was born. The 5 founding members were Iran, Iraq, Saudi Arabia, Kuwait, and Venezuela. OPEC sought to stabilize the price of oil, and knowing the non-renewable nature of their resource, they sought to increase market shares and profits. While OPEC nations wanted high oil prices to increase their profits, their consumers wanted lower oil prices to keep costs down instead.

After the Yom-Kippur War, the U.S. utilized the U.S. dollar position and remade its ties with Saudi Arabia. Thus, the "petrodollar union" was formed. In return for American military and political support to the Saudis, the Arab Kingdom would utilize its influence in OPEC to guarantee all oil exchanges would come in U.S. dollars. It would then reinvest its petrodollars in U.S. items and administrations, manage value levels, and forestall any oil ban from occurring.

Thus, all oil-exporting countries must get paid in U.S. dollars, making their national salary reliant upon the U.S. dollars' value. If the U.S. dollar falls, so does their nation's income. If the oil merchants are to, in some way or another, sabotage the U.S. dollar, such as making their oil less expensive, the providers will need to respond regardless of whether a lower price will be helpful or hurtful. It may appear to be monopolistic and unfair, yet this framework does some fantastic things.

Oil-trading countries get dollars for their goods, not their currency. That makes their national income subject to the dollars' worth. On the off chance that it falls, so does their government's revenue. Most oil-exporting nations had nationalized oil industries, leaving their economies vulnerable to fluctuations in price. As a result, these oil exporters decided to peg their currencies to the dollar, for more excellent stability.

Petrodollar recycling occurs when the dollars received by oil-producing nations are used by their Sovereign Wealth Funds to reinvest in American companies outside of the oil industry, leading to a decreased dependence on oil revenues[5]. However, by 1971, the American economy was feeling the effects of the long and drawn-out Vietnam War.

Another war of attrition took place between the major powers of America and its allies versus the Soviet and Chinese blocks. The U.S. was facing stagflation and had a run on the dollar as people rushed into relatively safe assets such as gold to protect their purchasing power. Many countries asked to redeem their U.S. dollars for gold, which led to a decrease in the U.S. gold reserves. To protect the gold reserves, President Richard Nixon famously took the U.S. off the gold standard in 1971, stunning the world. This was the start of profound impacts upon the economic and financial well-being of the world[6].

As a result of the U.S. dollar not being backed by gold, it fell to a free market equilibrium price, thus making American goods and services cheaper for the rest of the world and increasing demand and revenues for American companies. However, a falling dollar hurt the oil-exporting countries because their contracts were priced in U.S. dollars. So, they saw a decrease in revenues and an increase in import costs.

Following the Arab-Israeli wars and the oil embargo on Western nations, the United States and Saudi Arabia sat down to negotiate a new deal. In 1979, the Arabian Joint Commission on Economic Cooperation was established. This was when they remade the dollars for an oil deal, agreeing to recycle them back to the U.S. through contracts with U.S. companies to improve Saudi

---

[5] https://peakoil.com/publicpolicy/the-death-of-petrodollars-the-coming-renaissance-of-macro-investing
[6] The website www.wtfhappenedin1971.com, has some interesting charts for further reading.

infrastructure and technology transfer. This deal would, in turn, boost wages, increase imports, and help the economy. So now, the U.S. could seek any number of expansionist approaches and maintain a strategic distance from the reactions as nations are required to hold and use U.S. dollars, essentially financially backing the U.S.

During the most recent times, we had witnessed history in the making, when the cost of unrefined petroleum dipped below 0 to -$40 USD per barrel, and over the long haul, numerous experts think the worst is yet to come. After WTI oil-based agreements evaporated for May, contracts for June crumbled by 45%.

Economic analyst Kimberly Amadeo for The Balance wrote a report on April 8, 2020 titled *Petrodollars and the System that Created It: Will the Petrodollar Collapse?*, she wrote that the oil issues were not going away any time soon and we could see the U.S. dollar's eventual demise. Since 1944, the U.S. dollar was propped up by the petrodollar plot but with oil costs below 0, the dollar could undoubtedly crumble or lead to a decoupling of the petrodollar. The U.S. utilized petrodollars to authorize its international strategy.

For instance, Amadeo stated the U.S. punished Iran for refusing to end its advancement of potential atomic weapons by restricting access to U.S. dollars for trade. Similarly, it hit Russia with exchange embargoes for invading Crimea and causing a state of emergency in Ukraine. This had led China to seek a substitute to the U.S. dollar as a worldwide currency, with their recently issued digital yuan.

Still, ironically, according to official U.S. Treasury data, China is one of the largest foreign holders of the dollar. However, China insists on pegging the yuan to the dollar. In any case, numerous nations are not satisfied with the current situation and are actively seeking other options. Without access to dollars for trade and debt settlement, a nation or organization is isolated and with limited options. Furthermore, a dollar reserve currency forces the U.S. to run trade deficits with the rest of the world while gaining access to plentiful cheap goods which artificially inflates the lifestyle of its citizens.

A petrodollar is a U.S. dollar acquired through the offer of unrefined petroleum. For example, it is a term made to depict the circumstance of the

OPEC nations where the offer of this product permits these countries to thrive and reinvest its U.S. dollars in the countries which buy it. It is one of those simple aphorisms over which the world's energy, geopolitical, monetary, and financial frameworks are formed. The purchasing power of the petrodollar relies heavily on the value of the U.S. dollar and any shift to renewable resources can have profound effects. Changes to the system will produce huge impacts and costs in the geopolitical and monetary levels. Some excuse these impacts as a small probability while others guarantee them to be calamitous. Likely, the reality lies somewhere in the middle.

Over the past few years, the Saudis have been saber-rattling about dumping U.S. treasuries if the Americans continue to pursue them for their involvement in the September 11, 2001 (9/11) attacks. On April 5, 2019, Tom Luongo published an article titled *The Ultimate Pivot: Saudi Betrayal of the Petrodollar* detailing how the Saudis warned the Obama Administration that they would sell off hundreds of billions of dollars in U.S. assets. This would be in retaliation if Congress passed a bill that would allow the Saudi government to be held responsible in American courts for any role in the 9/11 attacks. While chances of the bill being passed were slim, the Saudis were heavily exposed to any fluctuations in U.S. dollar value and were seeking ways to become less reliant on it. Unsurprisingly, according to Statista, from 2009–2018, Saudi Arabia was by far the largest arms importer of American weapons[7].

Lately, according to an article published by Simon Watkins on April 27, 2020 titled *Trump Could Use "Nuclear Option" to Make Saudi Arabia Pay for Oil War*, Saudi Arabia was threatening to drop the U.S. dollar as a medium of exchange for their oil. The Americans had countered them with a No Oil Producing and Exporting Cartels Act (NOPEC) bill and anti-trust legislation which could hold them accountable and block imports from OPEC countries. Also, there had been threats to remove American troops and military protection from the gulf.

NOPEC, was first introduced in 2000 and aimed to remove sovereign immunity from U.S. anti-trust law, paving the way for OPEC states to be sued

---

[7] https://www.statista.com/chart/9509/saudi-arabia-is-the-biggest-buyer-of-us-arms/

for curbing output in a bid to raise oil prices. This bill was yet made into law despite numerous attempts but had recently become more popular under the Donald Trump Administration.

According to an article by Eli Okun in Politico on April 22, 2019, back in 2011, Trump declared that he supported NOPEC but was incredibly quiet since gaining office. Instead, he pushed for even closer relations with the Gulf states, especially Saudi Arabia, choosing to ignore the brutal killing of American-Saudi journalist Jamal Khashoggi. If the Saudis move forward with this plan, and would inevitably have to, there would be a lot of support amongst non-OPEC oil-producing nations like Russia, most especially with the significant consumer markets of China and the European Union.

According to a Peak Oil report titled *The Death of Petrodollars & the Coming Renaissance of Macro Investing* on October 15, 2017, these markets had shown strong support to move away from the dollar and to diversify global trade in a bid to dilute U.S. influence and hegemony over the world economy. Russia was one of several nations facing sanctions at the hands of the Americans that began selling oil in euros and yuan. Other nations included Iran and Venezuela that were under strict sanctions in their bid for regime change had diversified to several other kinds of oil swaps. However, when taken in the scheme of the global oil market, these were very insignificant and did little to threaten the dominance of the U.S. dollar.

For most people alive today, the dollar's dominance seems as natural as English as the unofficial second language of the world. But this has not always been the case. Cullen Roche brought forward a thought-provoking article titled *How Much Longer Will the Dollar Remain the Reserve Currency of the World?* According to him, if we go back to 1450, the Portuguese ruled the world as the global reserve currency where much of this was funded through colonialist expansion in Africa and Asia[8].

But after only 80 years, in 1530, the Spanish overtook them, thanks to their massive holdings in the New World and abroad. It was not until 110 years later,

---

[8] https://twitter.com/100trillionusd/status/1243115218043047938

in 1640, that the Netherlands began their rise as the world's reserve currency, but this only lasted for 80 years. In 1720, France rose to prominence, helped by several factors including colonization, but was replaced by the British after only 95 years. From 1815–1920, the world witnessed for the first time an empire where the sun never set. Indeed it was the first global empire, and during that time, it was also the world's reserve currency. However, following WWI and going into WWII, a massive shift took place where, for the first time in a long time, a global power outside Europe had taken the helm.

Since 1921 we have been under the leadership of the Americans as the world's reserve currency, which can be considered an extension of the British. Indeed, we have been in an Anglo-dominated world going back just over 200 years and eventually, like all things, this will have to come to an end. The average lifespan of a reserve currency is about 110 years and we are quickly approaching that time now for the U.S. dollar. When you are at the top, there is only one place you can go from there.

There are numerous different ideas about how the U.S. dollar will eventually collapse. Still, history has shown, unlike the sudden collapses of Zimbabwe, Venezuela, Argentina, or Germany, etc., global reserve currencies tend to go softly into the night. Over time, their dominance gently erodes and is replaced not in one piece but in sections.

The most probable threat to the U.S. dollar is the dual threat of high inflation and high debt. If rising consumer prices force the Fed to hike interest rates sharply, this will dramatically affect the short-term instruments such as adjustable-mortgage rates. Furthermore, if the U.S. government is forced to default on its interest payments, foreign creditors could start dumping dollars.

While some critics would be quick to blame the current Trump Administration for the massive increase in debt load, it would be wise to remember that under the Obama Administration, the U.S. doubled its debt by $10 trillion USD. Moving forward, given the massive stimulus needed by the government, the government's choice to increase spending year over year, coupled with its inability to downsize, it became clear that, whether a Republican or Democrat takes office in 2020, more spending and more debt are on the way.

If the U.S. enters a prolonged recession or depression, it will influence the petrodollar. Nations like Russia and China, along with central banks, have been stockpiling gold and silver over the last decade, with rumors swirling of a commodity-based standard making a return. Even if this is true, it will not necessarily collapse the dollar as foreign exporters like China and Japan enjoy the benefits of American consumers. Also, for any currency to be backed by gold and/or silver, such as a gold yuan or silver ruble, a massive global revaluation of the commodity will be needed.

One popular theory put forth by Brent Johnson, the CEO of Santiago Capital, a wealth fund manager specializing in gold, is "The Dollar Milkshake Theory." According to him, since the 2008-2009 financial crisis, central banks had teamed up to inject liquidity into the system through low rates, special purpose vehicles, asset purchases, quantitative easing, and money printing. All this liquidity came in many different forms and many different directions, frothing the financial markets and increasing stock valuations. But recently, the U.S. had inserted a proverbial straw into the milkshake of the world's markets and started to suck the liquidity out.

While the Fed hikes interest rates and reduces its balance sheet, central banks keep on pouring in liquidity. In a modern globalized world, capital can freely travel like people to where they are treated best. In Europe, Japan, and England, the central banks are running printing presses and devaluing their currencies while the U.S. dollar increases in purchasing power and leaves American investors at an advantage. While gold barely beat an all-time high in 2020, in the U.S. dollar, it has been on a moon shot for the past few years for almost all other currencies—an ominous sign of what investors have seen coming.

The Dollar Index, a basket of currencies priced against the dollar, was on a tear for the past decade, with no weakness insight. Outside of the U.S., there is over $11 trillion USD in debt that must be repaid by foreign companies that have borrowed in dollars and need to pay it back at much higher rates. What is worse is if any of these nations, like the recent case in Lebanon, end up defaulting on their loans, it would destroy the currency and decrease the monetary supply, leading to even more weakness against the dollar.

The U.S. dollar has not been this strong since the 1980s, which was stopped by the Plaza Accord, whereby France, Japan, West Germany, U.K., and the U.S. got together to devalue the dollar. The increased likelihood of this happening again is getting louder as we get nearer to this stage of dollar strength.

Simon Watkins put forth that, currently, the Saudis were hemorrhaging money. Their 2018 budget deficit was around 7% of GDP and since the 2014 oil price crash, they had gone from zero to $180 billion USD in debt to finance its budget or approximately 22% of GDP. He said that back in October 2016, the country's Deputy Economic Minister, Mohammed Al Tawaijri announced, "If we [Saudi Arabia] don't take any reform measures, and if the global economy stays the same, then we're doomed to bankruptcy in three to four years."

In March of 2020, Saudi Arabia's central bank depleted its foreign reserves at rates not seen since 2000. In that month alone, foreign reserves fell by 5%, or $27 billion USD, reaching the lowest level since 2011. It was left with just $164 billion USD in "fighting reserves" to utilize, with the other $300 billion USD was used for maintaining the peg to the U.S. dollar. Recently, the Saudis were forced to slash social welfare funding, triple the VAT, and stop monthly payments to its citizens. The citizens had begun to bear the burden for their government's fiscal adventurism—a situation which is not too far from the American citizen's future.

We are witnessing the slow replacement of the petrodollar as the world's reserve currency and, thus, American hegemony over the world's economies. The adversaries of Western dominance have become more vocal and have taken new steps to outdo the American policy in every corner of the world. In the past, nations had to be invaded, wars had to be fought, and populations needed to be swayed. In the brave new world which we live in, these actions have become covert and coordinated while people are blissfully unaware of their impending doom.

As citizens, we have put our financial security in the hands of governments which can make and break agreements at will. As oil prices become increasingly unstable, we see the economic and political fragility of the world around us start to crack. We have been born into this Anglo-hegemonic system, and it is easy to forget that the way things are have not always been the way things were.

Whether the dollar is crushed, devalued, or grows so strong it takes the world down with it, we will witness the end of the petrodollar as the world's reserve currency. These issues are set to continue as low oil prices mixed with high fiscal spending will endure for the near term. The economic crisis of today has its roots going back to 1971. When the U.S. removed the gold standard, the decline began but has since accelerated. We are seeing more debt and money being created this year in the U.S. than throughout its entire history. When we start to add up the unfunded liabilities, there is simply not enough to go around, which means that printing cannot slow down. It needs to speed up. If we look to historical examples, we will see that this has never ended well.

CHAPTER 3: THE ECONOMIC CRISIS

SECTION 1: INTRODUCTION

"Economic depression cannot be cured by legislative action or executive pronouncement. Economic wounds must be healed by the action of cells of the economic body – the producers and consumers themselves."

President Herbert C. Hoover

The world is experiencing one of the most exceedingly awful pandemics: COVID-19. The best safeguard to stop spreading this potentially lethal virus is to remain at home and avoid social contact. Practically all the nations of the world are forced into total lockdown for the wellbeing of their society. Due to these extreme measures, economies are starting to feel the devastating effects of the crisis.

The coronavirus has done what no wars or destruction has managed to accomplish—bringing the world economy to its knees. Supply lines are cut, travel restrictions and bans are in place, and consumer-based marketplaces are shut down. Surprisingly fast, the infectious calamity has pushed the world to the verge of an economic downturn—one that is more severe than the 2008 budgetary emergency. Record-high unemployment rates, government spending, delinquent payments, and foreclosures have become the "new normal." The length of the downturn will rely upon numerous components, including the conduct of the infection itself, general reactions, and monetary intercessions.

Given the exceptional situation of the pandemic-prompted emergency, financial and money related policymakers are working without a playbook. Some are pushing ahead with massive bailouts that could all in all top $10 trillion USD, spending trillions like they are billions. In contrast, others struggle to reopen their respective economy as soon as possible. The immediate effects of COVID-19 will be felt well into late 2020 and 2021, and the longer-term economic implications are just getting started.

Long before COVID-19 became an epidemic, the worldwide economy, specifically those of developed nations, is already cruising into a storm of biblical proportions. "We anticipate the worst economic fallout since the Great Depression," said Kristalina Georgieva, the overseeing chief of the International Monetary Fund. In the interim, the Organization for Economic Cooperation and Development said it had delivered the most grounded cautioning on record where most developed economies had entered a "sharp-log-jam." The World Trade Organization, as far as it mattered, estimated that about all districts of the world would endure two-fold digit decreases in exchange this year (2020), with North American and Asian exporters getting hit the hardest.

Most legislatures have successfully solidified social and monetary movements, in all or parts of their nations, to contain the flare-up, covering trivial organizations and requesting occupants to remain at home for weeks to months. Hence, billions of individuals have stayed under lockdown. Significant business industries, particularly aircraft and other travel-related market segments, are nearing the precarious edge of insolvency. The expectation is that economies can shut down without causing violent disturbances, such as bankruptcies or unemployment, and can rapidly return to an acceptable level when the pandemic is over afterwards. However, what we are witnessing are the apocalyptic conditions in the economic sector.

The brand name big box stores Millennials have grown up with are filing for bankruptcy in record amounts, part of the longer-term trend referred to as "retail-apocalypse." Without these anchor stores to drive traffic to malls, small businesses will face harsh economic conditions and be forced to close en masse. This has led to the landlords being left holding the bags as their tenants break their leases in record amounts, often spurred on by government policies.

After weeks of lockdowns, the areas which are struggling to reopen have been hit with riots and further delays, making matters even worse. Even as these areas attempt to reopen, the activity is not there in most sectors anymore and the restrictions put in place have hampered their income. The auto industry, which has yet to recover from the Great Recession of 2008, is being wiped out. The airline industry, which struggles at the best of times, is forced to see changes that make it economically unviable without significant increases in the traveling costs. The housing industry has been inflated and is facing a record-breaking correction.

Unemployment, income inequality, and social unrest have never been higher in the U.S. These effects are being felt around the world and not just in the U.S. All of this happened before the second wave of COVID-19. So, what will happen if this is just the beginning?

SECTION 2: UNEMPLOYMENT

"A recession is when your neighbor loses his job; it is a depression when you lose yours."

President Harry S. Truman, and later President Ronald W. Reagan

In an indication of the fantastic cost the infection was taking on the U.S. economy, more than 30 million Americans—around 1 out of 6 U.S. laborers—had filed for unemployment since March 2020. Before this emergency, the highest number of filings in a single week was 695,000 in 1982. Financial yield plunged by almost 5% in the initial 3 months of 2020, the steepest jump since 2008. Most investigators anticipated that the harm would be far more terrible in the subsequent quarter, with some suggesting that the unemployment rate could reach as high as 40%, which was fundamentally more elevated than its pinnacle of 25% during the Great Depression. To date, 36.5 million Americans have filed new unemployment benefits claims.

According to a group of prominent economists, Peter Ganong, Pascal Noel, and Joseph Vavra, from the Becker Friedman Institute for Economics at the University of Chicago, 68% of those currently unemployed could now bring home more money than when they were employed. According to their research, it was estimated from the 2019 government that "68% of unemployed workers who can receive benefits are eligible for payments that are greater than their lost earnings." They also found that "the share of a worker's original weekly salary that is being replaced by unemployment benefits—is 134%, or more than one-third above their original wage." With such a strong incentive to stay at home and receive "free money," it would be a wonder if anyone wanted to go back to work after this.

While the ever-shrinking population of high earners in the U.S. were indeed motivated to return to work, there was a significant, if not majority, percentage that was not. The less you made last year, the higher the temptation.

According to a post on CNBC on May 9, 2020 by Greg Iacurci, "The average unemployed worker in that [service] industry is now eligible to collect 182% of their previous wages. The average worker in this industry, which employs 14 million people, makes $13.45 USD an hour—the lowest compared with other industries. These workers would benefit most under the unemployment system when compared to others—collecting 182% of their previous wages, according to a CNBC analysis of Bureau of Labor Statistics and Labor Department data." However, it is essential to remember that many of their jobs might never be coming back[9], since the service sector industries are some of the hardest hit.

Hundreds of thousands of companies are expected to collapse so far, with the worst possibly yet to come. In a post from the Atlantic on May 18, 2020 by Derek Thompson, "Small-business activity has plunged nationwide by nearly 50%. Hundreds of thousands of companies have already failed. Big retailers such as J.Crew and Neiman Marcus have filed for bankruptcy, while others, including Macy's, are teetering. By some measures, scarcely one-third of Americans say they are working. Next month's jobs report will likely show that, for the first time since World War II, a majority of Americans aren't officially employed." So, the cold, harsh reality is that there are not enough jobs to go around, let alone those that can or are willing to afford what Leftists have been calling "a living wage."

Soon, it is expected that things will get more difficult for those hanging on by a thread. In an article by Emily Crane on May 18, 2020 for the Daily Mail, a recent Facebook survey of "86,000 small and medium sized business owners" found that "…[a]bout a third of small businesses forced to close due to the coronavirus pandemic say they won't be able to reopen due to an inability to pay bills or rent. More than half of the business owners surveyed by Facebook have also said they don't expect to rehire the same number of workers they employed before the pandemic."

Given the current fears and uncertainty over the COVID-19 crisis, it is unsurprising that business owners are cautious. Many are concerned about keeping what little they have left and have no interest in expanding anytime soon. It will be increasingly difficult for those unemployed to find work, which lends for more calls of free money. Since millions of Americans are still affected

---

[9] https://i.dailymail.co.uk/1s/2020/05/19/01/28546706-8332905-image-a-19_1589848303144.jpg

by unemployment in September 2020, it could force both President Trump and Representative Joe Biden to declare more free money to appease the masses. However, this will put the American administration and Congress in the unfortunate position to borrow money that they do not have, which inevitably puts only a band-aid over a serious wound.

This doesn't seem as far-fetched as it did a few months ago, especially since Joseph Zeballos-Roig of Business Insider reported on May 18, 2020 that the California government would be offering $500 USD cash payments to all unauthorized immigrants who didn't qualify for unemployment benefits or stimulus checks. All these poor decision choices have led the American economy, and thus the world's economies, down a path where most people are blissfully unaware of what is to come.

According to the National Bureau of Economic Research, the U.S. is officially in a recession for which they claimed was brought on by the COVID-19 pandemic. In their June 2020 report, they projected that this would be the "most severe economic recession in nearly a century," and was expected to last years. As COVID-19 conveniently takes the blame for what is being dubbed as a "global recession," many people are only beginning to realize what this means for them. Health officials have started to admit that a future vaccine is becoming unlikely, as economies try to find ways to reopen without endangering people's health.

If there is one thing that is detrimental to business, it is uncertainty. The trends towards a gig-based economy have allowed those able to work from home to do so and they will likely continue. The service and retail sectors have been racked as they are being forced to shift towards online models. Asian countries that have already established online ecosystems have noticed little difference, whereas their Western counterparts are just learning the ropes.

The way we do business and how we spend our money are fundamentally changing. The companies that recognize the trends will succeed while those that ignore them will fail. The developed economies of the world that have built their economies around consumers will be especially hard hit. Many of the jobs that went away will never come back, and those that do will not experience much difference from before. COVID-19 has taken a generational shift and condensed it into just a few months. One of the most visible sectors to this transition is the auto market.

SECTION 3: THE AUTO MARKET

"Nothing you will do in your lifetime, realistically, will waste more money than buying a new car. It's the single worst financial decision millennials will ever make."

David Bach, self-made millionaire and best-selling author

Over the past few decades, we have seen a growing trend away from new auto purchases, but never has it been as extreme as it is now. According to a report by HIS Markit on June 27, 2019, the average age of automobiles on the road in the U.S. was at a record high of 11.8 years[10]. While the industry has matured, with increased safety and quality, there has been stagnation in new auto sales despite the rising U.S. population. Wolf Richter of Wolf Street pointed out:

> "In 1999, new vehicle sales reached a record of 16.9 million units. This record was broken in 2000, with 17.3 million units. Then sales tapered off. By 2007, they dropped to 16.1 million units. Then the Financial Crisis hit, GM and Chrysler went bankrupt, Ford almost did, and peak-to-trough, sales plunged 40% to 10.4 million units by 2009. The recovery has been steep, and in 2015, finally the old record of the year 2000 was broken, but barely with 17.48 million units, and in 2016, the industry eked out another record of 17.55 million units. And that was it. Sales have fizzled since then. So far in 2019, the data[11] indicates that sales are likely to fall below 17 million units, according to my own estimates, bringing the industry right back where it had been 20 years ago in 1999."

Before the COVID-19 crisis, we had only just recently seen the sales numbers from 20 years ago. While new auto prices skyrocketed during this time, there were inadequate income distribution in the general population. However, we must keep in mind that the previous recovery was only maintained through new initiatives such as 0 down at or near-0 interest, cashback, warranty extensions, and other promotional tools to coax the consumer to buy a new car.

---

[10] https://wolfstreet.com/wp-content/uploads/2019/06/US-auto-average-age-2019.png
[11] https://wolfstree.com/wp-content-uploads/2019/06/US-auto-sales-annual-1977-2019-Est.png

According to Pew Research Center, in a report from August 2018, the average wage of workers in the U.S. had hardly risen when adjusted for inflation. With interest rates at all-time lows, this had forced consumers to go into debt for more extended periods to afford a new vehicle. "For many Americans, the availability of loans with longer terms has created an illusion of affordability," the center reported. However, this inevitably means that the consumer will be paying more for their car due to interest, bogging the consumer down from other purchases.

To make matters more complicated, the number of used automobiles in the U.S. market had never been higher at an estimated 279.3 million in 2019[12]. According to Richter, the rising average age of American automobiles did not necessarily mean that people drive the same cars longer, although many might do it. It represented the massive used market which had a strong demand for good quality, but older, vehicles.

In economic terms, this shows that consumers are highly price-sensitive when it comes to the auto industry. Cars are often considered the second most important purchase after a house, or possibly third after education. But this means that there is little room for growth in the industry, as there is often only one direction to travel once you have hit the top.

According to a report from J. D. Power on April 2019, "Inventory is starting to become a serious issue across all U.S. automakers. On average, new vehicles sold in May spent 74 days on dealer lots, the highest level for the month of May since 2009 when the industry was plagued with the looming effect of the Great Recession. 29% of vehicles sold so far in May have sat on lots for 90 days or longer, up from about 25% last year." This opinion was echoed in June 2019 when Bank of America stated that, "the auto cycle had peaked."

Over in China, the picture has been equally as bleak. A report from Statista by I. Wagner, published on March 17, 2020, listed China as the largest automobile market worldwide, in both terms of supply and demand. However, they found

---

[12] https://wolfstree.com/wp-content/uploads/2019/06/US-auto-sales-annual-vehicles-in-operation-2019.png

a reduction in the number of automobile registrations in 2019 with only 21 million—a decrease of 9%. According to The China Passenger Car Association (CPCA) report from February 2020, the auto industry has been in a recession for at least the previous 18 to 24 months. Then, battered by the effects of COVID-19, we saw historic figures produced.

While there had been efforts to "return to normalcy," the data was showing otherwise. Retail car sales in the country were down to 83% year over year for the third week in February. According to the CPCA, the country's auto sales had dropped to 5,411 units per day for the week. They also stated that vehicle production and sales would show a more noticeable drop-in February than in January. Chinese auto sales had gone into full collapse and fell to 92% in the first half of February.

During this time, the CPCA said, "Very few dealerships opened in the first weeks of February and they have had very little customer traffic." This was hardly surprising given the nature of the quarantine measures; which was why CPCA Secretary General Cui Dongshu stated, "There was barely anybody at car dealers in the first week of February as most people stayed at home."

The U.S. auto sector has been in trouble for some time and has failed to surpass the numbers seen nearly 20 years ago[13]. As the population increases, so too has the average age of the cars on the road, because many Americans feel that purchasing a new vehicle is unaffordable. In recent years, apps such as Uber and Lyft have sought to capitalize on this trend, allowing people to pay per use. These apps have become especially popular in major cities and even spawned copycat companies across the globe. Since younger generations prefer to live closer to the downtown core, they are turning their backs on traditional car ownership all the while gaining additional sources of income from these ride-sharing apps.

Also, the recent credit crunch and the subprime crisis are not helping people into purchasing new vehicles any time soon. Furthermore, because vehicles are depreciating assets, more people are finding that buying a new one will not

---

[13] https://pbs.twimg.com/media/ERRjjVvU4AE3Nek.jpg:large

make sense. What is going to happen to car companies when they run out of customers? The auto industry has shown signs of reimagining its purpose, with the rise of Tesla and others that offer up new possibilities to consumers.

In India, one of the largest vehicle manufacturers in the world, Tata Motors, has fully embraced smaller and much cheaper modes of travel. These options, along with others like electric scooters, have become massively popular across Asia and Europe. As society's progression means we become increasingly interconnected, the auto industry will be forced to adapt to the changing demands of their clientele or "go the way of the horse and buggy."

While the 2020 third quarter figures showed a modest rebound in the auto sector, with it being fueled by government stimulus and low interest rates, the question still remains: Will this be a sustained rebound or a dead cat bounce? Seeing how bleak the sector was during the longest economic expansions in U.S. history, what will happen when we start to feel the effects of the economic recession and social upheaval? Metropolitan centers and new smart cities of the future are turning their backs on the old ways of transportation, with these sectors are being replaced by exciting new technologies. Our freedom of mobility is under threat domestically and internationally and is tied directly to our economic mobility.

SECTION 4: THE YEILD CURVE INVERSION

"I never liked quantitative easing. It's misunderstood by almost everybody. Flattening the yield curve is not stimulative; flattening the yield curve is anti-stimulative."

Kenneth Fisher, businessman and author

The yield curve is a plot of the yields on all U.S. Treasury maturities, a form of debt sold by the U.S. government, which can range from 1-month bills to 30-year bonds. Under normal circumstances, the shape of the yield curve is upward sloping because bond investors expect to turn a profit and be rewarded more the longer they own the bonds. Mostly, these are loans to the government. So, the longer you loan the capital, the higher return you expect to receive. When yield curves further out are higher than those nearer, this is referred to as being steep.

For example, a 30-year bond may deliver a much higher percentage yield than a 2-year note. When the gap, sometimes referred to as the "spread," is narrow, the yield curve is referred to as "flat." A 10-year note may only offer a slightly higher percentage yield than a 3-year note.

So, what is a yield curve inversion? Well, on exceedingly rare occasions, some shorter-dated returns may be higher than the longer-dated ones. Many different market factors can produce these situations, but it generally shows an expectation for weaker future growth. Since 1950, there have been 9 major U.S. recessions and an inversion has preceded all 9 of them in the yield curve.

The yield curve is the spread between the long- and short-dated U.S. Treasury bonds and turns negative when the shorter-dated Treasury yield is more than the longer-dated ones. For instance, if we look at the difference between the 2-year and 10-year sovereign debts, the spread stood at -4 basis points, according to Tradeweb data.

In August 2019, the 10-year Treasury note yield, BX: TMUBMUSD10Y, slipped 5.2 basis points to 1.493%, the lowest since July 2016. The benchmark maturity was only 17 basis points away from its all-time low of 1.32%. The 2-year note rate, BX: TMUBMUSD02Y, was down 2.5 basis points to 1.533%, while the 30-year bond yield, BX: TMUBMUSD30Y, slumped 6.6 basis points to 1.975%, an all-time low[14].

While this movement could be considered one of the most precise indicators that a recession was coming, it could take up to 34 months for a recession to take place after the inversion. The yield curve inverted in March 2019 but, as with most things, we did not notice them until it was too late. Investors will turn to bonds as a safe asset when the stock market is seen as too volatile. But if we see too many investors moving into long-term bonds, then this is a sign for how Wall Street sees the economy will perform. We get inverted yield curves when short-term debt is seen as being riskier than long-term debt. While many investors will try to time the market, looking at these indicators can give us a clear picture of where they see things going.

The most recent data has shown that most developed economies are currently in a recession and is expected to last for several years. Generally, recessions are great for safe assets such as precious metals and bonds, but we have never seen returns this low before. As investors and speculators run out of areas to park their capital, they will be forced into riskier assets or simply sit in cash while they wait out the storm.

Precious metals and cryptocurrencies, often considered as "anti-fiats," have seen tremendous growth this year as they begin their new, multi-year bull markets. The premiums for physical precious metals have never been higher than before. As their spot prices plummeted in March 2020, premiums soared, but spot prices have since skyrocketed. As with the inverted yield curve, this is a clear sign of an impending recession which began in the retail sector through what is now being dubbed as the "retail-apocalypse."

---

[14] https://deighan.com/wp-content/uploads/2019-3-28-inverted-yeild-curve.jpg

SECTION 5: THE RETAIL APOCOLYPSE

"This is a death spiral. Once a department store goes vacant, that tends to be contagious because all those middle-mall stores—the nail salons and the jewelry stores—they are all depending on the traffic coming from the bigger retail stores."

John M. Clapp, a professor at the University of Connecticut's Center for Real Estate

Across the U.S., small businesses boarded up their windows as if a hurricane was going to roll through the city. This hurricane was not a natural weather event but a social and economic one that had been ravaging the country. Even as some cities tried to reopen, the traffic was not the same as before.

First came COVID-19, then came the uncertainty, and now, the rioting and looting. It seems like small businesses cannot catch a break this year. The places once packed with customers a few months ago—places where we would walk with our friends and families—are now looking like ghost towns. The big box stores that have become staples in the communities are facing bankruptcy, unable to pay rent and other dues.

As the big names close shop for good, the small mom and pop shops which are heavily reliant upon the traffic from the big box stores are finding it harder to open each day. The landlords are left holding the bag as tenants are forced into delinquency, renegotiating lower lease rates and refusing to pay. The protests sweeping across the U.S. have been hijacked by criminals in some places, looking to take advantage of those already finding it hard to keep their doors open. Some of the most desired real estate locations have become the most targeted. Victims of the economy have become victims of opportunists. As people stay home, the general trend towards online shopping has left the brick and mortar stores in the dust. These locations have come to resemble photo opportunities, instead of business opportunities.

How can anyone expect a recovery when the consumer-based U.S. economy cannot even protect their retail stores? Even Amazon drivers have been the victim of targeted attacks, leading Amazon to force some of their drivers to stay home. The slow and ominous decay of the U.S. has never been as evident as it is in the retail sector.

According to a report published by Coresight Research in April 2019 by Josh Bivens, an economist at the Economic Policy Institute, a whopping record of 9,300 retail stores were closed across the U.S. in 2019. The massive amounts of retail store closings across North America had become known as "retail-apocalypse."

According to the report, 5,844 stores were closed in 2018 and 9,302 in 2019, a 59% increase[15]. Payless Shoe Source shut down 2,100 stores, Fred's 564, Ascena Retail 781, Gymboree 740, Sears 210, and Charlotte Russe 512. 12 businesses had at least 200 locations shut down in 2019: Gamestop, Gap, Foot Locker, Walgreens, Destination Maternity, GNC, Bed Bath & Beyond, Victoria's Secret, CVS, Big Lots, Office Depot, and Pier 1 Imports. Rent-a-Center, and Abercrombie & Fitch also saw dozens of their stores closed.

In contrast, Dollar General opened nearly 1,000 new stores locations, Dollar Tree 348, and Family Dollar, according to the report. We witnessed how the more expensive, big-name retail stores slowly and quietly closing while low-priced retail stores too their place. But this had been going on for a long time and was alluded to by the great success that budget chains have seen over the past decade (whereas traditional brands have floundered)[16].

As the economic foundation of the country started to crumble, Trump boasted, "This is the greatest economy that we've had in our history, the best." If this is what the "best" looks like, I am not sure how we can handle mediocre.

"Despite a very favorable consumer spending environment, department stores have yet to catch a break," analyst Christina Boni said in her research report, stating that she expected to see online sales rise sharply in the future.

So far, in 2020, approximately 47,000 stores were closed temporarily across the U.S., with 25,000 estimated to stay closed, with most retailers struggling or refusing to pay rent. Long before the COVID-19 pandemic, old fashioned U.S.

---

[15] https://cdn.statcdn.com/Infographic/images/normal/20519.jpeg
[16] https://cdn.statcdn.com/Infographic/images/normal/13550.jpeg

brick and mortar retail was suffering from wave after wave of bankruptcies and mounting debts. While many were blaming Walmart and Amazon for destroying local businesses, both sectors had been growing for quite a while in a trend, which would only increase with time.

Companies in a free market need to adapt to future requirements from the consumer instead of living in the past. Those who have become over-leveraged are seeing their cash flows dwindle and are left to rethink their future strategies in an ever-changing market. Some are forced to choose bankruptcy, while others have been renegotiating their leases, with many of them still looking to the government for help. All of these are short-term solutions that do not address the economy and the source of the issues at large.

While the number of businesses forced to close is quite staggering, as time goes on, less and less will be able, or willing, to reopen after this crisis is averted. When looking to areas of the world that have tried to return to normal, they do not see the types of revenues or traffic as before. Many people are apprehensive about returning their children to school, let alone rack up the credit cards. Most consumers are facing overhanging debt levels and starting to question their spending habits during the quarantine. Reports showed that consumers had increasingly been paying down personal debts due to the uncertain future. While others were only relying on government assistance, all the while thinking: *Why work when I can enjoy life for free?*

In a report issued by Coresight Research, the forecasts moving forward in 2020 were grim. It was predicted that 25,000 retailers could close after lockdowns destroyed traffic, collapsed store sales, and forced businesses into delinquency on lease payments. Quarantine measures had accelerated the general trend towards online shopping, as fears in public health rose.

CEO of Coresight Research, Deborah Weinswig, stated in the report that the most dangerous effect was the "anchor tenants," consisting of big box stores being forced to shutter. When these "anchor tenants" closed, it meant certain death for the rest of the small businesses heavily reliant upon the traffic that the big names bring. This was already occurring across the U.S., and it would coincide with her prediction for an additional 20,000 to 25,000 shops to close by the end of 2020.

She added, "Department and large apparel-chain store closures in malls will, therefore, create a ripple effect that spells bad news for malls." As the big names in retail came under pressure, they would be forced to make tough decisions, none of which were good. One good example was when Simon Property Group, one of the largest mall operators in the U.S., sued one of their clients, GAP, for failing to pay more than $65.9 million USD in rent. The knock-on effects these closures were having on commercial real estate had been alarming.

According to Commercial Real Estate Brokerage, "Commercial real estate's recovery will lag that of the broader economy. The industrial and multifamily sectors should be the most resilient and largely recover within one year, followed by the office sector within two years and the retail sector within three." But according to the latest figures, the delinquency rate logged in April and May of 2020 by Trepp CMBS had been the highest since the Great Recession. Unless the debts could be forgiven, then even if the crisis were to end tomorrow, businesses would still need to find a way to pay back their loans and lease payments.

As businesses struggle to stay afloat during this crisis and beyond, many have and will be forced to change how they do business. The retail industry is quickly undergoing a transformative stage where big companies are getting bigger and pushing out the smaller ones. As more consumers do online shopping, this will push the retail sector to change their business models for the future to gain competitive advantage. 2020 has brought the death of department stores while solidifying e-commerce in the economy.

As income inequality ravage the U.S., the top 1% has grown more prosperous despite this crisis. Larger companies have several advantages over smaller ones during an emergency for they have more cash reserves, access to capital, and can rely upon their branding. Some even have relationships with the government, like Tesla, which can help them get bailouts if needed. The restaurant industry is already scrambling to shift to delivery services, which may offer a lifeline to many, with specific sectors like pizza already positioned well.

At no time in the past has it been more important to have an online presence. Initiatives like this have been supported by many jurisdictions offering bylaws to allow alcoholic drinks in deliveries or in places trying to open for service, quick and easy approvals, and funding for patios to enable social distancing. Since the start of this crisis, online shopping has gone from a recreational pastime to an obsession, with groceries being delivered, with no signs of slowing anytime soon. Online orders for Walmart and Amazon have skyrocketed, and thanks to their well-established delivery systems, they have been able to take advantage of this. An analyst from the Wall Street firm UBS noted that online shares of total retail sales had increased from 15% to 20% in recent weeks, representing a decade of change in just a few weeks.

One of the foundations of the American dream has been the small mom and pop shops. They are the backbone of the economy and provided valuable income for those at the lower end of the socio-economic scale. In parallel, without foreign investment, it is hard for a nation to develop; and without localized business investment, it is hard for a modern society to survive.

While many analysts consider these numbers as "just" figures, we need to remember how many lives are affected by each closing. How many jobs are being lost because businesses are just not profitable anymore? Where is recovery supposed to come from if only a few monopolies like Amazon and Walmart survive? With how these large corporations moving towards automation to reduce their costs of labor, how will people be able to afford to pay rent and mortgage payments considering the financial insecurity?

As we have seen by the rise of budget stores, the U.S.'s general population is facing more difficulties each day. In the decade since the Great Recession of 2008, cities within the U.S. have become more expensive at levels unaffordable to most Americans. As the general population tries to keep up with the bills, they have gone deeper into debt which is compounded by growing income inequality across the globe. Rents have soared in major cities and small businesses have been slowly pushed out of the market—a situation which is being accelerated under the current crisis. As the economic crisis begin to unfold, companies like Amazon and Walmart will see their business skyrocket while smaller companies close shops.

The retail industry will continue to collapse until the economic inequality is addressed, or until only a handful of monopolies are left standing. The economic stability of the U.S. and much of the developed world is collapsing with the death of the middle class. The divide economically has never been greater, and this is spilling over to the political realm. A war has been waged for decades against the middle class, and to understand it, we need to begin with income inequality.

SECTION 6: INCOME INEQUALITY

"An imbalance between rich and poor is the oldest and most fatal ailment of all republics."

Plutarch, Ancient Greek biographer

The U.S. is the land of economic opportunity, but it is also the land of consumption and "spend everything you've got." We do not have to look far to find out that Americans are generally poor savers. In a survey of more than 5,000 Americans by GoBankingRates in 2019, they found that 62% of Americans had less than $1,000 in savings. Later, they asked 7,052 people and found nearly 7 in 10 Americans or 69% had less than $1,000 USD in savings, including 34% who had $0 dollars saved for a rainy day. Of the remaining in the survey, only 11% had between $1,000 USD and $4,999 USD, 4% had between $5,000 USD and $9,9999 USD, while only 15% had more than $10,000 USD. These numbers were backed up by figures from Lendingtree, America's largest online lending marketplace, which found that 50% of Americans could not cover a $1,000 USD emergency, while 33% were still in debt from a previous emergency amounting to $1,000 USD or more.

If these numbers were remotely accurate, there would be over 108 million people in the U.S. with no income before COVID-19 arrived in the U.S., not to mention the longest stock market bull run in U.S. history. It was becoming obvious that the only growth seen over the last decade had not helped the average American, and what we had seen since the last financial crisis was an increase in the wealth gap across the developed world.

Ask those around you for their sentiment: Have things been getting easier or harder for them in recent years? Generally, those outside few key industries like the real estate and the financial market, as well as others like the medical field have not experienced the boom in growth as depicted in the official figures.

For most Americans, the economic situation declined for a decade due to a fundamentally broken system. According to the U.S. Census Bureau, in September 2015, 47 million Americans were found to fall below the poverty line, with a medium household income of less than $24,000 a year. Another data from the World Inequality Database showed that the bottom 50% of U.S. citizens saw a decline in income distribution over the past years while the top 1% saw an increase.

As Americans and the developed world suffer from more significant disparities in income inequality, we see little being done to curb the trend[17]. No doubt, these effects were felt in the increasing polarization of the American political sphere, with younger people shifting "ultra-left" and the older generation becoming "ultra-conservative."

Courtesy of Michael Snyder, published author and owner of the Economic Collapse Blog, we have the following information:

1) The U.S. Census Bureau says that nearly 47 million Americans are living in poverty right now.

2) Other numbers from the U.S. Census Bureau are also very disturbing. For example, in 2007 about one 1 of every 8 children in America was on food stamps. Today, that number is 1 out of every 5.

3) According to Kathryn J. Edin and H. Luke Shaefer, the authors of a new book entitled *$2.00 a Day: Living on Almost Nothing in America*, there are 1.5 million "ultra-poor" households in the United States that live on less than $2 dollars a day. That number has doubled since 1996.

4) 46 million Americans use food banks each year, and lines start forming at some U.S. food banks as early as 6:30 in the morning because people want to get something before the food supplies run out.

5) The number of homeless children in the U.S. has increased by 60% over the past 6 years.

6) According to Poverty USA, 1.6 million American children slept in a homeless shelter or some other form of emergency housing last year.

7) Police in New York City have identified 80 separate homeless

---

17 https://www.motherjones.com/wp-content/uploads/2018/06/blog_wid2018_top_10_percent_europe_us.jpg

encampments in the city, and the homeless crisis there has gotten so bad that it is being described as an "epidemic."

8) If you can believe it, more than half of all students in our public schools are poor enough to qualify for school lunch subsidies.

9) According to a Census Bureau report that was released a while back, 65% of all children in the U.S. are living in a home that receives some form of aid from the federal government.

10) According to a report that was published by UNICEF, almost one-third of all children in this country "live in households with an income below 60% of the national median income."

11) When it comes to child poverty, the United States ranks 36th out of the 41 "wealthy nations" that UNICEF looked at.

12) The number of Americans that are living in concentrated areas of high poverty has doubled since the year 2000.

13) An astounding 45% of all African American children in the United States live in areas of "concentrated poverty."

14) 40.9% of all children in the United States that are being raised by a single parent are living in poverty.

15) An astounding 48.8% of all 25-year-old Americans still live at home with their parents.

16) There are simply not enough good jobs to go around anymore. It may be hard to believe, but 51% of all American workers make less than $30,000 a year.

17) There are 7.9 million working age Americans that are "officially unemployed" right now and another 94.7 million working age Americans that are considered to be "not in the labor force." When you add those 2 numbers together, you get a grand total of 102.6 million working age Americans that do not have a job right now.

18) Owning a home has traditionally been a signal that you belong to the middle class. That is why it is so alarming that the rate of homeownership in the United States has been falling for eight years in a row.

19) According to a recent Pew survey, approximately 70% of all Americans believe that "debt is a necessity in their lives".

20) At this point, 25% of all Americans have a negative net worth. That means that the value of what they owe is greater than the value of everything that they own.

21) The top 0.1% of all American families have about as much wealth as the bottom 90% of all American families combined.

"If we truly are the greatest nation on the planet,' then why can't we even take care of our own people?" Michael Snyder said on May 7, 2020.

One area that has seen a massive growth over the last decade is the government sector, with "the greatest nation on the planet" becoming the greatest government leeches, sucking hundreds of billions out of the economy each quarter. According to a U.S. Treasury Department statement in 2019, the federal deficit hit $984 billion USD while revenues measured $3.46 trillion USD, with spending at $4.45 trillion USD. Never mind that these numbers did not precisely correlate with one another; that were just the processing fee. Unless the government downsized or reduced its foreign commitments and illegal wars, then balancing the budget would be a thing of the past. While the talking heads on TV and the political class debated about how to drive an economic turnaround in the U.S., they were actively doing everything possible to reduce that outcome instead.

According to the Keynesian economic theory, it is possible to spend your way into economic growth if the cause is a lack of demand or people are saving too much money. But this is not possible, when the market needs a correction, to fix the imbalances of the market and government, in a neoclassical business cycle theory approach. With the free market becoming diluted with socialist infections, it is unable to heal itself, especially when it is being weighed down by increasing burdens to satisfy the popular vote. Instead, we have been sold an illusion of a recovery since 2008 while special interest groups have used this time to siphon off trillions in revenues.

As they say, do not listen to what is being said. Follow the money instead. The narrative can easily be framed to suit the needs of the creator, while economic data can be twisted with double-speak effectiveness to create an illusion of economic recovery. If there has been a recovery, then where is all the wealth? It is undoubtedly not in most people's bank accounts.

In a report issued by Josh Bivens of the Economic Policy Institute in April 2019, we saw that the U.S. was poorly prepared for the next recession. While many people would automatically think this was due to high public debt and too-low interest rates, he stated that it was due to the inability to reduce inequality during the last economic expansion and increases in poorly managed public spending. While everyone was quick to jump on the Fed when it came to handling recessions, they were not able to fight them alone and their actions at best, were a reactionary measure instead of a proactive one.

He predicted that the U.S. would enter a recession within the next 18 months and, with the debt-to-GDP ratio so high, policymakers would be resistant to increase public spending when it was needed most. To stimulate what blood was left to be squeezed from the rock called the U.S. economy, the Fed had slashed interest rates to zero, with calls to go negative.

However, as history has shown, negative interest rates are not effective, and luckily, they are being resisted by the Fed. Biven has asserted that the Trump Administration has not proved smart or agile enough when it comes to macroeconomic management. Notably, the attempts to dismantle the financial system constraints put in place following the Great Recession of 2008, which is a threat to future macroeconomic stability. Inflation rates have been set too low to last and need to be increased in the future. He said that one of the essential lessons from the Great Recession of 2008 is that monetary policy can only lay the groundwork for fiscal policy. Still, it can only be relied upon as a supporting role for recovery, as there will not be anyone to save us if all the ships are sinking.

SECTION 7: THE CANADIAN ECONOMY

"Canada is in the midst of an historic economic contraction. The economy has largely shut down, paralyzed by measures to contain the coronavirus pandemic, free-falling financial markets, plunging oil prices, and plummeting confidence."

Tony Stillo, Director of Canadian Economics at Oxford Economics

When it came to Canada, the United States' largest trading partner, TD Bank's Economics division released a report forecasting 1.7% growth in 2020. They believed Canada, which escaped much of the last financial crisis along with Australia due to foreign investment, was on the verge of a recession. Growth was weak going into the end of 2019 but unusual weather, rail blockades, and other disputes before the pandemic hit had been causing harmful effects. As a major oil producer, especially in Alberta, they would be faced with hard times ahead. Canada was getting crushed from the collapse in oil revenues and, coupled with the knock-on effects of the coronavirus, their energy sector accounted for 10% of GDP. Since then, they updated their forecast for Canada to predict a 6.5% decrease in GDP for 2020. According to a report by Maclean's, Canada's economy had never been more dependent on household spending[18].

It was easy to see that readily available debt had fueled this consumption, even going beyond that of the U.S. Canadian households owed $2.16 trillion CAD in mortgage, credit card, and other consumer debts, representing an 80% increase since 2008. This amount was over the $1.74 trillion CAD the Canadian government spent in their economy in 2019. The Canada Mortgage and Housing Corporation (CMHC) expected average home prices in the country to decline as much as 18% in the next 12 months.

"Looking at debt multiples of disposable income, that measure will climb from 176% in late 2019 to well over 200% through 2021," Evan Siddall, Chief Executive Officer of CMHC, told a parliamentary committee in May 2020.

---

[18] https://www.macleans.ca/wp-content/uploads/2019/01/REAL_ESTATE_CHART0.jpg

"CMHC is now forecasting a decline in average house prices of 9–18% in the coming 12 months. The resulting combination of higher mortgage debt, declining house prices, and increased unemployment is cause for concern for Canada's longer-term financial stability."

Canadians' ratio of gross debt to GDP was already at elevated levels of 99% before COVID-19 struck earlier this year. That number was expected to climb to 130% by the third quarter of 2020 before declining, according to CMHC estimates. Siddall said that his agency was working to help manage a growing debt "deferral cliff" that loomed in the fall when the unemployed people would need to start paying their mortgages again. "As much as one-fifth of all mortgages could be in arrears if our economy has not recovered sufficiently."

In the hospitality and service sectors, which play a significant role in the Canadian economy, we have seen jobs evaporate overnight with no idea when or how strong they will return. Major cities have tried soft openings of businesses, only to close again. Still, even other occupations have not been immune to the situation.

In April 2020, Prime Minister Justin Trudeau announced the worst job loss figures in modern history and was expected to continue to rise. Since housing sales are a lagging indicator, it will not be until 2021 before we can begin to see the effects on the housing market which Canada relies upon; we can, however, expect it to be grim.

Simeon Siegel, an analyst at BMO Capital Markets, stated, "Even when companies are given the all-clear, we don't yet know when consumers are going to embrace that." Many people are likely to avoid large crowds, and significant events will likely be restricted until a vaccine is distributed, leaving many businesses to liquidate and disappear.

According to a survey done by the Canadian Federation of Independent Businesses, 55 % of small businesses needed government help to pay their June 2020 rent. Of the 6,000 companies it surveyed across Canada, half saw a 70% decline in revenues. The Canadian government had offered the Canada Emergency Commercial Rent Assistance program, but it had been criticized for not providing enough relief and was challenging to get approved. While some places had begun opening for business, as much as half were saying they could not afford to do so, or had already chosen to close for good, such as the large company Army & Navy.

As the Canadian economy begins to feel the effects of an over-inflated housing market and unmaintainable levels of debt, the results of COVID-19 are just starting to take shape. Canada's largest trading partner, the U.S., has been racked with crisis after crisis, with no easy solutions or end in sight.

While the world's developing economies are in a much more flexible position, developed nations have few options. The Canadian economy is too reliant upon energy sales, U.S. trades, and the housing market, all of which are overdue for corrections. In the coming months and into next year, delinquencies and bankruptcies will begin to rise, affecting the rest of the economy. The retail and service sectors have been hammered: first by lockdowns, then by restrictions, next by riots, before finally coming to uncertainty.

If there is one thing that can turn a credit application from good to bad, it is uncertainty. Canada will be in for a bumpy ride ahead as lenders restrict access to credit and tighten restrictions. When the stimulus checks stop rolling in and most businesses are unable to reopen, it will only lead to more requests for government intervention. We are seeing this with extensions to the Canadian Economic Relief Benefit and the transition to a new program. However, if there is one thing this economy needs, it is less government intervention.

SECTION 8: THE ASIAN ECONOMIES

"It says something about this new global economy that USA Today now reports every morning on the day's events in Asian markets."

Lawrence Summers, American economist, and advisor for the World Bank

In Southeast Asia, according to the Center for Strategic & International Studies (CSIS), the economies had been dramatically hit since the global pandemic began and the economic effects were expected to be at least on par with the 1997-1998 Asian Financial Crisis. While the economies of the Association of Southeast Asian Nations (ASEAN) were in much better macroeconomic states and had much larger foreign exchange reserves, the impact of the COVID-19 pandemic would be longer-lasting and felt in the much deeper aspects of society.

Currently, concerns that this virus may mutate or come back in waves (possibly like the seasonal flu), with risks of further quarantines and lockdowns in the future, are prevalent. We have seen the virus change but not fundamentally, while some areas are experiencing second summer waves. At the very least, according to the International Monetary Fund's (IMF) World Economic Outlook, sharp declines in regional growth and supply chain shocks were to be expected. The IMF projected the ASEAN-5's (Indonesia, Malaysia, Philippines, Thailand, and Vietnam) growth to be at -0.6% in 2020, a down from its earlier forecast of +4.8%.

The World Bank report, which was released at the beginning of April 2020, included a more pessimistic scenario, with the estimates projecting contractions of the major developing ASEAN countries in the -0.5% to -5.0% range, except for Vietnam which might maintain a positive (+1.5%) growth. Many private forecasts were even more pessimistic, with expectations of contractions in GDP across the board, in the range of -1.5% for 2020.

While the IMF predicted a strong rebound for ASEAN economies in 2021, The World Bank was not so optimistic. With questions looming of a potential resurgence of the virus, trade wars, protectionism, shifting of supply chains from one country to another, all of these were not conducive to doing business. CSIS had put forward 4 primary areas of concern for the economies of Southeast Asia.

First, ASEAN countries were highly exposed to and reliant upon trade, investment, and tourism—all 3 industries might never see a "return to normal." Increased levels of globalization had harmed these economies the most, as they were often specialized in exporting goods such as palm oil and mining in Indonesia, manufactured components from Malaysia, Vietnam and the Philippines, or textiles from Cambodia. Thailand relied heavily upon tourism which makes up one-fifth of their GDP and brought in much needed foreign reserves. Other tourism-dependent economies such as Indonesia, Malaysia, Vietnam, Singapore, and the Philippines had faced the double whammy of the U.S.-China trade conflict of 2019. The trade war reduced the demand for goods and services while their trade and tourism sectors declined.

Usually, ASEAN economies could turn to their various trade and investment partners such as the U.S., European Union (EU), and China for business. However, in a global pandemic, all these partners were in the same situations. For the first 3 quarters of 2020, China was expected to have 1% growth, the U.S. -6%, EU -7% to -8%, and Japan at -4%. While the near term is bleak, a positive future is projected for the ASEAN[19].

Second, the collapse in oil prices had caused an unexpected and sudden drop in energy consumption due to widespread lockdowns and travel restrictions. Oil and coal exports played a significant role in Indonesia's economy, making up one-quarter of total exports, while 90% of Brunei's economy relied on crude and natural gas exports. In contrast, oil and gas made up 16% of Malaysia's exports.

Third, with the full range of public health measures taken in various countries to protect against the spread of the virus, this had created an enormous impact upon consumption, which represented 60% of GDP for ASEAN economies.

---

[19] https://csis-prod.s3.amazonaws.com/s3fs-public/SEAsia_Table_v3_0jpg?VFmxwZUy7_pseuTj1SUZiGkME0rYirKo

The only exception to this would be Singapore.

Gareth Leather, a senior economist in the Emerging Asia team at Capital Economics, stated, "With exports collapsing and countries across the region implementing draconian restrictions on travel and commerce, economic activity in Emerging Asia will contract sharply this year. Parts of Southeast Asia and Hong Kong are likely to be the worst affected economies. Even if the virus is eventually brought under control, weak demand and impaired balance sheets mean recoveries will be gradual. Most economies are unlikely to regain their pre-crisis level of output until the middle of next year and will still be 2-4% smaller at the end of 2022 than if the crisis hadn't happened." While Leather mentioned some of the more developed economies explicitly, recent data showed that Asia's developing economies are in a much healthier place.

And finally, the COVID-19 crisis had a massive effect upon capital outflows, with investors driving large capital outflows from ASEAN economies as they seek safer places to park their money. According to the Institute of International Finance, over $100 billion USD had been drained from these economies so far in 2020, which caused for the depreciation of the Indonesian rupiah (+14%), Thai baht (+4%), Malaysian ringgit (+4%), and the Singaporean dollar (+4%). Central banks had been pressured to use dwindling foreign exchange reserves to shore up their currencies in the hope of an end to the crisis soon.

While the future is difficult to predict, this crisis will likely reshape the region's economies, if not the world. There are issues of national security coming into question regarding the production of pharmaceutical ingredients and medical supplies, which will inevitably alter the supply chains. Some countries like India and Vietnam have sectors greatly benefited from the trade war between China and the U.S., which has prompted the relocation of supply chains; but this has been rejected by many firms as it is costly and time-consuming. The compounding effects of the U.S.-China trade war and the global slowdown have mixed results for Asian nations.

While the effects of COVID-19 will be profound across Asia, thanks to the Belt and Road and other infrastructure and trade initiatives, Asia is ideally situated to recover quickly. As the main driver of growth and business over the past decade, Asian economies seek greater integration while the U.S. pushes for isolation. Countries that would typically be on the U.S. side are starting to lean toward Eurasia's.

As the trade war worsens and the U.S. becomes plagued with internal issues, Asia will continue to develop more integration which will drive more capital into different areas (economy, government projects, business, education, etc.) and see more prosperity and growth. As we will see a little further in this book, Westerners used to produce products to sell to Asia, but more recently, Asia has been making products for the West. Still, in the future, the West will once again look to Asia for business.

The reemergence of Asia as a key player in the world is among the most significant movements that will happen during our lives. One year from now, in purchasing power parity (PPP) terms, Asian economies will be larger than the remainder of the world combined for the first time since the 19th century. Not only is Asia growing richer; it is also coalescing as a constructive force for global governance the more integrated it becomes.

This emergence is timely. From climate change and demographic crises to technological disruption and yawning inequality, the world faces myriad challenges that require multilateral solutions. However, a lack of global leadership and consensus has stalled the reforms of global institutions, leaving severe governance deficits.

While Asia has profited tremendously from globalization, it additionally embodies a significant number of the world's issues. Luckily, there are developing signs that this lively, differing mainland can cooperate and ascend to offer a portion of the arrangements. If this is to be the Asian Century, it will be built by Asians working closely together on their continent. Despite Asia's striking ascent, its group of countries is regularly kept separated by troublesome geology and much more troublesome history. Luckily, as the shared advantages of participation become perpetually obvious, endeavors to conquer these boundaries and extend local reconciliation have picked up energy.

This is clear in the recovery of China's associations with India, Japan, and South Korea, just as the reboot of the China-Japan-ROK. Furthermore, provincial collaboration stages are increasing through the actions of the ASEAN, Asia-Pacific Economic Cooperation and Shanghai Cooperation Organization.

Asia is also bucking the global trend for trade fragmentation, becoming instead even more economically integrated via trade, investment, and tourism. Previously, this happened from the grassroots up without an overarching regional free trade agreement of the sort that spurred integration in Europe and North America.

Presently, Asia is at the core of the activity for multilateral exchange advancement. Surrendered by the U.S., the changed Trans-Pacific Partnership (TPP), otherwise called the Comprehensive and Progressive Agreement for Trans-Pacific Partnership (CPTPP), has been restored under the Asian initiative and came into power towards the beginning of 2020. Talks are additionally advancing towards the Regional Comprehensive Economic Partnership (RCEP). These living arrangements will proceed to develop and will probably pull in new players, offering an adaptable, multi-track way to financial reconciliation in Asia. For instance, the more thorough CPTPP can assist with setting principles for future exchange for cutting edge economies while the less-requesting RCEP will offer a path for creating nations to partake in streamlined commerce.

Knitting together infrastructure initiatives, trade pacts, and other groupings will boost pan-Asian coordination on connectivity and trade liberalization. In turn, this can help fuel a virtuous cycle of mutual gain and closer integration. A more integrated Asian community, one that brings together developed and developing countries and various economic systems, can also provide the momentum and modalities to reinvigorate multilateralism at the global level. Solutions that have been adapted to Asia's diverse conditions may well prove to be useful templates for the rest of the world.

Lying at the core of the territorial economy, China will without a doubt assume a focal function in the Asian Century. Notwithstanding, it is likewise a developing, multipolar century, one in which no single force can singularly direct standards and rules. China's worldwide methodology is solidly tied down to this reality, alongside the acknowledgment that multilateralism is the best way to address our transnational difficulties and continue an open, comprehensive worldwide economy.

As such, rather than a hegemon or revisionist power, China's role in Asia and the world will be to uphold the international order while offering innovative solutions to global governance, in line with its responsibility as a major global player. A key part of this role is to act as a catalyst for integration in Asia and beyond. Financially, China will remain the motor of development for Asia and the world. Its commitment to worldwide development will ascend to over 28% by 2023, as indicated by IMF projections. Notwithstanding, the idea of China's financial job will advance alongside homegrown rebalancing. In PPP terms, China's GDP has since quite a while ago exceeded that of the U.S.'s.

In the past period of globalization, Chinese fares drove worldwide exchange as an unfamiliar venture came in to help modernize the economy. In globalization 4.0, Chinese imports will assume an ever-bigger part as Chinese multinationals contribute across Asia and the world. From now until 2030, China's consumption growth is expected to exceed that of the U.S. and Western Europe's combined.

China-driven flows of goods, expertise, and capital will create opportunities for local communities and producers and help bring the Fourth Industrial Revolution to all corners of Asia. This links to China's role in the "systems upgrade" necessary to support deeper integration in Asia. The region still faces major infrastructure gaps that are impeding development and integration. The Belt and Road Initiative (BRI) offers an ideal vehicle to conquer these holes, acting like a venture capital fund to provide seed money and draw in additional resources for promising projects.

An ongoing report by the World Bank assesses that if completely actualized, BRI transport ventures can expand exchange somewhere in the range of 1.7% and 6.2% for the world, expanding worldwide genuine salary by 0.7% to 2.9% and assisting with lifting 7.6 million individuals from extreme poverty in the process. To genuinely satisfy its latent capacity, over the coming years, the BRI will move towards a more multilateral methodology. This will permit the activity to more likely pool assets, skill, and points of view from a differing scope of partners.

The Asian Infrastructure Investment Bank (AIIB), built up in 2015 and now posting very nearly 100 individuals, is a great representation of how the BRI can be multi-lateralized. Advancing the AIIB model and participation with other multilateral foundations can assist with tending to worries about the BRI being too Sinocentric and connect more members as significant partners.

For all its guarantees, the continued development of Asia in this century is not destined. The pioneers of China and its neighbors will face numerous dangers and difficulties en route. One of the loudest voices is coming from the U.S., since the past decade has seen Asian nations outclass their Western counterparts. So far, the current political crusade against China, Russia, Iran, and others in Asia has received mixed reviews. Many traditional U.S. allies wish to break their dependence upon the U.S. However, the unwavering position taken by the U.S. is forcing nations and companies into one of two camps. They are forced to choose between a waning superpower and a rising one. As the U.S. influence declines, the leaders of today and tomorrow can help ensure that the Asian Century brings fruits not only for Asians but for people around the world.

SECTION 9: EUROPE & WORLD ECONOMIES

Exactly when or how rapidly governments ought to unshackle their economies involves a serious discussion but has so far only promoted division. A few governments in Asia and Europe that think they have contained the infection or passed the peak have started to revive their economies gradually. More than 12 U.S. states have been reducing limitations, with President Trump not renewing government social-separating rules which ended on April 30, 2020.

Be that as it may, new episodes have just made a few nations reimpose restrictions. Many experts believed that coronavirus pandemic could be more economically destructive than any other outbreak and recovery would take a much longer time. In China, after only a little while of government-forced lockdowns on many urban communities, steep decreases in plant yield, local business, development, and other monetary movement was witnessed. GDP plunged nearly 7% in the first quarter, which was China's first monetary withdrawal in over 40 years.

Over in Europe, the picture was not much brighter. The German economy was expected to wither to levels not seen since 2009, somewhere in the range of 3% to 10% in 2020. Germany had the largest national economy in Europe, the fourth largest by nominal GDP in the world, and accounted for 28% of the Eurozone economy in 2017, according to the International Monetary Fund (IMF). The administration itself estimated a decrease of a little more than 6%, which would be the nation's worst economic decline in decades. In March 2020, about a half-million German organizations applied to have their representatives join a momentary government work program expected to forestall mass cutbacks.

Ciaran McGrath posted on May 19, 2020 in the U.K. paper Express, Italy, which already had a weak economy, should not rely on Germany to bail them out. Hans-Olaf Henkel, a former German Member of European Parliament (MEP) and economist, stated that Italy should look towards its wealthy citizens, rather than look to Germany. He added that "the best solution would be for Italy to leave the Eurozone and go back to their own currency, which he dubbed the 'new lira'". This essentially forced the Italians out of the European Union (EU).

The EU had passed a €500-billion EUR bundle to give crisis loaning and other help to nations, organizations, and laborers. Christine Lagarde, leader of the European Central Bank (ECB), guaranteed there would be "no restrictions" on the ECB's guard of the Eurozone. The bank was set to purchase €750 billion EUR in new bonds this year to help its individuals during the downturn. The IMF also put aside $100 billion USD to loan to nations that were confronting extreme monetary emergencies due to the coronavirus, with priority given to developing economies.

By early April 2020, more than 90 countries had mentioned bailouts. World Bank President David Malpass said the bank had submitted more than $150 billion USD to counter the pandemic's effects. More than 2-dozen infection-related advance solicitations had been optimized, with a lot more in the pipeline. India had received the most significant credit at $1 billion USD.

Developing economies throughout the world have been particularly hard hit, such as India and Pakistan. For instance, the Pakistan economy got caught in a vicious blow, resulting to an incomprehensible economic emergency that they had to request for another bailout from the IMF. During each significant financial emergency in Pakistan, the wheels of the casual economy chug along. Today, the casual segment stands to lose the most, especially the massive number of day-laborers, as they depend on this money to give them the absolute minimum pay required to meet their day-to-day needs. When you must go to work to be able to eat, what do you do when you cannot work?

The British, who were some of the last in Europe to announce quarantine, and admit there is a pandemic, are the worst-hit European nation. The pandemic is incapacitating the British economy; meanwhile, its pioneers are arranging a post-Brexit relationship with the EU. Before the current episode, there were worries about a downturn from a supposed hard Brexit. Business analysts stated that the coronavirus pandemic could take a 5% to 10% cut out of the economy in 2020.

But Japan may have it even worse. Financial experts anticipated that Japan's economy would recoil by around 3% in 2020, which would be its most devastating performance since 2008. The profound effect of the pandemic has been coupled with a zombification of the economy. The central banks have been propping up the stock market by purchasing assets that should have been left to free market devices for years. The pandemic also forced the cancelation of the Summer Olympics. If Japan were to lose the Olympic games, it would mean all the money invested would have been for nothing. Currently, there are rumors that Japan will proceed with the games in 2021, regardless of the pandemic.

While the EU's top diplomat, Josep Borrell, was forced to publicly declare to the U.S. that "we are not foes," the U.S. is becoming isolated on the world stage fast. As central banks struggle to keep liquidity in the global markets, nations are trying to reopen their economies, some more successful than others. COVID-19 has been a shock to the global economic system, giving many countries a clear wake-up call. While developing nations have been the hardest hit, they are in the best position to come out of this crisis more durable than before.

Across Eurasia and Africa, new independence and economic systems have begun to sprout up, giving us a glimpse into the future. The new world order is starting to take shape. This crisis provides the perfect backdrop for a shift away from the old and into the new. From London to Tokyo and Moscow to Sydney, the railways, roads, and trade routes being built today are the paths by which tomorrow's fortunes will flow. We are witnessing the remodeling of what it means to be modern, with the Eurasian continent reaping the benefits for becoming the ideal of true democratization that will be sweeping the world.

As we shift from a unipolar to a multipolar world, businesses, with emphasis on future transactions will be forced to adapt. Nations around the world are growing more confident in themselves and what they want for their futures. The age of American exceptionalism is coming to an end.

SECTION 10: THE HOUSING MARKET

Facing a tidal wave of insolvency, the U.S. housing market is barely staying afloat. According to a recent report, the Fed, and its money printer, came to the rescue with $1 trillion USD in liquidity to be injected into U.S. mortgage in real estate markets. Even though it may sound encouraging for investors, the effects of this stimulus are likely to turn out badly for the economy, and in the long run, it will only serve as one more needle that will press the U.S. debt bubble to burst and splatter blood all over the economy.

The effects of the unprecedented crisis we are living in are leaving scars in each one of the sectors of the U.S. economy. High unemployment rates with over 60 million jobless claims have been registered, but it is suspected the real numbers are even scarier than that. Due to the lockdowns, many businesses were compromised and either had their activities suspended or had to open their stores for the flies to sit on causing many families to struggle in paying their rent or mortgage. Ultimately that created major insolvency in business rental payment leading some of them to bankruptcy and others to massive debts. Thereby, with missed rental payments and mortgage defaults piling up like never before, amid the looming real estate chaos, the Centers for Disease Control and Prevention (CDC) enacted public health emergency powers to impede landlords across the country from evicting tenants.

The amount of mortgage bonds the Federal had been purchasing since March stacked up to $1 trillion USD, capturing 30% of the country's outstanding mortgage bonds. The winter will be shortly coming and will bring with it many more challenges for the Americans to handle, mostly due to the government decrees to shut down more than 60% of the nation's businesses and the lockdown mandates giving them no choice of reinsertion into the job market.

Now, unwilling to continue to assist its citizens with unemployment checks, it is safe to say that the abrupt and ill-thought-through shutdowns were one of the least efficient government moves, on the assumption that it supposedly had the intention to support its economy and the population. What happened because of that was the complete opposite. Instead of developing ways to keep things on track safely, the government just left these businesses to die and people to lose their jobs so it could justify their decision of feeding the financial markets continuously.

That was when the Fed stepped in and attempted to salvage the country by saving the rich and leaving the rest in a free fall. Our leaders had let the economy fail in so many segments so far just to keep finding excuses to boost the financial markets. The same is true for the real estate sector. The real economy is not based on delusional Wall Street forecasts or on wealthy investors who believe everything is going to be just fine just because they are profiting from this catastrophic crisis and they will probably be the only ones who will be safe and sound when hell breaks loose.

While the stock market stays resilient through ups and downs, millions of Americans are struggling to pay rent because of the U.S. government's harsh lockdown tactics. Many of them cannot afford rent at all because it has been impossible to make ends meet with all the overwhelming impacts of this multifaceted crisis. Country homeowners and rental tenants are facing meltdown across the country and the signs are showing in several hard-hit states.

The obstruction in the economic activity, as a consequence of a lack of practical measures to manage the health outbreak-induced shutdowns had caused the neutering of 60% of the U.S. economy and causing serious distress for many renters and homeowners nationwide, especially those living in many major cities like New York and San Francisco. The real estate market is in pure agony as rents plunged to all-time lows. For instance, San Francisco is seeing rents drop tremendously to levels not seen over the past 6 years. Meanwhile, several reports have been shifting their attention to the affliction of international investors who invested in U.S. real estate before the beginning of the crisis that are now left holding the bag.

The Fed is trying to keep the real estate market afloat, so it is doing whatever it takes to make it look good and appealing for investors to keep coming. Since March, the Fed has dropped $1 trillion USD into the mortgage bond system. Although some analysts had defended that the stimulus had helped some homeowners with their refinancing, the Fed's balance sheet of U.S. properties also allowed the central bank to have a dishonest advantage when it came to set lending rates.

Recently, a Bloomberg report had shown that the Fed was on a mortgage buying spree with no end in sight, capturing around 30% of outstanding agency mortgage bonds to date. The Fed bought around $300 billion USD of bonds in March and April, respectively, and had been buying out about a hundred billion dollars a month since then. It now owned almost a third of bonds backed by home loans in the U.S. As a result, it had lowered mortgage rates with the average 30-year rate falling to 2.91% as of September from its 3.3% in early February.

According to Bloomberg, on one hand, that decline had made it possible for homeowners to refinance their mortgages, which basically was the same as giving them a raise by counting their monthly loan payments, as well as some consumers to buy homes which seemed very generous and unusual for their part. This was where those tricky factors lied because on the other hand, the central bank's efforts were making its balance sheet balloon; and by owning so many U.S. home loans, they gained an abnormally high power over selling mortgage rates. In simple terms, they could set the rates accordingly to their will.

Keep in mind that the money they used to purchase these real estate holdings was printed out of thin air, and inflation is not something an economy can hide from forever. As the central bank leverages massive purchases of outstanding mortgage bonds and the CDC's latest emergency powers emerge, it is hard not to envision the U.S. real estate market as a house of cards getting ready to collapse.

As one thing or another begins to crumble in the wake of this pandemic, we see mismanagement, bipartisan politics, and bureaucratic red tape leading to what could be the "largest real estate crash" consumers will see in their lifetimes. The worst housing-bubble the world has ever seen is well underway in the U.S., Canada, Australia, and many other nations that have only been kept afloat thanks to foreign investments.

This housing crisis will make what happened in 2008 look like the pre-game warmup. Not only has nothing been done to fix the issues, but governments have encouraged growth with no liabilities since those inflating the bubble will be bailed out. Political institutions in agreement with financial institutions have done little outside of encouraging consumer spending, overleverage of the population, cheap corporate debt, and virtually "free money"—all of which equates to the perfect recipe for collapse. In recent years, younger generations have found it increasingly difficult to become homeowners as, when you factor inflation, wages have decreased versus assets since going off the gold standard in 1971.

All of these in a bid to resist the potent effects a recession will have on the economy and to promote an ever-increasing GDP. While government and financial policymakers have managed to kick the proverbial can down the road, it will only mean that a typical 2- to 3-year recession can quickly turn into a decade or more depression.

Unemployment has been shattering records across nations as people are forced to stay at home since the first half of 2020. Businesses such as those in the food industry have tried to remain open by converting to take-out only models are not seeing revenues or government support to stay profitable. Hundreds of millions of workers worldwide have found themselves out of work, with no idea when they can resume an income.

In developing nations such as India and Pakistan, this has an especially harsh effect upon migrant workers. However, even in the developed countries of North America and Europe, they are not immune to the plight of migrant workers. Travel restrictions have seen those who usually work in the agricultural industries, stuck at home, unable to go where they are needed. Overnight, service sector jobs were wiped out with many restaurants and bars unable to open and would be unable to reopen. If they did manage to do so, they could lose potential earnings to enforce social distancing.

While many banks and landlords have been giving mortgage and rent deferrals, these are only temporary solutions to be dealt with after the crisis. Those able to work from home are not sure if they can or will return to their respective workplace after the disaster, while others have been given a choice to be laid off and look for government assistance. Unemployment assistance has been skyrocketing, with governments looking to stimulus checks to soften the impact. All these things can be summed up in one simple word: insecurity—the one thing that creditors hate the most. There is nothing worse than job insecurity if you have outstanding loans or need to be refinanced on a mortgage or car loan.

According to Jesse Columbo, an economic analyst for Forbes Magazine, we are in the "U.S. Housing Bubble 2.0" which was formed from the Fed's zero-interest-rate policy and quantitative easing[20]. The Great Recession of 2008 was caused by the bursting of the housing market bubble, causing significant damage to the U.S. financial and banking systems. As a quick fix to this problem, the Fed bailed out the banks, re-inflated house prices, and kept interest rates at record lows through the Obama Administration. According to the Case-Shiller U.S. National Home Price Index, this had caused housing prices to skyrocket by 59% since their low in 2012.

As with all artificial bubbles, the Housing Bubble 2.0 is not supported by any fundamentals. As we have seen previously, in fact, there has been growing income inequality throughout the developed world. Citizens are left to work longer hours, take on second jobs, increasing debt loads often from shadow-creditors, to maintain their standard of living.

All the while, in major cities around the world, foreign investment has been pouring in, leading to increased house prices for the haves and rising rents for the have-nots. This situation has been exacerbated by new online platforms like Airbnb which experienced a massive decline in revenues due to cancellations. According to Airbnb, one-third of their hosts have 24 or more properties that they are responsible for; these people are often referred to as "super hosts."

In recent years, these companies, and others like them have come under fire for lowering available rental units on the market and increasing rents. The financial troubles for landlords and lease-letters have only begun since,

---

[20] https://specials-images.forbesimg.com/imageserve/5e84091e5f192f00068bee40/960x0.jpg?fit=scale

eventually, all outstanding payments to creditors will subsequently have to be resolved one way or another.

Wolf Richer, the CEO of Wolf Street Corp. and Fed policy expert, had called attention to the ordinarily robust areas of the housing sector, such as in San Francisco and New York, where things had come to a screeching halt. In the Spring of 2020, he stated, "This is supposed to be the Spring selling season, and new listings are supposed to surge, but sellers aren't interested in having potentially infected people traipsing through their home, and they know that buyers are woefully absent, and it doesn't make that much sense to list the home because previously listed homes are still languishing on the market."

According to real estate listing firm Redfin, home sale prices were on a 22.7% decline in April 2020, with new listings plunging to 41% and inventory declining to 21%. Weiss Analytics stated that 30% of homes, listed at $200,000 USD or less, were falling to 6.3%, while 37% of homes valued at $600,000 USD or more were discounted at 7.7% since February 2020.

While the buying and selling markets have been struck, homeowners will not escape the effects due to the pandemic. A recent report from Oxford Economics estimated that 15% of homeowners would fall behind on their monthly mortgage payments, causing delinquencies to surpass numbers seen during the Great Recession of 2008. Currently, mortgage holders who have missed 3 or more payments are at a 10-year high.

Oxford Economics added, "The uncertainty in the mortgage market has contributed to a significant tightening of lending standards that may persist even once a recover is underway." With household debt-to-income ratios at all-time highs across the developed world, this would be especially dangerous for those who needed to refinance their mortgages. For example, Australia, Canada, New Zealand, and the U.K. have hazardous levels of household debt[21].

The residential mortgage market in the U.S. is worth over $11 trillion USD and will leave homeowners feeling the effects of the crash for years. In Japan, house

---

[21] https://www.abc.net.au/cm/lb/11286678/data/australia-leads-the-world-in-household-debt-data.jpg

prices have still not recovered from the crash that took place in 1991-92. What followed this period was referred to as the "Lost Decade"—10 years of stagnation and deflation in Japanese asset prices.

While low-interest rates across North America can attract buyers, major cities where the demand is have seen runaway prices and stricter lending criteria. Central banks have ignored privately issued residential mortgage-backed securities, letting them proliferate, and have refused to purchase them, denying liquidity where it is needed most. While there has been some government assistance to homeowners, the majority of this equates to a delay in foreclosure on their properties. Thomas Barrack, a commercial real estate voice in the U.S., warned that that sector was close to collapse due to a lack of rent payments and the large numbers of forbearance requests.

In fact, by the end of April 2020, 7.3% of all mortgages were in forbearance, with the number expected to rise. After the Great Recession of 2008, many small lenders were left to fill the void left by the larger institutions in the U.S. credit markets. Now, these organizations are responsible for half of all the single-family home mortgages in the U.S. Credit institutions like these are responsible for 80% of all Federal Housing Administration loans, catering specifically to low-income or high-risk borrowers and 64% of all minority group borrowers.

As the tsunami of evictions and delinquencies begin to sweep across the U.S., and much of the developed world, what is already a housing shortage will soon become a housing crisis. Recent trends showed that due to the rising costs of homes and rents in major cities, people had begun to move as economies shifted towards more remote gig-based work. For decades, the purchasing power of consumers has shrunk while asset prices have only gone up. This has led to many young people, the future of the economy, to give up hope of ever owning a house. Many are abandoning major cities for much more affordable smaller towns. In places such as California or New York, a mass exodus has happened, mostly caused by government regulations. This pandemic has thrown a wrench into what little parts of the economy are still churning in what is already a challenging economic climate. COVID-19 has exposed the fatal flaws within the current financial and economic systems.

As people struggle to find solutions for the future, the time for those receiving help from the government is running out. While evictions and rent hikes may be temporarily frozen, they have only managed to delay the inevitable. When the economy tries to get back to normal, and the flood gates are opened, we will start to see the real costs to bear. One of these costs may be the loss of mobility options, with the travel industry being one of the worst hit sectors.

SECTION 11: THE AIRLINE INDUSTRY

If you have spent any reasonable amount of time on YouTube, or other forms of social media, you surely would come across travel vlog. Traveling to exotic places, eating exotic foods, and experiencing foreign cultures have become the way of life for many Westerners. I am an expat myself and have lived in several countries over the past few years. Traveling is as intoxicating as any drug and a staple for Millennials. If you take a stroll through the seedier parts of East Asia, you will find more Australians than locals sometimes (just look for the bars). Whether you are an Instagram influencer or just looking for a quick trip to Mexico with the family, traveling has become a part of our lives. However, this has not always been the case.

In the past, you had to be rich to travel; but these days, it is easily accessible for everyone. Over the past 100 years, we have seen traveling go from reading a book to the tourism industry that provides a livelihood for millions of people. Today, this industry is under attack by the crippling restrictions upon one of the major arteries of mobility, the airline industry.

In a matter of only a few months, COVID-19 has sent the airline industry, one of the most significant cultural and economic phenomena of the postwar boom, back decades. Higher fares, much fewer routes, multiple health checks, increased sanitization, masks, and social distancing, are all part of the new era of air travel. A seismic shift is underway in the sector which looks to transform it as much or even more than the events of the 9/11 attacks. The cabins of airplanes will look more like hospitals, with goggles, gowns, gloves, and masks, than the warm and inviting atmosphere we are accustomed with.

To further complicate things, health tickets and phone apps may be required before we can board. Many airlines only profited a few dollars per customer during the best of times, which means all these extra costs will have to be made up somewhere. All these factors will change how and how often we travel, which will have knock-on effects for numerous other industries. The way we travel will be quite different in the future and the old ways will not be coming back soon.

With trouble brewing in the domestic markets, the airline industry has been particularly hard hit due to the COVID-19 crisis. An already tricky sector must deal with refunds, cancellations, layoffs, and travel restrictions, not to mention the new measures that will need to be in place to operate in a new environment. Calls for social distancing on planes leave the airlines with limited options, with some smaller companies like Ryanair being particularly hard hit.

According to a recent analysis from the International Air Transport Association (IATA), they expected that the COVID-19 pandemic might extend to 2023. Long-distance travel and international flights would be the most significantly affected. The report published on May 15, 2020 detailed a slight increase in domestic travel but would not see pre-COVID-19 travel levels until 2023 due to a variety of factors. "Global GDP growth is expected to fall by around 5% this year, before rebounding and returning to its 2019 level in 2021," the report explained. "To put this decline into context, it is around 4x larger than that of the global financial crisis, where world GDP fell by 1.3% in 2009." This translated to an approximate 50% decline in travel throughout 2020. "The recovery is such that a return to the level of 2019 does not occur until 2023, taking around two years longer than global GDP," according to the report.

The steep decline in consumer confidence is one of the leading factors, coupled with mobility restrictions, economic factors such as income cuts, and finally a threat from multiple waves of the virus. Given the nature of how easily the virus is transferred and how interconnected the global community truly is, it will be a long time before health and safety measures are lifted and consumer confidence is restored.

The following figures were calculated in Revenue Passenger Kilometers (RPKs), "Domestic RPKs are expected to decline by around 40% this year, while international RPKs are likely to decline by around 60%," the report explained. "As a consequence, we expect the average trip length will decline sharply this year, by around 8.5%, before gradually recovering thereafter." While there was a chance that the government would intervene in the airline industry, as we saw in other areas, it might be too little too late.

"The impacts of the crisis on long-haul travel will be much more severe and of a longer duration than what is expected in domestic markets," Alexandre de Juniac, Director General and CEO of IATA, said in a press release on May 13, 2020. "This makes globally agreed and implemented biosecurity standards for the travel process all the more critical. We have a small window to avoid the consequences of uncoordinated unilateral measures that marked the post-9/11 period. We must act fast. We need a solution for safe travel that addresses two challenges. It must give passengers the confidence to travel safely and without undue hassle. And it must give governments confidence that they are protected from importing the virus."

According to a survey conducted by IATA in 2020, 69% of travelers stated that they would not consider traveling if they had to quarantine for 14 days when they arrived at their destination. Overall, IATA's data showed that there were challenging times ahead for the airline industry, which would not be resolved in the near term.

If you knew the average profit margins for an industry was just 3.26%, would you want to go into that industry? This was the case for the airline industry, as reported by CSI Market, for the first quarter of 2020. This low percentage spoke volumes about the sector's durability, but their troubles were far from over. As people were forced under lockdown and travel restrictions came into effect, the airline industry had struggled to adapt. The calls for social distancing made it nearly impossible to function in the closed cabin of an aircraft. Amid waves of cancellations, airlines had been forced to hike what little ticket prices they have through the roof.

Calin Rovinescu, the CEO of Air Canada, mentioned, "We're now moving through the darkest period ever in the history of commercial aviation-significantly worse than the aftermath of 9/11, SARS, and the 2008 financial crisis." These troubling times had forced some airlines to sell aircraft in order to generate capital, while others were looking to revamp their fleets for smaller and more economical models. On the bright side, since more people were shopping online, this meant that cargo volumes had increased during the pandemic.

Emirates became the world's first airline to cover medical expenses and quarantine costs related to COVID-19. Under the directive of Sheikh Mohammed, UAE Vice President and Prime Minister and Ruler of Dubai, the airline is now covering medical expenses of up to €150,000 EUR (approx. $230,000 CAD) and quarantine costs of €100 EUR (approx. $155 CAD) per day for 14 days, should they be diagnosed with COVID-19 during their travels.

This cover is provided by Emirates free of cost to its customers, regardless of travel class or destination. Effective immediately, the policy is available to customers flying on Emirates until October 31, 2020, with the first flight to be completed on or before October 31. It is valid for 31 days from the moment they fly the first sector of their journey, meaning customers can continue to benefit from the added assurance of this cover even if they travel onwards to another city after arriving at their Emirates destination.

Passengers do not need to register or fill in any forms before travel nor are they obligated to utilize this cover. Any impacted customer who has been diagnosed with COVID-19 during their travel simply has to contact a dedicated hotline to avail of assistance and cover. However, as airlines struggle to adapt to the changing climate of travel, higher prices and less variety are on the way for consumers. Over the summer of 2020, airlines continued to lay off employees and made cuts to their staff. Continued travel restrictions across the globe are limiting the economic viability of the industry.

While North America struggles geographically and demographically to produce economically viable airline companies, Eurasia will likely see the quickest rebound. There have been travel bubbles open between European countries and another in East Asia. The European and Asian continents are home to most of the world's populations and not far apart in condensed areas. While the picture is bleak for North America, with estimates ranging up to 3 or 4 years before we see pre-COVID-19 travel levels, Eurasia provides a glimmer of hope in the pending financial crisis.

CHAPTER 4: THE FINANCIAL CRISIS

SECTION 1: INTRODUCTION

"If you tell a lie big enough and keep repeating it, people will eventually come to believe it. The lie can be maintained only for such time as the State can shield the people from the political, economic, and/or military consequences of the lie. It thus becomes vitally important for the State to use all of its powers to repress dissent, for the truth is the mortal enemy of the lie, and thus by extension, the truth is the greatest enemy of the State."

Paul Joseph Goebbels, Reich Minister of Propaganda of Nazi Germany

In classical Greek literature, the tragedy of Cassandra is a famous tale. She was born to the King Priam, the last king of Troy, and was one of his most loved and beautiful daughters. According to Aeschylus's tragedy, Cassandra was loved by the god Apollo who had promised her the power of divination only if she complied with his desires.

While Cassandra accepted his proposal and received the gift, she later refused to hold up her end of the agreement. This mortal angered Apollo for her defiance and he ordained that while her prophecies were accurate, nobody would believe her. She accurately predicted Troy's fall and even the death of King Agamemnon but, as wise as she was, she was ignored. Even though Cassandra was blessed with the foresight to warn those around them of their impending doom, their blissful ignorance condemned them to destruction as they would not heed her warnings.

During the battle of Troy, Ajax the Lesser dragged her from the altar of Athena and proceeded to rape her. For this insult to the gods, Athena sent a massive storm to sink the Greek fleet loaded with bounty on their way home. Eventually, Cassandra was stolen as a prize by King Agamemnon, the leader of the campaign against Troy, but was later murdered with him.

2500 hundred years later, human nature has persisted in the same fallacies; it is easier to ignore a problem than to solve it. Most people go about their daily lives blissfully unwilling to be aware of reality. The thing about truth is that it does not care who you are, what you think, or how you feel. Reality will persist when our times have passed, and it is as immutable as the forces of physics. They say you cannot fight the Fed, but a more accurate term would be you cannot fight human nature.

If you are to turn on the TV and listen to the narrative of any mainstream media, you will hear terms such as "pent up demand," "back to normal," "recovery," and "green shoots." While the consensus is that the COVID-19 pandemic will pass and then we will get back to business as usual, let's not forget that these are the same "experts" who said COVID-19 would not come to America. They said it was just a flu and would go away before finally admitting that we were grossly unprepared and ill-informed.

How was it that the CIA, the best-funded and best-equipped intelligence service in the world, had no idea what was coming? Understandably, governments did not want to create panic or mass hysteria. Look at what happened over toilet papers. But aren't so-called democratic governments supposed to be transparent?

On February 20, 2020, one of the most massive stock market crashes in history began. Despite the relief rally and federal liquidity injections, all 3 Wall Street indexes fell more than 12% when markets reopened on March 16, 2020. As Peter Schiff put it, "We have an economy based on credit, based on debt. So, not people spending the money they earned, but spending the money they did not earn, but they borrowed."

Consumer debt has become one of the central issues with the financial system. Defaults and delinquent payments have started to trickle up the credit streams to their issuers. Long before COVID-19, there were unresolved issues with subprime borrowers, subprime mortgages, subprime credit cards, and subprime auto loans. Hence, the financial system became proliferated in junk debt, and even the major institutions were in a furry to create as much junk debt as possible to saturate the markets.

It got to the point where newborn infants and the dead were being approved for credit. Is this what a healthy financial system looks like? All the while, those considered alternative to the official narrative who have been warning the public for years, some going well back before the Great Recession of 2008-09, were ignored, marginalized and called a conspiracy theorist, or a "doomsayer."

As a day trader and technical analyst myself, I am reminded of a phrase that all traders continuously tell themselves: "Follow the smart money." If Warren Buffet is any indicator, that means they are on the sidelines in cash. Buffett had shed airline stocks such as United Airlines and American Airlines. He also reduced holdings in financial institutions such as JPMorgan and Wells Fargo. Buffett was not a fan of gold, often deriding the precious metal. To the dismay of gold bugs, Buffett became the de facto leader of the "anti-gold crowd." There has been a belief that investing in gold is akin to betting against America.

Buffett deserves credit for shifting his stance to the new reality because of the irrational policies of massive borrowing and money printing by U.S. leaders. Berkshire Hathaway, Inc. bought about 21 million shares of gold miner, Barrick Gold, spending about $563 million USD according to a filing released on August 14. He famously stated in the past: "Gold has no earnings and does not pay a dividend." The importance of this move could not be overstated. Buffet foresaw how global central banks had completely lost control with the way they were printing trillions and killing fiat money. If he and the central banks are any indicators, then you'd better own gold. In a world awash in liquidity, credit, and debt, it is not gold that goes up but the value of fiat currencies that keeps collapsing.

SECTION 2: THE SUBPRIME MARKETS

"Whoever controls the volume of money in any country is absolute master of all industry and commerce."

James A. Garfield, 20th President of the United States.

Mainstream media has been pushing the narrative that we will not face a recession; everything will go back to normal once the lockdowns are lifted. But there are those who would say differently. Peter Schiff might already be a familiar name for you. He is an American stockbroker, financial commentator and forecaster, economist, public personality, and author known as "the man who predicted the economic meltdown of 2008." After years of warning about the economic and financial systems, he gained notoriety after the fact.

Currently, Schiff is the CEO and Chief Global Strategist of Euro Pacific Capital Inc. and a broker-dealer. Since the Great Recession, he has relentlessly been advocating the same message; but as stock markets inflates and housing prices rise, his warning have increasingly fallen upon deaf ears. As stated by Peter Schiff on April 16, 2020:

> "If you shut down the economy, how do all the people with debt pay their debt? And if the debt isn't being paid, then by definition, you have a financial crisis. That's why the real estate crisis was a financial crisis. It wasn't because real estate prices went down. It's because real estate prices going down meant loans that were collateralized by real estate weren't getting repaid. And to the extent that the banks had to foreclose, the collateral wasn't there to make the banks whole."

The same thing is happening now in 2020. The banks are even more exposed today than they were in 2008. This is an even bigger crisis than it was in 2008 because we have a lot more debt. We have a lot more borrowers who are in trouble. One would think that banks would have learned from their mistakes in 2008, but they were bailed out by the taxpayers, those who were "too big to fail," were just that. Today, the picture is bleaker with even higher market saturation and greater credit risk. Schiff said that the Fed's response was a clear indication that this would be worse than 2008 despite their best efforts. "The

Fed is doing everything it did during the last financial crisis, except way bigger and way sooner. So, if they're doing all the same stuff, only they're having to do more of it, they're having to do it at even greater excess, then what does that tell you? That tells you this is a financial crisis just like the last one, except it's bigger. It's a worse financial crisis."

When consumer spending is needed the most to restart the economy, consumers have and will be using what little stimulus they receive for outstanding bills. The economy is not a light switch that can be turned on and off at will. It takes time to build consumer confidence but, like trust, it can easily be broken overnight and takes a long time to repair.

According to Wolf Richter of Wolf Street, credit card balances, which were 30 days or more delinquent, were skyrocketing at the highest rate since the 1980s. The rates of delinquencies for smaller banks have risen especially since the Great Recession of 2008[22]. Consumers who had obtained credit cards issued by smaller banks were particularly in trouble and were falling behind in historic proportions.

Similarly, as of February 2020, auto loans had become seriously delinquent at 4.94% on total auto loans and leases outstanding. This represented the highest delinquency rate since the Great Depression and higher than the Great Recession of 2008. At that time, 23% of all subprime loans were 90 days or more delinquent and the numbers continued to increase since then. How can consumers be in such bad shape after the longest economic expansion in U.S. history? Isn't the stock market correlated with the health of the average citizens?

What is worse, since this is a lagging indicator, these numbers represented a pre-COVID-19 crisis, with unemployment in the U.S. near historic lows. So, when people were still working and times were good, somehow a large portion of consumers were falling behind on their loan payments. Why would creditors make loans when they know these can probably never be repaid?

---

[22] https://wolfstreet.com/wp-content/uploads/2020/02/US-consumer-credit-card-delinquency-2019-q4.png

Consumers with a credit score below 620 are considered subprime. While they could receive subprime loans from smaller creditors, they are faced with exorbitant interest rates of 25% to 30%. In the traditional markets, according to the 2019 Federal Deposit Insurance Corporation Quarterly, the banks' average cost to borrow was around 1%. This represented a lucrative markup for subprime loans, making them one of the most profitable assets for financial institutions. As the hunt for profits become harder in recent years, banks are turning to riskier assets to keep the revenues rolling.

The Western consumer-based society has pushed people into record levels of debts in a failed effort to keep the economy going. As an effect, people have been loaned money they should have never been eligible for. All that was needed was an event like COVID-19 to push the financial system past the breaking point. While many analysts have been warning for years that we are on the verge of a financial collapse much greater than the Great Recession of 2008, they have been ignored.

Instead of rectifying the situation made evident by the Great Recession of 2008, the banking system has only managed to kick the can further down the line. This means that when we have to deal with the consequences, they will be much worse than if we hadn't ignored the issue. How can a society function without a healthy economic and financial environment? Is it any wonder we are seeing more calls for debt jubilees, student loan forgiveness, basic income, and other socialist policies now? While the situation for most developed economies is downright dreadful, the developing world is poised for a quick rebound.

In the U.S., the Fed and the government have enacted socialist policies to fix the problems from the previous socialist policies, and this will not end well. What we see out of Washington is nothing more than simple solutions to try and tide things over until the next election. However, people's rage has started to show as they take to the streets demanding changes. Those in charge have forgotten their duty to provide policies that allow people to thrive. Instead, we are seeing too many hands in the cookie jar, complicating the crises we face today. As the world slowly steps out of lockdowns, they will see the financial crisis begin to unfold, and the unrest in the streets will become more common.

The real enemy is not those in the Oval Office but those who have corrupted our economic and financial systems.

SECTION 3: THE FEDERAL RESERVE

"Prices are going up. Unemployment continues to go up. And we have not had the necessary correction for the financial bubble created by our Federal Reserve system."

Ron Paul, American politician, author, and physician

The U.S. is a sick man walking. A virus did not cause the Great Crash of 2020; it merely triggered it. The economic and financial fragility already existed. The most exceptional economy in the world is essentially popping OxyContin to get through the day; a shell of its former self. If anything, a crash is long overdue and should have happened a decade ago. But like all junkies hooked on a fix, the Fed could not allow their best customer to get clean.

When it looked like the U.S. would finally go into rehab, the Fed injected more corporate stimulus, more special purpose vehicles, more "helicopter money." Too much debt, malinvestment, fear, and greed have taken control of a market that has been manipulated to fail. Just like how it is for the dealer, it is not just about keeping your customers hooked and buying your product. It is also for the extra benefits you get when they run out of ways to pay.

Crashes are the most exceptional opportunities of a lifetime, and what is coming will be the most significant wealth transfer in history. Central banks and the Fed are responsible for the vulnerabilities in the markets, enabled by populist government policies. This uncomfortable truth cannot afford to come to light. So, we are bombarded by false narratives blaming the virus among others when, in fact, we should be looking at ourselves.

While the media seeks to distract us and analysts pretend to act surprised that we are in this predicament, it is essential to remember that history has already proven that this will not end well. Printing more money has never translated into prosperity for the general population; it only made things worst. While there are several ways things can unfold, none of them are great for the 99%. Meanwhile, recent figures showed that the top 1% had gained massively so far during this crisis. The stock market had become so disconnected from reality that we are seeing bankrupted companies selling billions in shares to the retail market through "dumb money." When the music finally comes to a stop, and it will, the retail investors will be left holding the bag in this cruel and manipulated game. Is it any wonder why apps such as Robinhood have become so popular recently?

The striking image provided by Visual Capitalist, laid out the details on the Fed's monetary policies[23]. Currently, the Fed is making history, lending $600 billion USD directly to companies that need it. According to the Wall Street Journal article published on May 18, 2020, the goal of this program was to give cash to the companies that were too large to get small business loans but too small to benefit from the Fed's other interventions, such as buying hunk bond Exchange Traded Funds (ETFs).

Former Fed Chair Ben Bernanke believed that the Fed's most significant challenge now was "making these programs work" in un-freezing the credit markets. But how do you avoid the Fed's balance sheet from becoming filled with junk loans that nobody wants? The Fed's asset holdings are already at record highs, currently reaching $7 trillion USD, with plans to go up to $10 trillion USD in 2020.

Another former Fed Chair, Janet Yellen, said, "The Main Street program is going to be tremendously complicated. One of the problems with this program is that it may turn out to be insufficiently generous." The Main Street program, which was conceived through the discussions of Jay Powell and Steven Mnuchin, was designed for "companies with up to 15,000 employees or less than $5 billion revenue. More than 19,000 companies had between 500 and 15,000 employees in 2017 and they collectively employed between 30 and 40 million people." Under this program, banks can lend up to $25 million USD in new loans or refinance up to $200 million USD of existing investment in a company's total debt.

Meanwhile Senator Mark Warner had been advocating for loan forgiveness, also known as giving away free money for bad investments. But so far, the Fed

---

[23] https://2oqz471sa19h3vbwa53m33yj-wpengine.netdna-ssl.com/wp-content/uploads/2020/04/fed-balance-sheet-exponential-covid-19.jpg

was resisting. Some economists suggested that the Fed should loosen the terms of eligibility and lower borrower's rates, to which Powell replied, "The Fed has lending powers, not spending powers."

On April 9, 2020, the Fed decided to announce some remarkable stimulus packages, and these were in addition to the myriad of operations in March and prior months. In what was being coined as "monetary lightspeed" by economists, the Fed's balance sheet rose from $3.76 trillion USD at the end of August 2019 to $4.16 trillion USD by February 2020. By May 13, 2020, it was at $6.93 trillion USD, a shocking increase of $2.77 trillion USD in just 10 weeks, which dwarfed anything seen during the Great Recession of 2008.

The Fed has been a blank check for malinvestment within the U.S. They have promised to purchase mortgages, treasuries, and municipal bonds in any amount necessary, including investment-grade corporate securities, high yield junk bonds, and even collateralized loan obligations (CLOs). All of which are facilitated through a newly created Secondary Market Corporate Credit Facility (SMCCF). As one of the basic tenants of Economics: if there is demand, there will be supply.

According to the Federal Reserve Act, the Fed is only responsible for purchasing or lending securities with a government guarantee, which is one of the safest forms of assets. So how did the Fed become the mom and pop of Millennials for corporate America? The Treasury has enabled the Fed to break the law by side-stepping regulations. The Treasury Department provided $75 billion USD of initial funding from the Exchange Stabilization Fund, acting as an accomplice to the Fed. Those funds were directly deposited into a special purpose vehicle (SPV), specifically used to purchase corporate bonds in the secondary market.

With the Fed entering through the back door, they acted as an intermediary and employing asset manager BlackRock to leverage the funds 10 times, allowing the Fed to buy an additional $675 billion USD in securities and select ETFs.

On April 20, 2020, John Hussman, professor of Economics and Hedge Fund manager, described this maneuver as illegal in which Congress never granted authority for:

> "…additional purchases to 'leverage' that funding are neither secured by non-financial collateral, nor have security sufficient to protect taxpayers from losses. They are illegal, both under Section 13(3) of the Federal Reserve Act, and under Section 4003(c)(3)(B) of the CARES act, which 'for the avoidance of doubt' specifically invokes 13(3) 'requirements relating to loan collateralization, taxpayer protection, and borrower solvency.'"

With the amount of leverage and speculation in securities, the Fed was putting the taxpayers at risk. A 10% drop or more in the value of an SPV asset would result in immediate insolvency. These assets did not meet the requirements of sufficient security intended "for the avoidance of doubt" about a potential loss for the taxpayer, making them illegal.

The current economic realities are not bright within the U.S. and other countries. Unemployment in April stood at 14.8%, with consumer spending, confidence, and industrial production at all-time lows. No industry or sector is unaffected by the current crisis and everyone has their hands out to the government looking for a bailout that was courtesy of generous taxpayers. GDP was expected to drop by 12% to 15% in the second quarter, which might be an optimistic prediction. On May 17, 2020, Fed Chairman Jerome Powell said it could be as much as 30%.

Across all industries, depression-era data is being released with little hope on the horizon because a cure is not expected for another year at best. Even if there is a rush to mass vaccinations in the following months, the damage has already been done. The chances of seeing corporate losses on the Treasury's balance sheet exceeding 10% are highly probable. Even as some areas try to open, there is continued distrust and uncertainty.

John Hussman pointed out, "As a result, the newly created SMCCF is either a Ponzi scheme at public expense (if the Fed plans to allow portfolio losses to exceed 10%) or a 1987-style portfolio insurance scheme (if the Fed plans to liquidate securities into a falling market in order to cap its losses at 10%)." Would the Fed lead or follow the markets? According to the *Fed Uncertainty Principle* by Mike "Mish" Shedlock, "If the Fed is following market expectations, can the Fed be to blame for the consequences? More pointedly, why isn't the market to blame if the Fed is following market expectations? This is a fascinating theoretical question."

This principle states that the Fed has distorted the market via self-reinforcing observer/participant feedback loops. It is flawed logic to assume the Fed is merely following the markets and the market should be blamed for following the Fed's actions. This is not a free market; this is a heavily manipulated market directed in the same way the Greek gods intervened on life in Ancient Greece.

Mike Shedlock provided us with the 4 Uncertainty Principal Corollaries:

- **Uncertainty Principle Corollary Number 1:** The Fed has no idea where interest rates should be. Only a free market does. The Fed will be disingenuous about what it knows (nothing of use) and doesn't know (much more than it wants to admit), particularly in times of economic stress.

- **Uncertainty Principle Corollary Number 2:** The government/quasi-government body most responsible for creating this mess (the Fed), will attempt a big power grab, purportedly to fix whatever problems it creates. The bigger the mess it creates, the more power it will attempt to grab. Over time this leads to dangerously concentrated power into the hands of those who have already proven they do not know what they are doing.

- **Uncertainty Principle Corollary Number 3:** Don't expect the Fed to learn from past mistakes. Instead, expect the Fed to repeat them with bigger and bigger doses of exactly what created the initial problem.

- **Uncertainty Principle Corollary Number 4:** The Fed does not care whether its actions are illegal or not. The Fed is operating under the principle that it's easier to get forgiveness than permission. And forgiveness is just another means to the desired power grab it is seeking.

While the Fed managed to learn from the mistakes of negative interest rates in Japan, they ignored the lessons from European Central Banks in bailing out the perpetrators. We are in this mess due to the Fed's direct actions of holding interest rates too low for too long, inflating multiple asset bubbles. Instead of letting a natural recession take its course, they bailed out the companies responsible, allowing them to irresponsibly use the funds for corporate stock buybacks, increase the bonuses of CEOs, and proliferate junk debt.

While it is beyond the Fed's legal authority to purchase junk bonds, the Fed is responsible for creating the demand that has saturated the markets with people who should have never received credit. While all these measures are sold to the public temporarily, their track record has shown that nothing is brief and the lies are permanent.

The Fed will now do what was unthinkable to many at the start of the year and start buying high-yield or junk debt. While this might be good news for the stock market in the short term, the long-term structural implications are destructive. Powell is making it clear he will do everything it takes to keep the economy moving forward. But with every downturn, he is absorbing more and more risk.

SECTION 4: JUNK BONDS

"Did anyone of those bullish investors ever think what would happen to the Treasury market if the Fed ever became a net seller of bonds?"

Ziad K. Abdelnour, author, financial advisor, and President & CEO of Blackhawk Partners, Inc.

In the latter part of the 20th century, Charles Saatchi became extremely famous and wealthy, for buying up nondescript British artists, such as Damien Hirst, Sarah Lucas, Jay Jopling, and Karsten Schubert. At the time, these artists were unknown, with little to no exposure, but he monopolized the market for their works. After displaying their works in his galleries, and putting on shows, he created a buzz around their work, gaining them notoriety. Saatchi even managed to convince Sir Norman Rosenthal, a famous art historian and curator, to feature their works at the Royal Academy.

With such a limited market and their growing acclaim, Saatchi single-handedly took these struggling artists and made them a sensation. This was the first example of buying "junk art" that resulted to massive profits through sheer marketing. Saatchi made a fortune selling these works he picked up for next to nothing. Was it a genius move or was it an art of deception? One man's junk is another man's treasure.

According to an article published on Bloomberg by Paula Seligson and Claire Boston on May 19, 2020, Herbalife sold $600 million USD of junk bonds at a yield of 7.875%, to do stock buybacks. Herbalife Nutrition Ltd is a producer of weight-loss shakes and supplements, with Carl Icahn as its largest shareholder.

Icahn had explicitly stated to creditors that they were funding his next several homes and he would be pocketing the proceeds. This new 5.25-year bond would yield slightly more than the company's current $400 million USD of 7.25% unsecured notes due in 2020. Moody's Credit Rating Agency (Moody's) had rated these bonds at B1, or just 4 notches below investment grade. Icahn had used the Fed's buying spree to flood the starving junk bond market with more of what they want and had also authorized an ongoing 5-year $1.5 billion USD buyback program.

If we refer to the Great Recession of 2008, as reported by David Segal of the New York Times on March 17, 2009, those credit agencies were complicit in the subprime securities and ratings of big corporations. At least 10 of these companies failed or were bailed out but had an investment-grade rating from a primary credit agency. This could be likened to a dying patient being given a clean health bill. But what could be the motivation behind the deception?

While some claimed that these agencies were simply paid by the corporations that were earning billions in fees, it did not take long to notice there was a connection between Warren Buffet and these rating agencies. One of the richest men in the world, known as "the Oracle of Omaha," owned as much as 20% of Moody's but that figure had declined to 12.8%, according to recent Berkshire Hathaway's filings. Some of the companies rated by Moody's were owned by Buffet himself, which was a conflict of interest. In 2010, Buffet was forced to go in front of a hearing, where he said he did not rely on the opinions of rating agencies when he made investment decisions, but what about the rest of the market?

As reported by the Financial Times on May 21, 2020, America's largest shopping mall, Mall of America, missed its second mortgage-backed bond payment. The payments were scheduled for April and May of 2020. Since March 2020, the mall was shut down due to the pandemic, notifying its mortgage servicer Wells Fargo. The complex featured more than 500 stores across 2 million square feet. The $1.4 billion USD mortgage posed a severe risk to the broader bond market. Mall owner, Don Ghermezian of Triple Five Group, said that "many malls will be headed into a default" if they could not secure government assistance.

According to Erin Hudson of The Real Deal, a New York Real Estate publisher, on May 18, 2020, "A mystery investor blew out more than 10.5 million shares of an S&P 500 Real Estate fund last week representing a $333 million sale." This totaled about 7.4% of outstanding shares in the Real Estate Sector Fund, which is a macro indicator of the industry's largest companies.

This resulted to an obscene amount of investment capital liquidated at a time when markets had supposedly stabilized. This only meant that increased difficulties were at least perceived, if not ahead.

There was a hot debate about whether to follow Europe's lead in the U.K. with negative interest rates, but it appeared their bond market had already decided for them. According to the Financial Times on May 20, 2020, they sold, "£3.75 billion in 2023 gilts at a negative yield of -0.003% for the first time," to prop up the economy[24]. A negative yield means that for the investors who hold the debt to maturity, they will get a fraction less than what they paid. They were essentially paying for the privilege to lend the U.K. government money, which worked great when Japan tried this. This represented the first time that the U.K. had sold a longer-term bond at a yield rate below 0.

"I can't think of an economy where negative rates are a worse idea than the U.K.," said SocGen FX strategist Kit Juckes. "The economic benefits are dubious but the power of a cocktail of negative rates and massive quantitative easing to weaken the currency seems clear and if the pound falls enough, it will make QE harder." When this is considered, after the fact that the Consumer Price Index crashed below the 1% target, halving to 0.8% from 1.5%, the lowest level in almost 4 years, economists began warning of a broader deflationary trend.

"With inflation now more than 1 percentage point below target, the governor of the Bank of England will have to write a letter to the Chancellor explaining why inflation is so far below target and what he intends to do about it," said Melanie Baker, senior economist at Royal London Asset Management. "The next step we expect to see is more asset purchases."

What comes first: supply or demand? In classical economics, the supply is created, and demand is created through advertising. But what we see here is how the central banks are creating demand for junk bonds while the corporate world is manufacturing the supply. This is not a sign of a healthy or functional

---

[24] ttps://www.zerohedge.com/s3/files/inline-images/3Y%20gilt%20auction.jpg?itok=qG_eSwhV

financial system, or a sustainable one. What happens when the bank buys up everything that nobody wants and is then left holding the bags?

We saw this example take place in Japan with the zombification of their financial system. According to Mio Tomita of the Asian Nikkei Review on June 27, 2018, "…[t]he Bank of Japan has become a majority shareholder in nearly 40% of listed companies as the central bank keeps buying stocks under its ultraloose monetary policy. The BOJ has amassed an estimated ¥25 trillion JPY ($227 billion USD) of equities as a result of purchasing exchange-traded funds. The tally is equal to nearly 4% of the roughly ¥652 trillion JPY aggregate market value of stocks traded on the first section of the Tokyo Stock Exchange."

These purchases began in 2010 when BOJ Governor Haruhiko Kuroda took office in 2013, pushing for aggressive monetary easing. These annual purchases had amassed a total of ¥6 trillion JPY, since 2016. So, what happens when the central bank eventually starts unloading these positions?

Quantitative easing and stimulus packages do not fight deflation. In fact, they create deflation. This, in turn, creates zombie companies and banks that are half alive and addicted to central bank stimuli to stay afloat. This leaves no room for new companies, better organized and even profitable, to gain market share, which is the innovation that has moved developed economies for decades.

The grassroots entrepreneurs are the foundation of any stable economy. But they are being shoved into bankruptcy while those who should not be in the business get bailouts. The market used to represent the actions of an economy, but it has been transformed into a video game whereby anyone can win. However, assets cannot inflate forever without consequences Eventually, like all Ponzi schemes, they will run out of new money. The definition of insanity is trying the same thing over and over and expecting different results. The mistakes being made today are repetitions of the past and, as we have seen before, the results will be the same. A bubble can only inflate so far before it is forced to pop; and what we have today is the largest bubble ever created in history, "the Everything Bubble."

SECTION 5: THE EVERYTHING BUBBLE

"'The only thing we learn from history, it has been said, 'is that men never learn from history', a sweeping generalization perhaps, but one which the chaos in the world today goes far to confirm."

Lieutenant-General Sir John Bagot Glubb, British soldier, scholar, and author

In the mid-1600s, the Dutch enjoyed a period of unmatched wealth and prosperity. Newly independent from Spain, Dutch merchants grew rich on trade through the Dutch East India Company. In the 17th century tulips, originally cultivated in the Ottoman Empire, were a new arrival in the Netherlands and their changing colors made them a hot product for the aesthetically attuned.

With money to spend, art and exotica became fashionable collector's items. This was how the Dutch became fascinated with rare "broken" tulips, bulbs that produced striped and speckled flowers. Unknown to them, these pigmentations were caused by diseases. First, these prized tulips were bought as showy display pieces and it did not take long for tulip trading to become a market of its own.

Tulip prices spiked from December 1636 to February 1637, with some of the most prized bulbs like the coveted Switzer experiencing a 12-fold price jump. The most expensive tulip receipts were for 5,000 guilders, the going rate for a nice house in 1637. But those exorbitant prices were outliers. 37 people paid more than 300 guilders for a tulip bulb, the equivalent of what a skilled craftsman earned in a year.

But even if a form of "Tulip Mania" did strike Holland in 1636, did it reach every rung of society—from landed gentry to chimneysweeps? Most of the buyers were the sort you would expect to be speculating in luxury goods, people who could afford it. They were successful merchants and artisans, not chambermaids and peasants.

Tulip Mania was popularized by an account written by the 19th century Scottish writer Charles Mackay, who loved a juicy story. He was not taken seriously as a historian, but his vivid tales have caught on. Ironically, Mackay himself was caught up in a bona fide financial mania: the British railway bubble of the 1840s which some scholars regard as the "biggest technology bubble" in history, followed by one of the biggest financial crashes.

The "Tulip Bubble" of the 1600s is considered the first modern-era bubble, and this period had been dubbed as the Tulip Mania. This is a lesson for us all. It is extremely easy to scoff at past bubbles and even to exaggerate the stupidity of those caught up in them. But it is not so easy to know how to react when one may, or may not, be involved in one.

Sir John Glubb wrote a detailed essay, titled *The Fate of Empires*, wherein he described the stages of development (then eventual decay) that commonly led to collapses in all leading societies. He listed the order as follows:

1)   The Age of Pioneers
2)   The Age of Conquests
3)   The Age of Commerce
4)   The Age of Affluence
5)   The Age of Intellect
6)   The Age of Decadence

While Glubb was British and had lived in a period where, after centuries of colonization, Europeans had dominated the world, his perspective could be considered Eurocentric (but it still provides an interesting analysis). He described "The Age of Decadence" as a period marked with defensiveness, pessimism, materialism, and frivolity. In this age, a massive influx of foreigners or a weakening of religion and the ideals the empire was founded upon is often seen.

The cause of this decadence stems from the extended period of wealth, power, selfishness, love of money, and a loss of sense of duty. Overall, as societies become more prosperous, they tend to push cultural boundaries, leading to some improvements but also undermining society. In time, greed takes over people and the lack of confidence can unravel even the mightiest of empires. If we look back through history, the empires that rose the quickest tended to fall the fastest, whereas those who built up over long periods generally fell through a long and drawn-out process. Many times, citizens will not notice how their lives gradually degraded like a frog left in a frying pan with the heat slowly turned up. As Michael Hopf stated in the book *Those Who Remain*, "Hard times create strong men. Strong men create good times. Good times create weak men. And, weak men create hard times."

Charles Hugh Smith published an article titled *The Taxonomy of Collapse* on December 9, 2019 where he built upon Glubb's analysis. According to Smith, "The higher up the wealth-power pyramid the observer is, the more prone they are to a magical-thinking belief that the empire is forever, even as it is crumbling around them." Smith believed that if we could understand the processes that led to the collapse of the empires of the past, we would know where we stand and possibly avoid the same scenario. Furthermore, he said that the U.S. was currently entering The Age of Decadence and was on the verge of collapse[25].

What causes a civilization which is seemingly at the top of the world to begin to descend into oblivion? Smith suggested that several common factors were at play throughout history, and we see them today. Smith listed these as:

1) **Bolt from the blue.** A fast-moving, unexpected crisis that overwhelms the usual defenses and responses of the empire. An invasion by previously unknown forces with superior technology and/or organization fits the bill: the Mongols in Eurasia, the Spanish in the New World, etc. Extremely contagious and previously unknown infectious diseases like plague and smallpox are also bolts from the blue, devastating populations with no immunity.

   It is estimated that 80% or more of the population of North America died from exposure to smallpox and other European diseases, in many cases long before the victims had ever seen a European, as the diseases spread much faster than the invaders themselves. A drought that never ends is another unexpected catastrophe that quickly depletes food stores. These bolts from the blue can strike at the same time: one reason why the small-in-number Spanish forces conquered vast

---

[25] www.oftwominds.com

empires in the New World was the empires had already been fatally weakened by diseases introduced by Columbus decades earlier.

2) **Irreplaceable declines in essential resources.** Food tops the list, as a decline in calories leads to weakened immune systems and heightened odds of pandemics spreading and a subsequent drop in the number of workers needed to support the empire's vast infrastructure.

The book *The Fate of Rome: Climate, Disease, and the End of an Empire* makes a compelling case that the Western Roman Empire centered around the Mediterranean suffered from a slow environmental transition from an unusually wet era that enabled grain to be grown in previously marginal areas to a drier era that no longer supported the immense grain harvests needed to feed the empire.

Other forms of depletion can also sap the empire of essentials: forests are cut down, silver mines are tapped out, nearby sources of slaves (labor) are no longer available, and so on. The imperial machinery that is accustomed to there's always more somewhere, refuses to trim its expenses, elites refuse to lessen their skim, and since the fat of elite excess is retained, eventually the muscle of military power and trade decay, leaving a hollowed out empire on the edge of a precipice awaiting one final kick into the abyss.

3) **Reversal of fortune.** Military misadventures top the list, as invasions of nearby competing powers are in effect last-ditch gambles to acquire desperately needed wealth and resources to prop up the status quo. When the imperial army is defeated and destroyed, there are no longer sufficient resources and recruits to rebuild the army.

4) **Internal civil conflict.** Civil wars and political conflicts that break out into society and the economy end up consuming the last of the empire's seed corn, just like an invasion of a bordering empire that fails. Once the conflict is resolved, there are no longer enough resources left to support the imperial infrastructure.

Like nature, history offers a near-infinite variety. But just as nature fits into taxonomies of organisms, history can be shuffled into its own taxonomy however messy and imperfect it might be.

Smith stated that these triggers could overlap, contributing to what is called a "perfect storm" accelerating a societal collapse. "All complex hierarchical systems are intrinsically fragile and prone to disruption; we don't see the fragility or vulnerabilities until the decline has reached the terminal phase… even as it is crumbling around them." Smith warned that the COVID-19 pandemic is a final trigger, exposing the fragile economic and financial systems we have built up.

In a book titled *Ages of Discord: A Structural-Demographic Analysis of American History* by Peter Turchin, he identified 25-year, 50-year, 150-year, and 200-year cycles, comparable to Kondratieff's economic cycles, being repeated through human history. While these cycle lengths do not have to be exact, they provide a rough guideline to the waxing and waning of certain events.

Turchin's model identified 3 primary forces at play within these cycles:

1) An oversupply of labor that suppresses real (inflation-adjusted) wages.
2) An overproduction of parasitic elites.
3) A deterioration in central state finances (over-indebtedness, decline in tax revenues, increase in state dependents, fiscal burdens of war, etc.).

As these forces combine and impact social order, it eventually leads to societal collapse. The 4 cycles listed by Turchin are:

1) **The cycle of credit expansion and contraction**, which is now in the final blow-off stage of unsustainable credit expansion (bubble) which will inevitably lead to renunciation of debt (credit collapse) and global depression.
2) **The generational cycle (4 generations or approximately 80 years)** of American history which leads to nation-changing social, political and economic upheaval (The American Revolution: 1781 +80 years = Civil War, 1861 +80 years = 1941, World War II + 80 years = 2021).

3) **The 100+ year cycle of price inflation and stagnation of wages' purchasing power** which began around 1901 is now reaching the final stage of widespread turmoil, shortages, famine, conflict, and crisis.

4) **The demographic cycle**: the workforce stops expanding and starts shrinking while the population of dependent elderly explodes higher, triggering a decline in earnings and the tax base just as taxes must increase to pay for the care of the rising population of elderly.

As Smith and Turchin put it, during the Great Recession of 2008, all these cycles aligned; and instead of dealing with the issues at hand, the inevitable was delayed. Smith claimed the demographic cycle had only accelerated since then and the expansion of credit had reached levels not thought possible only a few years ago. The generational cycle had manifested in the popularity of Trump, Brexit, and the Yellow Vest movements before the expected terminal crisis of 2021.

Smith stated that since the 1990s, one asset class after another had been inflated, culminating in what was referred to as the "Everything Bubble." While official figures claimed low inflation, the costs of childcare, healthcare, rent, higher education, and other essentials had skyrocketed over the last decade. The cost of consumer goods began to increase as globalization and the free movement of trade became threatened. Smith saw resource depletion and geopolitical conflicts at the center of what could become scarcities in consumer food and goods. While the media would be quick to pin the current situation on the Black Swan event of COVID-19, Smith and Turchin asserted that these forces were already at play and a part of the culmination of these cycles. Even the vaccine could not save us from what was to come.

Chamath Palihapitiya, Social Capital's founder and Facebook's former executive, suggested in his interviews with CNBC in April and May 2020 that the airline industry and other sectors should be allowed to fail. He warned that the economy was in serious trouble and the COVID-19 response by the White House and Fed had added to it. "There should be no doubt now that we've completely divorced the economy from stock and bond markets. All this money going in to prop of companies-what you are going to start or accelerate is a really bad deflationary super cycle" Palihapitiya stated. While the Federal

Reserve's balance sheet had swelled by trillions of dollars, he said that the equity market rebound has not done anything to put food on people's plates or help resolve small business owners' anxieties.

"This is a lie that's been propagated by Wall Street. When a company fails, it does not fire its employees... it goes through a packaged bankruptcy... if anything, what happens is the employees end up owning more of the company. The people who get wiped out are the people who own the unsecured debt and the equity... but the employees don't get wiped out and the pensions don't get wiped out... And if a bunch of hedge funds get wiped out – what's the big deal? Let them fail. So they don't get the summer in the Hamptons - who cares?" Palihapitiya stated heatedly. "Asset inflation does not solve income disparity. It actually doesn't solve full employment. It doesn't do any of the things we need it to do for it to be a robust economy. What it does is it allows people who play in the financial markets to make money," Palihapitiya further explained.

He stated that by handing out money to massive corporations that spent the last 10 years using borrowed money to buy back stocks and paying workers more in unemployment benefits than they earned in wages, the same economic situation that occurred in Japan during the 1990s could play out in the U.S. after the crisis. Consumers would rush to save more, even in the face of low to no interest; growth would slow, forcing price instability as productivity decreases; and high unemployment would proliferate.

A lack of confidence, mixed with increased income inequality, would have destabilizing effects on other markets such as stocks, housing, etc. "If you don't break this cycle and teach a new pattern of behavior, we're going to be looking at a Japanese-style deflationary period," he added. Be it bankruptcies, credit events, natural disasters, or terrorist attacks, there has been a growing bubble present looking for an excuse to pop. Markets have become so fragile that it is only a matter of time before it cracks. Since the Great Recession of 2008, loose monetary policy has led all asset classes to reach all-time highs. Out of control debt and credit creation, stock buybacks, corrupt credit rating agencies, and more has led the financial markets to skate on thin ice. Creditors have dug deep to find anybody or anything to lend money, all in a failed effort to drive growth in the economy.

With companies in the energy sector already filing for bankruptcy, the retail and hospitality sectors are not far behind. The real estate and the auto sector are all set up to fall off a cliff. Landlords are being left out to dry, with some areas forcing no rental increases or evictions, and allowing tenants not to pay. At some point, this will put pressure on the creditors, who will either get bailed out or face Lehman-style defaults. While the quantitative easing and stimulus packages may have delayed the bulk of the disaster until after the election, eventually, the bills will have to be paid.

To all these problems, the answer again and again is to print more money and create more debt, both of which can never be paid back. With restricted global output and falling demands, it is only a matter of time before the inflation gets out of hand, especially with the increases in money supply. In the middle of all this, and looking at the relationship between the central banks' balance sheets and the world stock markets, don't you wonder who is buying the dip?[26]

Charles Hugh Smith stated, "The Everything Bubble will finally pop, stripping the system of phantom speculative wealth and fictitious capital. Price discovery will once again be possible, as all the central bank-inflated bubbles will deflate, and real demand and supply will set the price of assets." He predicted millions will lose their jobs, solid businesses will crumble, and 'everyone on the edge of insolvency gets a hard push over the cliff.'"

"The bottom line," he said, "is that the U.S. economy needs a reset to 'lift all boats' and, as painful as it will be, the sooner the better." When this day arrives, we will be forced to return to precious metals as a standard for exchange. But by then, they will be too expensive or impossible to obtain.

---

[26] https://www.zerohedge.com/s3/files/inline-images/2020-05-09.jpg?itok=vcHC1iEo

SECTION 6: DUMP THE DOLLAR

"A democracy cannot exist as a permanent form of government. It can only exist until the voters discover that they can vote themselves largesse from the public treasury. From that moment on, the majority always votes for the candidates promising the most benefits the public treasury with the result that a democracy always collapses over lousy fiscal policy, always followed by a dictatorship. The average of the world's great civilizations before they decline has been 200 years. These nations have progressed in this sequence: From bondage to spiritual faith; from faith to great courage; from courage to liberty; from liberty to abundance; from abundance to selfishness; from selfishness to complacency; from complacency to apathy; from apathy to dependency; from dependency back again to bondage."

Excerpt from *Cycle of Democracy* by Alexander Fraser Tytler, a Scottish lawyer and professor in 1700

In the mountains of Asia Minor, on the western part of the Armenian Plateau, existed the famous and wealthy Kingdom of Lydia. During the 6th and 7th centuries BCE, they set up some of the first retail shops that sold electrum in permanent positions. The Pactolus River ran through their heartland and was one of the largest sources of electrum in the ancient world.

Electrum is a natural mix of gold, silver, and trace amounts of copper. Referred to by the Greeks as "white gold," the fame of the wealth in this region grew to mythic proportions. Its kings gained massive fortunes, being the first to create coinage from this magical new metal, and this concept was quickly copied by the Athenian Greeks.

As referenced from Encyclopedia Britannica, it was not long before the Athenian Greeks plundered the region, not unlike that of the Battle of Troy and Homer's *The Iliad* and *Odyssey*. But it was in Robert Hussey's work, *An Essay of the Ancient Weights and Money and the Roman and Greek Liquid Measures*, that we were able to know how the Greeks always admired the "wealth of the East."

Later, the Persians, having copied the same model from the Greeks for a gold and silver standard, stole from the Lydians and set out to establish their standard. Roughly a medium of exchange was set at 10 silver pieces for 1 gold piece, and the Lydians became famous for their purity.

In William E. Metcalf's work, *The Oxford Handbook of Greek and Roman Coins*, we learned that in the middle of the 6th century BCE, King Croesus of Lydia replaced electrum coins with that of pure gold and silver called Croeseids, information coming to us by Herodotus. According to Hussey, the purity of the gold produced by the Lydians was around 23 karats fine, allowing this gold to silver ratio to work effectively. Still, we learned from ancient writers that counterfeiting began to take place.

For Ancient Greece, silver became the chosen medium because of their ample silver mines and gold was scarce. Over time, copper slowly came to be used for lesser values but eventually worked its way back to the gold. Burdened by the costs of state affairs and ravaged by constant and expensive foreign campaigns, politicians and kings of Ancient Greece, Lydia, Persia, and even Rome made the choice to eventually debase their gold and silver. The debasement was done through a variety of means, such as mixing gold with copper or clipping the edges of coins to make more coins.

While the styles of counterfeiting money for currency varied, they all ended up with a similar effect: loss of purchasing power, inflation, and eventual loss of confidence in the monetary system. Why spend my silver coin today when next month it will be worth more? This realization has led to hoarding and the crippling of the economic and financial systems. Once it crashes and burns, we will pick up the pieces and start back to when we realized that money cannot be created, only debt.

According to a report by Russia Today on May 18, 2020, Moscow had cut its stockpile of U.S. Treasury Securities by $8.73 billion USD. This move was in line with a longer-term move away from reliance upon the U.S. dollar. The report stated that Moscow liquidated 96% of its U.S. debt holdings over the past 3 years. Currently, according to official figures, Japan remained the largest holder of U.S. state debt since June 2019, with China a close second. Both

Russia and China had been pursuing de-dollarization policies in response to the sanctions imposed by Washington.

The report stated, "As a matter of state policy, Moscow has also been diversifying its reserves, increasing bullion purchases to record levels, and earning the title of the world's most committed purchaser of gold. According to the latest data from the Central Bank of Russia, the country's total gold holdings amounted to 73.9 million troy ounces (2,298 tons) as of March and worth around $120 billion [USD]."

On August 7, 2019, Anna Golubova published an article for Kitco News stating that China's central bank had been stockpiling gold for the last eight months. According to Colin Hamilton, Managing Director of Commodities Research at BMO Capital Markets, this move showed that there was a desire to move away from the dollar and diversify at the central bank level. But why would anyone want to move away from the dollar? Isn't it the most accessible medium of business transactions?

The U.S. government always has vested interest in the health and welfare of its economy. The Department of Treasury works together with the Fed to "maintain economic stability." While the U.S. Treasury is known for printing currency and giving financial advice to presidents, the Fed and central banks' role are to provide credit and loans to borrowers. Both organizations are essential when fighting recessions and promoting healthy economic growth.

It is not surprising that what was once considered as "gas money," is deemed virtually worthless today—just look at the drop in purchasing power experienced by the dollar over the last 100 years[27]. This visualization was created to demonstrate the effect inflation has upon fiat currency based on the Consumer Price Index (CPI). It depicted major events, such as the creation of the Fed, the Black Thursday Wall Street Crash, and the Bretton Woods Agreement to name a few. But regardless of how people voted, whether Republican or Democrat, the effect would still be the same: their currency would become less valuable. But it is important to remember that it is not gold,

---

[27] https://cdn.howmuch.net/articles/Rise-and-Fall-of-the-USD-688d.jpg

silver, Bitcoin, and other assets that has become more valuable; it is our fiat currencies that are losing their purchasing power.

No one articulated it best than Friedrich A. Hayek, a Nobel prizewinner and economist, "With the exception only of the period of the gold standard, practically all governments of history have used their exclusive power to issue money to defraud and plunder the people." Or, as Sir John Dalberg-Acton put it, "Power tends to corrupt, and absolute power corrupts absolutely. Great men are almost always bad men..." So, are these organizations issuing money or debt?

Mike Maloney's *Guide to Investing in Gold and Silver*, and Robert Kiyosaki's *Rich Dad's Advisors* book series gave us a concise definition of money. Maloney defined money as having the following characteristics: a medium of exchange, a unit of account, durable, divisible, portable, fungible, and, most importantly, a store of value.

A medium of exchange is the ability to be used as an intermediary in trade. A unit of account is the ability to be numbered and counted. Durability refers to how long its usable life is. Divisibility means it can be divided into smaller parts without losing any value. Portability is the ability to take it with you anywhere. Fungibility means that each unit of equal value is the same and capable of being mutually substituted. However, Maloney pointed out that while fiat currency retains all these criteria for the definition of money, it is not a store of value. Store of value is something that can retain its purchasing power over long periods, which all fiat currencies do not have.

In fact, according to Jerry Robinson in his New York Times bestseller, *Bankruptcy of Our Nation*, he stated, "...today's U.S. dollar is a completely worthless piece of paper that derives its value through the faith of the public and the policies dictated in Washington. Isn't it amazing that after all of the fiat failures throughout history, here we are standing at the same cliff of disaster yet again?"

Ever since fiat currency was created in Ancient China around 1000 CE, we have repeatedly made the same mistakes. In Richard von Glahn's book,

Fountain of Fortune: Money and Monetary Policy in China, 1000–1700, we can see still the same mistakes being made with currency today.

- **In stage 1**, greed takes over, and the monetary supply is slowly debased, losing value at a slow and unnoticeable rate at first.
- **In stage 2**, this eventually leads to the perpetuation of more greed, often to pay debts, more currency is minted, [and] the monetary supply is debased, essentially taxing the citizens.
- **In stage 3**, those holding currency during these periods will see their purchasing power collapse, and the wise ones will opt for hard assets.
- **In step 4**, when the needs for even more currency arise, as they inevitably always do, then inflation begins to take over, now the effects are noticeable by the general population, often leading to a scramble for assets.
- **By stage 5,** there is hyperinflation, as people struggle to purchase necessities. By this time, economic productivity has halted, because the supply chains have collapsed.
- Finally, in **stage 6,** people have learned the lessons and go back to what history has shown is a reliable model, gold and silver standard based on real money, which restarts the cycle again.

What is $100 worth in 1913 over time?

1913:	$100
1923:	$57.89
1933:	$76.15
1943:	$57.23
1953:	$37.08
1963:	$32.35
1973:	$22.30
1983:	$9.94
1993:	$6.85
2003:	$5.38
2013:	$4.25
2019:	$3.87

What stage do you think we are in with the U.S. dollar? If you had $100 USD in 1913, Howmuch.net calculated you would have about $3.87 USD today—a 97% loss of purchasing power of. As we can see in the chart, while the purchasing power can go up and down, it never came close to regaining what it once had.

Inflation, which is the constant rise in prices each year, has diminished the purchasing power of all fiat currencies in circulation. Carlos stated, "As demonstrated by the data, dollar purchasing power has a negative correlation with the CPI. As the CPI increases, the purchasing power of the dollar decreases over time." While controlled inflation can have a positive effect in an economic environment, during recessions and other major financial events, these can have a drastic impact on inflation. As governments borrow more money and hand out economic stimulus, and central banks bail out corporations, the more the economy props up, increasing the monetary supply.

Instead of basing on real economic growth, the global economies, since the Great Recession of 2008, have relied heavily upon financial services and assets. Instead of letting unprofitable companies fail as we have seen in Iceland, they were bailed out with massive amounts of funds, using it to buy back stocks and give corporate bonuses when it could have been used to promote economic growth. But the calls for bailouts did not stop at the corporations. Now, whether you are a student, elderly pensioner, business owner, etc., you are qualified for a bailout.

As the famous, but not an actual quote from, Benjamin Franklin (even though it was posted as such on Forbes), once said, "When the people find they can vote themselves money, that will herald the end of the republic." As the stock market becomes heavily zombified, the real tradable value of these institutions becomes hidden. Eventually, there is nothing worth investing in, and investors will be left to secure safe assets to preserve their wealth, including central banks around the world. The "smart money" is preparing for what is coming, but it will be too late by the time the "dumb money" wakes up. If you have not begun preparing, it is not too late to do so. But time is running out.

SECTION 7: THE NEW GOLD RUSH

"Gold is the money of kings, silver is the money of gentlemen, barter is the money of peasants – but debt is the money of slaves."

Norm Franz, best-selling author, and economist.

If we were to go back to the bustling markets of Babylon, we would receive 2.1 grams of silver for a day of hard labor; and while prices ranged, it would take one to eight days' worth, for us to buy a sheep. In Ancient Greece, it would be better if we were unskilled laborer. One attic *drachma*, about 4.3 grams of silver, was a day's wage in the 5th century BCE and increased to 2.5 *drachma* by 377 BCE.

In the 5th century BCE, if you were to go to the market in Ancient Greece, one *drachma* could buy about 3 kilograms of olive oil, while 3 *drachma* could get about one *medimnos* or 52 liters of wheat. Even though the price of one *medimnos* of wheat increased to 5 *drachma*, if you only lived on bread and foraged, a day's labor could still feed you for 2 weeks.

During the Roman Empire, a day of unskilled labor was 1.2 *denarii* or 4.2 grams of silver, not unlike that of the Greeks. But due to inflation, especially during and after the times of Emperor Nero, the currency slowly debased, lowering the silver amount and mixing in other metals. Eventually, this led to the prices of hard assets to skyrocket, as trust in the currency failed.

During Medieval England, a laborer was expected to receive 2 pounds sterling a year or 672 grams of silver, equating about 2.1 grams of silver per day since they were on a different work schedule. A thatcher of the time, a form of roofer, would earn about 2 pence or 2.8 grams of silver a day, which would rise to 4 pence in 1381 and then to 6 pence by 1481. In the 14th century, wine would cost between 3 and 10 pence a gallon and 2 dozen eggs would be one penny. In the 15th century, an ax would go for 5 pence, whereas a liter of wheat would be 0.2 grams of silver—not far off from Ancient Greece's.

With the rise of the Industrial Revolution, we had more fiat currency introduced alongside gold and silver coins. The price of gold, which Sir Isaac Newton fixed in 1717, stayed relatively the same until WWI. Silver also stayed about the same at $1.30 USD per ounce when the U.S. was founded, except for the turbulence of the Civil War, until the last of the 1870s. During the 19th century, the prices declined until WWI. Throughout most human civilizations, we have valued silver to gold ratio with eight to 13 ounces of silver for 1 ounce of gold.

More recently, in 1792, the U.S. fixed it to 15 to one, which stayed that way until the 20th century. A day's worth of unskilled labor averaged nearly one-tenth an ounce of silver throughout most of history and still does in many parts of the developing world.

On June 24, 2015, Daniela Pylypczak-Wasylyszyn brought us the historical analysis, in a piece titled *The Historical Value of Silver: A 2000-Year Overview*. This historical perspective of valuations can help provide a reference point for our understandings of the future. A troy ounce[28] is an international form of measuring the weight of metals, which is 31.1 grams to a troy ounce. Since ancient times, gold has had a central role in financial systems. This had remained the case until President Nixon decided to end the convertibility of the U.S. dollar into gold at a fixed rate of $35 USD a troy ounce.

After a strong inflation surge throughout the 1970s, gold prices declined, leading many central banks to start selling their gold reserves[29]. Without the price increase in gold, there were much more attractive investments elsewhere. However, since the Great Recession of 2008, we have seen nations and central banks increase their reserves faster than ever before.

While many individual investors have turned to digital versions of gold and silver, such as ETFs, there has been increased accumulation from private investors, hedgers, nations, and central banks in the physical forms. As the adage goes, "If you don't hold it, you don't own it."[30]

According to an article in Bloomberg News by Elena Mazneva on July 19, 2019 titled *Central Banks' Gold-Buying Spree is Far from Over, Poll Shows*, over the last

---

[28] https://macrotrends.net/1333/historical-gold-prices-100-year-chart
[29] https://bmg-group.com/wp-content/uploads/2016/04/DOLLAR-VS-GOLD-1024x614.jpg
[30] https://static.seekingalpha.com/uploads/2019/7/31/410007-15645934659948127.png

decade, central banks had been increasing their investments in gold. She stated that this gold buying spree would likely continue as financial instability was bullish for gold. "In a survey of central banks conducted by the World Gold Council and YouGov, 54% of respondents expect global holdings to climb in the next 12 months amid concerns about risks in other reserve assets. Looking further ahead, two-thirds see gold's share of reserves staying the same or rising in 5 years' time."

According to the data from the International Monetary Fund, nations around the world had increased their strategic gold reserves, up about 14% since 2009. Countries, such as China, Russia, and Poland, facing slowing economic growth, rising geopolitical tensions, and seeking diversification away from the U.S. dollar had seen the most significant increases. Mazneva stated that in 2018, bullion holdings rose the most on record since 1971 by an estimated 651.5 tons. As the price of gold began to rise in 2018, so had silver since it usually rises after and much faster than gold.

According to the 2019 Central Bank Gold Reserve Survey published on July 18, 2019 by the World Gold Council (WGC), there had been a robust demand for gold by central banks, with plans to expand gold purchases. The levels reached 651 tons of demand, the highest on record during the current international monetary system. The driving force behind these purchases was the perceived economic risks in reserve currencies and instability.

The survey stated, "In the next 12 months, heightened economic risks in reserve currency issuing countries are seen as the main factor driving these purchases, but in the medium-term structural changes in the global economy may also play a role."

With more purchases planned on the horizon and the geopolitical landscape getting more treacherous, central banks have been rushing to safe assets in the hopes for financial changes. Rising national tendencies helped play a part in the rush for gold as countries try to reduce dependence upon the U.S. dollar. This was illustrated in a comment by President Erdogan of Turkey, "Gold has never been an instrument of oppression." As more and more nations face the sanctions of economic reality, we see more "oil for gold" schemes, such as between Iran, India, and Turkey, which helped the Iranians counter American sanctions.

Similarly, the Russians have been selling oil to China, priced in Chinese yuan, which is then used to buy gold on the Shanghai Gold Exchange with yuan-denominated gold futures contracts. In the face of American unilateralism, the central banks of some countries such as Poland and Hungary have been stepping up purchases of gold. It is not surprising that some of the largest purchasers of gold among central banks since 1999 are developing nations such as China, India, Russia, and Turkey.[31]

While the past 50 years has seen several generations of investors grow up with the thought that gold is a "barbarous relic," we see this change as global financial systems come under pressure. It has been said that gold travels to where it is best appreciated. Throughout history, that has usually been Asia and that is no different today. The rapid development and rising incomes in Asia have helped facilitate increased gold buying. Countries such as Vietnam, Turkey, Iran, Thailand, India, and China have been buying, saving, and using gold as money for thousands of years. For instance, it is still a common practice for the groom to purchase ฿6 THB of gold (3 troy ounces), as gift to the parents of the bride.

Marin Katusa, of Katusa Research, a leader in resource-based research and investment, issued a report on February 10, 2020 titled *Red Gold: China's Stealth Plan to Use Gold for World Domination*. In the report, he stated that during the last quarter of 2018, central banks bought more gold than any other quarter recorded and possessed 1.064 billion troy ounces of gold or 33,200 tons. This colossal figure equated to about one-fifth of all the gold mined on Earth, ever. The thing about gold is that the vast majority that has ever been mined is still in existence today thanks to its value and use in financial systems.

Katusa said, "In the first half of 2019, central banks purchased 11.97 million ounces of gold (374 tons). Once again, that was far more than ever before. And

---

[31] http://www.usfunds.com/media/images/frank-talk-images/2019_ft/JAN-JUN/top-10-gold-producing-countries-2017-06-2018.png

it's equivalent to one-sixth of total gold demand in that period. And total central bank gold purchases for 2019 were the second highest they've been in the last 50 years (2018 being the first)." He found the most exciting part of the data, was that most of the gold buying came from just 4 nations: Russia, China, Kazakhstan, and Turkey. While Asia has been on a gold-buying spree, most Western governments have been asleep (but some countries have taken notice).

In recent years, we have seen Russia hit with sanctions which helped kick-start de-dollarization policies. It included selling off all U.S. dollar-denominated assets and using the proceeds to invest in gold.

According to the World Silver Survey issued in 2019, "Asia accounts for approximately half of silver held by governments, spread over a few different countries. Contrary to gold, which is actively purchased by Asian and other central banks, silver enjoys little attention regarding diversifying foreign exchange reserves. At two-thirds, China accounts for the largest share." Katusa said that in 2019, the gold purchased by Russia had increased from $86 billion USD to over $112 billion USD, resulting not only in profits but also leverage for the Russians.

Data provided by Katusa Research[32] shows the percentage of foreign exchange reserves held in gold has been increasing. As the saying goes, "He who has the gold makes the rules." While the chart from Katusa Research showed the official gold reserves in U.S. dollars[33], we could see Russia and China lagging the Western nations. Still, China held much larger foreign reserves, so gold was thus a smaller percentage overall. Katusa stated that for China to match official figures with the U.S., it would take 14 years of gold production worldwide (1.98 billion troy ounces or 62,000 tons of gold) to do so.

While this may be a near-impossible feat for some nations, official figures showed China is both the largest producer and consumer of gold and has been actively buying mines around the world. While this stockpiling will not have an immediate effect upon the spot gold prices, if it is consumed at the production stage with lower costs, it will restrict supply to the physical markets.

---

[32] https://katusaresearch.com/wp-content/uploads/2020/02/Gold-as-percentage-of-foreign-exchange-reserves-min-768x562.png
[33] https://www.zerohedge.com/s3/files/inline-images/world%20gold%20holdings%20may%202020.jpg?itok=OpPHcuns

Complicating the issue is the fact that China does not regularly update its official gold figures and it is not easy to verify independently. As Katusa pointed out, "From 2009 to 2015, the Chinese government didn't provide any updates about its gold holdings. Then it suddenly announced a massive 57% jump in its reserves."

While official figures portrayed one part of the story, we need to consider the history of Asia as gold-buying consumers. Asian countries such as India and China have a tradition going back thousands of years of investing in and gifting gold. Gold jewelry is more common and in purer forms than their counterparts in Western countries. It is a standard part of any Indian wedding and is often sold during financial difficulty.

As we can see in the charts provided by Smaulgld, both gold and silver imports have been on the rise in India since 1999[34][35]. In recent years, the push towards a cashless society has helped drive demand for gold and silver in India. With the recent rise in gold prices, this has made silver a much cheaper and attractive investment.

A survey conducted by the World Gold Council in 2016 produced the following responses with Indian consumers: 63% of respondents agreed with the statement: "I trust gold more than the currencies of countries." Meanwhile, 73% agreed with "Gold makes me feel secure for the long-term."

Pierre Lassonde, the cofounder of the first publicly traded gold royalty company Franco-Nevada Corporation, had seen a transition in the gold market in recent years. 30 years ago, central banks were net sellers of gold and the West dominated the markets; but now, we see gold shift towards the East. The demand had grown significantly in China and India, which, together in 1989, just made up 10% of the gold demand. But by 2018, they account for 53%. Essentially, the Eastern markets were draining the West of gold for years.

According to an article published in Kitco News by Anna Golubova on

---

[34] https://il.wp.com/smaulgld.com/wp-content/uploads/2020/01/Indian-Gold-Imports-1999-2019.png?resize=580%2C357&ssl=1
[35] https://il.wp.com/smaulgld.com/wp-content/uploads/2020/01/Indian-Silver-imports-1999-2019-november.png?resize=580%2C356&ssl=1

October 17, 2019, China had more gold than they were letting on. She stated that while official figures showed China as the 6th largest gold holding nation, this did not consider the large population's holdings. It was not until 2003 that the ban on owning gold was lifted for the citizens of China; and since then, the government began encouraging its citizens to actively own gold.

Based on my personal experiences living in China, Chinese banks offer programs to give information and advertise gold and silver. There are advertisements in public places like the subways and malls. It is not difficult to find a jewelry store or bank to purchase coins or bars as these are plentiful in most cities. It is well known that the holiday buying of both India and China are so great that it can affect market prices.

In contrast, the only advertisements we see about gold and silver in the West are "cash for gold" and selling what little they have as fast as possible. These days, you do not even need to know how much you are going to get. You simply need to mail it in and then receive your check., resulting to the increasing unawareness people have on the daily price of gold. Whereas in Asia, every jewelry store or place that sells bullion usually have the daily spot prices listed, generally in large signs. As investing and saving play a more significant role in Asian consumers, so does gold and silver.

Wells Fargo's Head of Real Asset Strategy John LaForge said, "China and Chinese citizens are quite keen to hold gold. Gold holdings, however, are one component of economic data that can be hard to come by and can be confusing. China, and Chinese citizens, likely hold more gold than official numbers would indicate." He believed Chinese consumers had accumulated more gold than official figures let on and imported data from Hong Kong to Mainland China could prove this[36].

"The chart shows gold flows over the past year, from Hong Kong to Mainland China. At 400 tons (blue bars), gold flows from Hong Kong into Mainland China were nearly 4 times higher than official PBoC (People's Bank of China) statistics. Precisely where this gold is going, once it makes it into Mainland

---

[36] https://www.kitco.com/news/2019-10-17/images/WellsFargoOctChina.png

China, is anyone's guess," LaForge said.

While Asians have come to dominate the precious metals markets, Europeans have begun to share their views regarding them. Not only is gold considered a strategic asset by central banks and governments, but it is also essential for individual investors.

On May 29, 2020 WGC issued a report titled *Safety and expected returns attract German investors to gold* by Louise Street. They conducted a survey in 2019 with 2,000 German investors, as part of a much bigger study of 12,000 investors, across the U.S., China, India, Canada, Russia, and Germany. According to the survey, "The research revealed that almost half of German retail investors buying gold bars and coins felt that the main role of their gold investment was to protect their wealth, with around one-third focusing on good long-term returns (in excess of inflation)." The survey showed that 31% of participants thought gold would produce the best returns over the next 3 years ahead of stocks at the global level with risk management as its main driver[37].

Since 2020, given the developments involving the COVID-19 pandemic, physical bullion sales have managed to clean out most dealers' inventories. Throughout history, and even around the world today, when nations face economic uncertainty, precious metals have acted as a safe asset to preserve wealth and purchasing power. As we have seen, foreign currencies come under increased pressures against the dollar; the flight to gold is likely only to increase. However, by the time everyone wants it, the supply will be gone.

With the world distracted by COVID-19, something unusual was happening in the gold and silver markets. As global supply chains were collapsing and markets churned in turmoil, precious metals were especially feeling the effects. Gold and silver futures contracts began to decouple from the physical prices of bullion. The trade price of gold and silver fell drastically with the market, whereas the physical price rose. Seemingly overnight, all the dealers for physical metals were either closing shops, refusing to sell, or charging steep premiums well above the spot price.

---

[37] https://www.gold.org/sites/default/files/2020-05/louise_1.png

Under normal circumstances, dealers might charge 1% to 2% for the run of the mill bullion products; but suddenly we saw premiums as high as 5% to 10% on these same items. Not only was it challenging to buy, but it was also expensive. The closures of many refiners made the situation even more difficult. On top of high prices, dealers were not selling much stock, and what was for sale was 6 weeks or more away. A lot can happen in 6 weeks.

As reported by Elena Mazneva and Jack Farchy of Bloomberg on May 29, 2020, there was a record divergence in gold futures versus spot prices which opened a flood of physical metal transfers to the U.S. It was reported that this "may be one of the largest ever physical transfers of the metal."

In New York, as commodity traders scramble to cover their positions, there is an unprecedented demand for physical gold. According to a report from Reuters on May 26, 2020, official customs data showed that Swiss exports of gold to the U.S. were 111.7 tons in April, the most significant month on record.

During this same period, supplies to other countries dwindled, with India only receiving 0.5 tons and Hong Kong and China only receiving one kilogram. Allan Fin, the Global Commodities Director for Malca-Amit, told Bloomberg that since late March, at least 550 tons of gold valued at $30 billion USD, which was about the same amount mined during this period, was added to the Comex. That amount accounted for the 11th largest sovereign gold holding, even more significant than the European Central Bank's total of 504.8 tons.

To meet the demands for physical bullion, refineries worldwide must increase their production of kilobars, the size used for delivery to the Comex. Brink's Managing Director Mark Woolley said that the recent surge in demand was unlike anything he had seen over the last 20 years.

"The amount of metal that we've successfully moved into New York is pretty significant," he said on a webinar hosted by the London Bullion Market Association. "It's probably not far off the total amount of metal that's been mined in this period."

Michael Hartnett, Chief Investment Strategist at Bank of America Merrill Lynch Global Research, stated that the current trend for the "smart money" was to sell stocks and buy gold. During that period of several weeks, he witnessed high net worth clients selling equities and buying gold; a trend which has only continued since then. Mislav Matejka, JP Morgan's Head of Global and European Equity Strategy, mentioned that while technology shares were expected to do well, gold would outperform the market during deflation and relation.

As stated earlier, the silver to gold ratio for most of the human civilization varied from eight to 15 ounces of silver to one ounce of gold. If we take the ratio gold and silver are extracted from the ground, current mining figures put the silver-gold ratio at about 9 to 1. However, if you look at spot prices or gold-silver ratio charts, you will see history in the making.

On March 26, 2020, the silver-gold ratio hit an all-time high of 126 to 1. This meant that 126 troy ounces of silver was worth 1 troy ounce of gold. Since then, the ratio had declined back down to 96 to one as of May 31, 2020 and was around 70 to one as of September 1, 2020. Personally, I would not consider trading my silver for gold for anything less than 15 to 20 to 1.

But if we are to look at the 100-year chart[38], we will see that gold generally trades in an average band of 40 to 60 to 1, and for as low as 30 to 1 as of April 26, 2011 upon market closure. As we overshot to the upside on the ratio, it is common market behavior to overshoot to the downside, which I am patiently waiting for. In the past, when gold rallied, silver would languish for a bit before running with much more intensity. While I am not a financial advisor and cannot legally give financial advice, given the current price action, silver would be an excellent choice compared to gold. Assuming silver sees more robust demand than gold in the future, the silver-gold ratio could come back down to sub 40 to one, as price action tends to overshoot before finding an equilibrium.

In theory, if you were to buy 99 troy ounces of silver when the ratio was 99 to one, then traded them for gold when the ratio was 33 to one in the future, you would receive 3 troy ounces of gold for the same value as you would originally have for one troy ounce. While there are dealer premiums, and the silver to

---

38 https://www.macrotrends.net/1441/gold-to-silver-ratio

gold ratio does not reflect the exact exchange rate of dealers, it does provide a thought-provoking guide to the market.

If we were to look back through the history of the banking system, we could see that gold and silver have been valued and has played a central role for thousands of years. Gold and silver provide a check and balance for monetary policy and give value to the currency because we cannot produce gold and silver. The actual cost of each troy ounce of gold and silver not only relies on its price but also on how many hours of labor and resources go into the searching, extracting, and processing of each troy ounce.

As societies have shifted from what can only be considered as real money to a currency-based system, we see the same results repeatedly. As currencies get overproduced, they begin to lose purchasing power, resulting to inflation. During an inflationary environment, real asset prices skyrocket leading everyone to hold what they have and not sell. In our current financial climate, we are witnessing currency creation at rates which the world has never seen. As central banks, nations, and private investors rush to safe assets, such as gold and silver, this will only cause shortages.

As someone who began training in technical analysis in 2016, I am reminded of some foundational rules of trade. One of the most important things I learned is to "follow the smart money." Smart money is a term that refers to institutional investors, such as whales, banks, hedge funds, etc. advisors, with deep pockets and possible insider information.

Opposite this is the "dumb money" which refers to retail investors and the public. Anyone who has day traded knows that by the time the news hits, it is too late, and the market has already reacted. This is because it is theorized that two emotions, fear and greed, control people so people see a price move and chase the high. The term for this is FOMO or fear of missing out. Why is it that people repeatedly sell at the worst possible time? To this point, Warren Buffet, arguably the most investment-minded person of all time, once said, "Be fearful when others are greedy and greedy when others are fearful."

In the case of gold, the smart money has been rapidly accumulating gold and silver with no plans to stop. We have even seen governments such as China encourage their citizens to have more physical gold and silver. All the while, Western citizens have been herded towards the stock market as the big players cashes out.

So, the question is: Who are you going to follow—the "smart money" or the "dumb money?"

CHAPTER 5: UNRESTRICTED WARFARE

SECTION 1: INTRODUCTION

"On avait oublié toute à fait que sous l'homme, même le plus civilisé, on attient vite le sauvage."

(It has been completely forgotten that if you scratch the surface of man, even at his most civilized, you quickly reach the savage.)

Anne Louise Germaine de Staël-Holstein, Genevan political theorist and witness of the French Revolution, Napoleonic Era, and French Restoration

"A new generation of *Unrestricted Warfare* is upon us" was a concept created in 1999. It is known as 超限战 in simplified Chinese and 超限戰 in traditional Chinese, respectively, which both translate to "warfare beyond bounds." This is a modern form of military doctrine written by 2 colonels in the People's Liberation Army, Qiao Liang (乔良) and Wang Xiangsui (王湘穗).

As the American proverb points out, generals are always prepared to fight the last war. The concept focused on the 4 critical areas of offensive actions: Lawfare, Economic Warfare, Network Warfare, and Terrorism. With technology advancing at lightspeed, mainly thanks to Moore's law, the theatre of war is dynamic. What may have been a check and balance a few years ago can be upended and change the direction of military investments for the next decade.

In recent times, we have seen drones become perfected for use, mainly for light recon and heavy drones for autonomous missions. We even have suicide drones now. In a few short years, drones became an invaluable part of the military, playing crucial roles in the current conflicts in Africa and the Middle East. But what does it mean to go to war? Are economic sanctions a form of war? How about cyber terrorism?

The nature of warfare has undergone as much transformation as the technologies that facilitate it, and so has its definition. The book *Unrestricted Warfare* set out to not only define these methods but also exhibit how China, from an underdog position, can defeat a technologically superior opponent such as the U.S. through a variety of untraditional means. Though, as we see, these methods have been deployed by various actors on the world stage. In the book, these methods can "have the same and even greater destructive force than military warfare, and they have already produced serious threats different from the past and in many directions for...national security."

First, the book detailed an alternative form of warfare called "Lawfare". It is a term that is often considered to date back to an essay by Charles J. Dunlap, Jr. in 2001, a now-retired Major General in the U.S. Airforce. Dunlap defined the term as "the use of law as a weapon of war." He later elaborated on it, saying it is "the exploitation of real, perceived, or even orchestrated incidents of law-of-war violations being employed as an unconventional means of confronting a superior military power." Hence, Lawfare uses political actions, either officially or unofficially, through transnationals and NGOs to cause policy change.

This reminded me of George Soros, the famous billionaire who likes to dabble in societal change. By using private organizations like NGO's, the need for an expensive and troublesome organization, such as the CIA, becomes unnecessary. Effectively, these are boots on the ground, without the legal backlash and plausible deniability.

Furthermore, if these organizations are persecuted, it will give the media an excellent narrative. Isn't it surprising that so many organizations have received large amounts of funding over the last decade, leading to many nations banning their activities? Under a guise of activism, it is much easier to enact policy changes in a country through "grass-roots" proxies. The use of these proxies eliminates the need to use direct military actions to achieve end goals.

Next, there is "Economic Warfare" which has a severe effect within an interconnected, globalized society. We have seen nations like America and her allies put economic sanctions on countries as a form of punishment to anyone who opposes them. According to the U.S. Department of the Treasury (USDT), as of May 2020, the U.S. has 32 active sanction programs against numerous counties—some dating back decades like Cuba (1958). These countries include Afghanistan, Belarus, Burundi, Central African Republic, China (PR), Côte d'Ivoire, Crimea Region, Cuba, Cyprus, the Democratic

Republic of the Congo, Eritrea, Fiji, Haiti, Iran, Iraq, Kyrgyzstan, Laos, Lebanon, Liberia, Libya, Myanmar, North Korea, Palestinian Territories, Russia, Rwanda, Somalia, South Sudan, Sri Lanka, Sudan, Syria, Venezuela, Yemen, and Zimbabwe.

Furthermore, this does not account for the numerous individuals that the U.S. has identified and put under sanction. According to USDT, economic sanctions can take a variety of forms and come in varying degrees. It can involve a ban on arms imports or exports, restricting technology access, economic assistance, waiving diplomatic immunity, and, most of all, the restriction of access to financial institutions. In fact, we are witnessing the Bank of England being pressured by the U.S. to refuse the return of Venezuela's gold stored in their vaults. As well as the oil restrictions the U.S. imposed on Venezuela and Iran, effectively cutting them off from the world's markets.

Then, we come to "Network Warfare," a severe threat to nations and a critical part of any modern warfare strategy. This involves government, public and private satellites, telephone and other communication mediums, internet access, apps, and power grids. In the case of Israel and Iran, it means nuclear energy.

In a technology-based society, access to reliable electricity and communication are necessary. Cyberwarfare is the new hot spot in military doctrine, even though it generally goes unreported. While forms of electronic warfare have existed since WWII, it was only in recent years, with the development of the internet and jamming technologies, that this previously shadowed and highly specified sector became better known to the public.

Increasingly, shutting down power networks, along with other vital areas, have become parts of a coordinated attack strategy. As early as 2014, we heard reports of Russian media claims about jamming technologies being used to disable American warships. On April 12, 2016, these claims became evident when 2 Russian SU-24s made as many as 12 close passes with the destroyer U.S.S. Donald Cook. However, the Americans refuted this. Regardless, it is well known that the U.S., Russia, China, Iran, North Korea, and many more have active electronic warfare units already integrated in their respective militaries.

At the same time, there are numerous private contractors in the arena. Hence the reason why there are so much controversy over 5G networks and apps such as Ticktock and WeChat.

Finally, we have the traditional form of "Terrorism," updated and modernized. The Oxford dictionary defines terrorism as "the unlawful use of violence and intimidation, especially against civilians, in the pursuit of political aims." Terrorism has become popularized in modern terms but has a proven and public track record. One nation's terrorist is another nation's freedom fighter. The book detailed that terrorism can be used to achieve one's end goals and can have an especially brutal effect on a nation's social fabric.

Simply take a look at the U.S. after the 9/11 attacks with the extensive security measures put in place that changed many aspects of daily life. A nation's sense of security and well-being can come into question after a terrorist attack. These attacks are exceedingly difficult to predict and even more challenging to stop. To top it all off, we have seen how anything can be used as weapons: from a mere kitchen knife to everyday vehicles. However, as we see in the Middle East, too many terrorist events can desensitize people to atrocities. But terrorism can be a useful tool, especially if the goal is general chaos, which is a much easier target than full regime change.

While the nature of warfare has changed with technology, the complexities it amounted to create challenges in identifying adversaries and predicting possible attacks. Gone are the days when a nation's leader will declare war with the public's approval. Instead, we live in a world where we are always unknowingly under attack in one form or another. We live in a state of perpetual warfare, a concept made famous by George Orwell in his book *1984*.

Warfare has come to mean something different in the 20th century than it did in the past. It is not a matter of "if we are at war," it is with "who and how much." War is part of human nature since the dawn of humankind. There has been no part of the world able to live without it for prolonged periods. The period of prosperity the developed nations experienced following WWI and WWII was only made possible because of the bloodshed left by these terrible events.

Let us not forget the 26 million Soviet citizens who gave their lives during WWII. For many North Americans, and even some Europeans, warfare may be a distant problem for nations that does not affect us. But in our interconnected world, we see supply chains shut down, resulting to job losses in domestic markets. Food and consumer goods shipments, along with migrant agricultural workers, are restricted in numerous countries. When the GDP of nations begins to drop respectively and the population looks for someone to blame, war becomes the easy way out.

While many think the Cold War ended with the fall of the Soviet Union, it only transformed into something different. Today, we are in the Cold War 2.0, meaning, the war never stopped.

SECTION 2: GLOBAL SOCIAL UNREST

"Hunger makes a thief of any man."

Pearl S. Buck, a recipient of the Nobel Prize for Literature in 1938

"Anyone can become a barbarian; it requires a terrible effort to remain a civilized man."

Leonard Wolf, annotative author of the mid-20th century

Americans see themselves as the torch bearers and inheritors of a long line of dominant western European civilizations and, as such, their history textbooks always begin with the Romans and Greeks. As if Europe had not stolen almost everything, they have that which can be considered part of their identity from Asia. Even more ironically, Greco-Romans labeled the ancestors of these Anglo-Germanic peoples as barbarians. However, since the mighty Roman Empire is so fond in the hearts and minds of Americans, let us begin there.

Without a doubt, numerous factors contributed to the decline of the Roman Empire, but the ones often overlooked were the social-economic ones. Near the end of the Roman Empire, a great shift took place. Income inequality was rampant, with the elites in control of large amounts of the wealth. The archeological record showed those who were wise began to flee the cities and building large, fortified villas far away from others. One of the more famous examples was Diocletian's Palace in modern-day Croatia. Built in the 4th century, it housed around 9000 people behind towers and tall walls.

In his book, *The Decline and Fall of the Roman Empire*, James Ermatinger stated, "Their disinclination to lead may have been caused by forced exactions, confiscations, business concerns, tax pressured, or general economic fears, which made protecting one's own interests seem more prudent than looking out for the interests of others."

In their selfishness, the Roman upper class abandoned their people when they needed them most, only further destabilizing Rome. Soldiers and common citizens could no longer trust that they would get what was "theirs," as the ruling upper class tended to keep all of their wealth to themselves, while maintaining slaves who did all of the work of the typical middle working class. An economic system built upon endless wars began to break down. All that was left for citizens and soldiers was economic squalor as wealth continued to be inherited by the rich and labor was taken by the slaves of war.

By every metric, the U.S. is even more divided and unfair than Rome before its fall. The effects are perfectly evident as well as there is increasing inclination from the rich to build fallout bunkers and withdraw from civilization and politics just as the Roman elites did centuries before. Across the U.S., major cities are being abandoned en mass. Democratic states like California have seen a population exodus for the past few years. Record levels of people are renouncing their citizenship, with more and more moving overseas. Citizenship for investment schemes have never been easier or more popular as recent figures showed overseas property markets are booming.

Worsening matters is the evidence of extreme racism towards migrant workers who, like the slaves in Rome, "take the labor from the hardworking middle class". Increasingly, the middle class shrinks as social unrest and bigotry grows. It is a scary combination that could potentially spell the end of civilization as we know it, just like it did for the Romans centuries ago.

Nations of the world are experiencing unprecedented social unrest, in which this COVID-19 pandemic helped fuel the fire of change. Versik Maplecroft, a data modeling, risk analysis, and strategic forecasting company, offered a perspective on complex issues in a global risk landscape for businesses and investors. They stated, "Global organizations can no longer afford to view environmental, political, social and economic risks in isolation—the lines have blurred." This had never been more apparent than in 2019.

In the report published on January 16, 2020 by Miha Hribernik and Sam Haynes, the dramatic increase in protests around the world in 2019 was detailed. These protests swept across a quarter of all countries and were expected to increase through 2020 and beyond. They developed a Civil Rights

Index (CRI) which assessed more than "150 political, human rights and environmental risks."[39]

In their report, nearly 40%, or about 75 out of 195 nations, would see some form of civil unrest or riots in 2020. This was approximately a 100% increase from the 47 countries that experienced civil unrest in 2019[40]. This directly correlates with the increase in human rights abuses against protesters, fanning the flames even more. Even corporations will not be spared They will be viewed with suspicion, especially with the increased pressure to cooperate with authoritarian regimes. The economic toll this causes to nations can amount to tens of billions.

The report also stated, "The number of countries rated extreme risk in the Civil Unrest Index has also jumped by 66.7%; from 12[%] in 2019 to 20[%] by early 2020. Countries dropping into this category include Ethiopia, India, Lebanon, Nigeria, Pakistan and Zimbabwe. Sudan, meanwhile, has overtaken Yemen to become the highest risk country globally."

Nations in the extreme risk category will face business risks, transport disruptions, damage to public or private assets, and physical risks to employees due to violent protests. These nations will see essential sectors such as mining, tourism, energy, retail, and financial services crippled. The effect on national economies will cause billions of dollars in losses.

"In Chile, the first month of unrest alone caused an estimated USD4.6 billion worth of infrastructure damage, and cost the Chilean economy around USD3 billion, or 1.1% of its GDP." While the toll was already being felt, the report did not see any relief coming in the near term. They expected Chile, a nation previously praised for its stability and prosperity, to remain in the extreme risk category until at least 2022.

While each protest may be a unique case with individual factors, on the macro stage, they all share the same key themes. Income inequality, warfare, inflation,

[39] https://www.maplecroft.com/siteassets/images/insight-images/analysis/2020/pro-2020/civil-unrest/figure-1-the-Civil-Unrest-Index-reveals-widespread-increases-in-risk-during-2019-jpg
[40] https://www.maplecroft.com/siteassets/images/insight-images/analysis/2020/pro-2020/civil-unrest/Figure-2-A-quarter-of-all-the-worlds-countries-saw-significant-increases-in-civil-unrest-during-2019-Index-2019.jpg

erosion of social liberties and increased authoritarianism are all on the rise and well documented across nations. If people are willing to riot over a cut in government subsidies, what do you think their financial situation is?

In a report depicting countries which were most likely to commit human rights abuses, it detailed, "In Chile, protests have been driven by income inequality and high living costs but were triggered by a seemingly trivial [$]30-peso [CLP] ($0.04 USD) increase in the price of metro tickets."[41]

As protests seem to wash across the globe, unabated, both the intensity of these protests and the number of actors involved is expected to increase over 2020. While businesses struggle to continue operating in emerging economies, they will face increased security concerns such as natural resource extraction and energy projects. These companies will be forced to seek increased protection, employing the state of private contractors, which may perpetuate the violence and anger. The report also said, "From an investment perspective, the use of state-sanctioned violence is a significant risk to any country's sovereign environmental, social and governance (ESG) profile, and is no less a risk to the ESG profiles of complicit companies."

According to the report, what began in 2019 was expected to be the "new normal." Companies, along with investors, would have to adapt to this unfavorable climate. While policymakers had responded with limited concessions in general, the impact of COVID-19 added fuel to these already hot fires of discontent. The report stated that the vast majority of these "grievances are deeply entrenched and would take years to address."

As indicated by a report in Agence France-Presse on May 18, 2020, the International Monetary Fund (IMF) cautioned about the financial destruction brought about by the coronavirus pandemic, adding social distress far and wide, and encouraged governments to find a way to forestall the unsettling influences. The report described how the IMF was ready to assist many nations

---

[41] https://www.maplecroft.com/siteassets/images/insight-images/analysis/2020/pro-2020/civil-unrest/Figure-6-A-look-at-our-Security-Forces-and-Human-Rights-Index-and-our-Civil-Unrest-Index-projections-for-2020-identifies-jurisdictions-where-protesters-are-most-likely-to-face-abuses-jpg

in tackling unemployment, income inequality, and the risk of warfare. Still, it warned that global economic recovery is unlikely in 2021.

In a New York Times opinion-editorial published on December 16, 2008, the former U.S. National Security Advisor and Center for Strategic and International Studies, Zbigniew Brzezinski, warned the following:

> "For the first time in human history almost all of humanity is politically activated, politically conscious and politically interactive. Global activism is generating a surge in the quest for cultural respect and economic opportunity in a world scarred by memories of colonial or imperial domination… There are only a few pockets of humanity left in the remotest corners of the world that are not politically alert and engaged with the political turmoil and stirrings that are so widespread today around the world."

Indeed, it seems that technology helped facilitate the needs and desires of a more accountable world community. It was at this moment the term "global political awakening" was coined. Since then, we have seen restfulness and resentment transcend borders, evident by the cases of refugees and migrants.

> "America needs to face head-on a centrally important new global reality: that the world's population is experiencing a political awakening unprecedented in scope and intensity, with the result that the politics of populism are transforming the politics of power. The need to respond to that massive phenomenon poses a historic dilemma to the American sovereign: What should be the central definition of America's global role?"

Since the end of WWII, global powers, such as the U.S. and her allies and the Soviet Union and her allies, have been battling over spheres of influence. These battles would take place indirectly through smaller states referred to as proxies. This is reminiscent to George Orwell's book, *1984*.

Recently, China has emerged as a growing competitor across a wide range of fields such as diplomacy, financial assistance, arms sales, and economic relations. Ever since Putin took office in Russia, Russian foreign diplomacy has increased its consolidation over former Soviet republics. The Americans have invaded past the agreed-upon boundaries of influence, expanding NATO, and stepping up involvement in the South China Sea. But have had their focus on the Middle East, especially since the events of 9/11 attacks. This has left room for China and Russia to expand their spheres of influence, unburdened by the severe effects of terrorism.

> "[T]he central challenge of our time is posed not by global terrorism, but rather by the intensifying turbulence caused by the phenomenon of global political awakening. That awakening is socially massive and politically radicalizing."

Developing countries that may have previously viewed Western nations in a positive light have become increasingly distrustful and, thus, turned to the East. The more nations the Americans bomb, sanction, and invade, the more they are isolating themselves on the global stage. In addition, they waste resources and go deeper into debt while their opponents grow stronger.

According to a *Eurasian Times* report on December 21, 2017, China had surpassed Americans in trade with Africa back in 2009, doing business with 40 countries. Each following year showed increasing volumes, surpassing that of the U.S., U.K., and France combined.

> "It is no overstatement to assert that in the 21st century, much of the population of the developing world is politically stirring and, in many places, seething with unrest. This population is acutely conscious of social injustice to an unprecedented degree and often resentful of its perceived lack of political dignity. The nearly universal access to radio, television and the Internet is creating a community of shared perceptions and envy that can be galvanized and channeled by demagogic political or religious passions. These energies transcend sovereign borders and pose a challenge both to existing states as well as to the existing global hierarchy, a place in which the U.S. still perches on."

Cellphone usage has ballooned to encompass the whole globe, enabling more interconnection between people. We have increasingly seen new technologies, such as social media apps and virtual private networks, play leading roles in the spread of information and the organization of discontent.

> "That turmoil is the product of the political awakening: the fact that, today, vast masses of the world are not politically neutered as they have been throughout history. They have political consciousness. Politically awakened mankind craves political dignity enhanced by democracy. But, in a world acutely aware of economic, racial and ethnic inequities, political dignity has come to encompass ethnic or national self-determination, religious self-definition, and human and social rights."

The quest for political dignity, especially through national self-determination and social transformation, is part of the pulse for self-assertion by the world's underprivileged. We live in an age where mankind writ large is becoming politically conscious and politically activated to an unprecedented degree. It is this condition that produces great deal of international turmoil. That turmoil is the product of the political awakening, the fact that today vast masses of the world are not politically neutered, as they have been throughout history. They have political consciousness.

This powerful and prophetic piece clearly describes our current dilemma. Population around the world is stirring, seeking a "new deal" with their governments, corporations, and foreign powers. The saturation of media, thanks to progress in technologies, has increased its already tremendous reach. Nowhere are people more restless than in developing nations where we have seen record levels of seemingly unstoppable waves of humanity looking for a better life. American hegemony and globalization have not had desirable effects upon much of the world and can be likened to legalized colonialism.

Now in a bid to break the shackles, the descendants of those formally enslaved by their corrupt leaders and corrupt policies have nothing to lose and are seeking to get their share of the pie. The U.S. and their regime-change system in Latin America dated back to the early 1800s where they politically considered the region as their "backyard." But now, after years of interventions and political manipulations, these people have been fleeing to the U.S. and leave behind the social unrest of American interventionist policies.

Unless there are economic prosperity, freedom, and stabilization, then, whether the U.S. builds a wall or not, illegal migration will not stop. The migrants will not stop arriving on European shores without solving the social and economic issues, along with the political corruption in Africa. Until the Western states stop their interventions in the Middle East, those people will keep on being funneled through Turkey. The old way is not working, and people want a better way.

In a world of growing inequalities, the intergenerational gap is likely to trigger the reconstruction of the social-economic and political structures, reshaping the future and founding a whole new era. This is what Deutsche Bank's Jim Reid defended on his latest study "Age of Disorder." This piece caused shocks across the financial world, revealing the Millennials' and Gen Z's discontentment with the current configuration of the world economy endorsed by the Baby Boomers, as well as highlighting their willingness to engage in a stronger political presence to minimize wealth disparities, allowing them to turn the page and build a new age—"one that will be characterized initially by disorder".

As a banker, Reid focuses on the market aspects that such extensive socio-economic and political implications will have at the coming "new age"; more specifically on how current record-high global valuations are threatened, outlining 8 major global themes that will boost the transition to this new phase, such as the deterioration of US-China relations, the explosion of global debt levels, to the imminent runaway inflation, the worsening of wealth and income inequality, and, of course, the looming generational conflict between the Millennials and Gen-Z and the Baby Boomers.

In his study, he identified 5 different economic cycles over the last 160 years:

1) **1860 to 1914,** the first era of globalization

2) **1914 to 1945,** the Great Wars and the Great Depression

3) **1945 to 1971,** Bretton Woods and the return to a gold-based monetary system

4) **1971 to 1980,** the start of fiat money and the high-inflation era of the 1970s

5) **1980 to 2020,** the second era of globalization

From 2020 onwards, we will experience the Age of Disorder, the moment where we, as a society, will face a sharp shift in the global financial world and social organization. He asserted that economic cycles come and go, "but sitting above them are the wider structural super-cycles that shape everything from economies to asset prices, politics, and our general way of life."

In that sense, when considering that inequality is a multifaceted area, one of the subareas that could emerge out of it, causing a critical disorder in the system, is the intergenerational divide that has been expanding recently and likely to develop and receive even more attention in the immediate future. At the moment, the generational divergence is at extreme levels because, as the study pointed out, over the last decade, those who graduated into the labor market already experienced 2 massive shocks: the Global Financial Crisis and, currently, the global virus outbreak, both of which are considered to be the 2 worst economic collapses since the 1930s Great Depression. Meaning: the younger generation have been left behind economically compared to the past generation on various issues—from homeownership to student debt levels.

For now, what we know is that the prospects to the 2020 decade indicate that the Gen Z and Millennials are going to gradually take the electoral base from the hands of the older generation. An electoral victory in their favor could mean all-round redistributive policies, starting with the feared redistribution of wealth of the rich amongst the less favored classes, higher corporate and property taxes, more preference to commodities rather than stocks, and more tolerance of inflation "insofar as it will erode the debt burden it is inheriting and put the pain on bondholders, which tend to have a bias towards the pensioner generation," according to Reid.

In this direction, with increasingly high disparities and a world scenery in crisis, while an economic collapse is still unfolding, younger generations are likely to keep fueling this force of reaction to the oppressive policies that have been enacted over the past decades. As they are elected into positions of power, they will disrupt society as we know it—rebuilding it and shifting the world's attention to topics that were once left aside such as the consumption model and the level of carbon emissions.

The more our leaders suppress the necessities of this group, the larger the reacting force becomes. The Age of Disorder is on the horizon and will transform reality in unprecedented ways. That being said, do not expect this transition to happen smoothly. Much more turbulence will come with it. Are you ready?

SECTION 3: CYBERWARFARE

"It was the rise of Athens and the fear that this instilled in Sparta that made war inevitable."

Thucydides, Ancient Greek historian

While people fought wars of the past face-to-face, the wars of the future will be aided with technology changing the nature of battlefields forever and have already begun. Foreign wars no longer happen on foreign soil. They are now fought from the comfort and safety of digital command centers. This is known as "digital fighting" or "cyberwarfare" which utilizes technological innovation to assault different countries' military, as well as their public and private, networks.

Even though no full-scale cyberwarfare has occurred between nations to date, there were reports of state-supported assaults received each year. Countries like Russia, China, Iran, Israel, and North Korea regularly show up in these reports, while those of the Western nations go largely ignored. With President Donald Trump stepping up the pressure with trade wars, economic and financial sanctions, and political rhetoric, the *Unrestricted Warfare* doctrine opened another layer of adversity.

The new Cold War began years ago when Russia, China, and their vast allies worldwide became fed up with American interventionist policies, feeling encroached. As permanent member-nations of the UN Security Council, they offer valuable partnership. However, they have made a play by taking oppositional stances to the U.S. In what many people thought was a unipolar world, it is evident that we are increasingly becoming multipolar. Inevitably, while constrained in the public domain, this would lead to increased hostilities in the cyber sector.

Bertrand Venard, a Professor at Audencia Business School and the University of Oxford, became the supervisor of a significant research project funded by the European Union on cybersecurity. In an article published by *The Conversation* on October 16, 2019, he detailed the effects of an alleged Russian cyberspace attack on Estonia in 2007. He said the attackers were able to cripple the government functions, banks, hospitals, media, and telecommunications companies of Baltic state for several days.

Regardless of who was responsible, the fact remains that it is possible to cripple a nation anonymously. This style of penetration on networks and computers to extract information and exploit vulnerabilities has since been used in much smaller but highly effective ways. Operation Stuxnet was jointly developed by the U.S. and Israel to slow down the Iranian nuclear program "by remotely damaging uranium-enrichment centrifuges through a complex attack involving, inter alia, a computer virus."

He also pointed out a valuable lesson from history: "Thucydides Trap." This trap happens when a dominant nation feels threatened by an up and coming rival nation and the results are not promising. The past 500 years saw 16 cases in which a rising power threatened to displace a ruling one, and 12 of them ended in war. In the modern age, this war has begun and is being slowly ratcheted up over time. By the time we realize it, it will be too late.

In this battle for cyber supremacy, new cyberwarfare doctrines have been established. After the incident in Estonia, Venard stated that the U.S. and China have been actively developing their cyberwarfare organizations, procedures, defense, and offensive capabilities. Under the Obama Administration, the role of cyber strategy claimed to be defensive; whereas under the Trump Administration, it became proactive. These shifts in strategies correlate directly to the rising in tensions in the political arena.

"This cyberwarfare, or Cold War 2.0, is based on the development of technical and human resources, intelligence gathering, sabotage and influence operations," Venard said.

We see leading technological companies at the forefront of these tensions. Each side tries to get ahead of the other, putting significant strain on the profit maximization of companies in these sectors. Effectively, these multinational and even smaller-scale organizations are left to choose a side in the new cold war. An "us vs. them" mentality has prevailed, with 5G technology and semiconductors at the heart of this. This has forced both sides to pour resources into these sectors with the U.S. creating a new military command center: the U.S. Cyber Command in 2010. In response, China created "the Strategic Support Force, which brings together the resources of the People's Army in the field of cyber, space and electronic warfare."

Venard believed that these actions only caused a dramatic increase in espionage between the two rivals, as well as increased tensions. As former FBI Director Robert Mueller stated in 2012, "…there are only two types of companies: those that have been hacked and those that will be."

On March 15, 2020, the magazine *TruePublica* published that due to government inaction and underfunding in the cybersecurity sector, private companies would be forced to bear the brunt of an estimated $1 trillion USD in digital security operations in 2020 and 2021. As American foreign policy has created many enemies abroad, the American taxpayers funded $620 billion USD on defense in 2019, but only $10 billion USD on cybersecurity. This has left American citizens and private and public organizations vulnerable.

It is assumed that there will be increased tensions and hostilities throughout 2020 and beyond, and China, the originator of the *Unrestricted Warfare* concept, is already feeling the effects. Chinese leaders see their country under attack on all fronts, especially since late 2019. They claimed "China has been beset with a massive swine flu outbreak, a severe bird flu outbreak, and a coronavirus epidemic that has destabilized the entire workings its economy. The trade war is financially damaging and unpopular at home. Political unrest in Hong Kong, the re-election of Taiwan's pro-independence president, combined with stepped-up U.S. naval operations in the East and South China Seas, also adds to keeping Chinese leaders awake at night."

During the Clinton Administration, Nouriel Roubini was a Professor of Economics at New York University and the Senior Economist for International Affairs in the White House's Council of Economic Advisers. In the past, he worked with the IMF, Federal Reserve, and the World Bank. In his view, China had had enough and was ready to fight back. He stated, "China's immediate response to U.S. containment efforts (the trade war) will likely take the form of cyberwarfare. There are several obvious targets. Chinese hackers (and their Russian, North Korean, and Iranian counterparts) could interfere in the U.S. election by flooding Americans with misinformation and deep fakes. With the U.S. electorate already so polarized, it is not difficult to imagine armed partisans taking to the streets to challenge the results, leading to serious violence and chaos."

While these were merely predictions of possible outcomes, he has made reliable forecasts for the years ahead: "…the U.S.-China conflict could have escalated from cold war to a near-hot one. A Chinese regime with its economy severely damaged by the COVID-19 crisis and facing restless masses will need an external scapegoat, and will likely set its sights on Taiwan, Hong Kong, Vietnam, and U.S. naval positions in the East and South China Seas; confrontation could creep into escalating military accidents."

The South China Sea may be one of the key hot spots for any future war. We are already seeing President Trump use the conflict with China as a deflection and distraction for the failures and inefficiencies within the U.S. If President Trump continues his aggressive stance against China, instead of trying to resolve the situation, he will be cornering and forcing himself to travel down a road none of us want to see.

Roubini added, "U.S. cyberattacks against the four rivals will continue to intensify this year, raising the risk of the first-ever cyber world war and massive economic, financial, and political disorder." These "four rivals" referred to Russia, China, Iran, North Korea, and Venezuela to a lesser extent.

Asymmetrical warfare is defined as using unconventional strategies and tactics, especially when opposing military forces are unequal or significantly different enough, to avoid making the same kinds of attacks on each other. Often considered as the "underdog approach," all 4 principals of *Unrestricted Warfare*—Lawfare, Economic Warfare, Network Warfare, and Terrorism—fall in this category. It also includes foreign operations like regime change, corruption, and others that generally circumvents law and order. These are all useful tools for the U.S. However, they have increasingly faced push back from those who have been forced to "fire with fire."

Roubini said, "As of early 2020, this is where we stand: the U.S. and Iran have already had a military confrontation that will likely soon escalate; China is in the grip of a viral outbreak that will become a global pandemic; cyberwarfare is ongoing; major holders of U.S. Treasuries are pursuing diversification strategies; the Democratic presidential primary is exposing rifts in the opposition to Trump and already casting doubt on vote-counting processes; rivalries between the U.S. and four revisionist powers are escalating; and the real-world costs of climate change and other environmental trends are mounting."

According to him, 2020 is the best time for further escalations on all fronts, with opponents to the U.S. hegemony looking to roll back U.S. influence and replace it with that of their own.

In recent times, we have seen increased cooperation between the "four rivals" and they are only expected to grow closer. While nations line up to choose sides in the new Cold War, the effects of COVID-19 and the collapse in energy markets will send shockwaves throughout the global economic, financial, and political sectors. All of which, are fueling the fires of discontent, setting the stage for a final confrontation, if not multiple clashes, as each sphere of influence struggles to maintain hegemony.

Amid the uncertainty, there are only 8 countries remotely prepared for cyberwarfare. According to Roubini, "...the Western allies consist of the United States, United Kingdom, India and Israel on the one side – China, Russia, Iran, and North Korea on the other. These 2 opposing sides are the only countries that have significant and active cyber operations for offensive and defensive operations. Both sides are currently experiencing many political and economic challenges that are surging in 2020."

While India is considered a Western ally, they have taken a more neutral stance in recent years, enjoying warm relations with both Russia and Iran while also opposing China due to its support to Pakistan.

As modern humans, we live in a 2-lane world—the physical realm and the digital realm—and is the case for the countries we live in. An attack in the digital realm can cause real damage to our physical world, such as power supplies, financial hubs, and health systems, affecting the civilian and military sectors alike. We are all on the front lines and nobody is immune—even Hillary

Clinton became a target of an email hack. While on the surface the U.S. seems to be refraining from attacking other nations, it has, in fact, continued behind closed doors.

On June 20, 2019, *BBC* reported that Iran accused the Americans of invading their airspace with a surveillance drone, flying near the Strait of Hormuz. The Iranians shot a missile at the drone, sending it crashing out of the sky. In response, the Americans launched cyberattacks on Iran, focusing on computer systems that control missiles and rocket launchers. This led to alleged cyberattacks against U.S. businesses.

They also reported back on February 7, 2013 that one of the RQ-170 Sentinel drones used by the U.S. Air Force and the CIA had been remotely hacked and landed safely in Iran. The Iranians claimed that these drones illegally crossed over their airspace and allegedly released the video from the drone to prove it. Also, they vowed to reverse engineer and produce their versions of the drone to which the U.S. claimed was beyond their capabilities. Be that as it may, it would not be beyond the capabilities of Russia and China, who both showed interest in studying the technology.

On February 10, 2018, *The Times* of Israel reported that Israel had shot down a drone linked to the Syrian conflict which resembled a copy of the RQ-170 and was surprisingly sophisticated. North Korea, which has been under scrutiny over its atomic program and tempestuous relationship with the U.S., was accused of being active over the internet. According to the U.S. Department of the Treasury, the North Korean state was connected to the dangerous hacking association code-named HIDDEN COBRA, otherwise called the Lazarus Group. It was alleged that this group was responsible for the WannaCry 2.0 ransomware attacks, the Sony hack in 2014, and the hack of a Bangladeshi bank in 2016.

Physical sabotage played a vital role with the U.S.'s cyberattacks against North Korea, as Business Insider reported on April 17, 2017, where several North Korean missiles got disabled by U.S. cyberattacks which prevented their launch.

As nations continue to conduct Cold-War-2.0-style guerrilla warfare against one another, it leaves their respective citizens in the middle of hot tit-for-tat escalations and it is only one miscalculation away from the point of no return. If these clandestine operations continue out of public scrutiny, and the U.S. pursues its aggressive domination, we are well on track for Thucydides' Trap.

In contrast to standard weapons of devastation, cyberwarfare is harder to track as components like malware can be installed to evade detection. State-supported assaults often go unclaimed, leaving room for theories to run rampant while the general public is forced to believe false narratives. We realize that Russia and China are creating digital weapons to use in any future cyberwars, with the US, France, and Israel not far behind. Be that as it may, we cannot really say for certain that any of these nations are utilizing them, even though we know they have the capacity and have done so previously.

While Operation Stuxnet was probably the best example of digital fighting in real life, other critical occasions can be ascribed to state-level assaults. One ongoing model originated from Russia: a nation that has been blamed for several state-level cyberattacks. According to the U.S. narrative, Russia was responsible for mounting various digital assaults against Ukraine, including the Black Energy assault—the distributed denial-of-service (DDoS) cyber espionage that left 700,000 homes without power. Also, in 2015, they were blamed for the NotPetya malware, a Trojan Horse planned to decimate the frameworks it contaminated disguised as a ransomware.

Cyberattacks are now the new hybrid warfare. As clarified by The Conversation, the term "hybrid warfare" was, to some degree, poorly characterized and had changed in importance in recent years or so since it came into utilization. Progressively, it is utilized to depict the daily cyberwarfare around the globe and endeavors to disturb law-based procedures.

For instance, just like in a political race, "Group A" may take part in endeavors through channels like online networking all the while focusing on the sites of its primary rivals, "Group B" and "Group C," with DDoS attacks or cyber vandalism. Normally, it will not be Group A itself that participates in these exercises. Instead, it will delegate experienced organizations to spread misinformation, as well as recruit programmers. As a result, it will be difficult to track the responsible party and creates plausible deniability. This is a strategy often used in state-sponsored cyberattacks, where nations guarantee an attack starting from "devoted programmers", following up on their terms and influence from the state.

Currently, the world's population is in self-isolation and is reliant on the web. This colossal reliance on the internet and online systems only created vulnerabilities to which information-hungry lawbreakers can prey upon.

At this advanced time, the world is looking at quite a bit of danger from cybercriminals, all the while confronting the physical risks from the pandemic. An ever-increasing number of administrations are getting on the web. For example, specialists advancing telemedicine in smaller towns in Pakistan; private organizations and organizations' representatives telecommunicating and utilizing online applications for video conferencing; understudies and instructors conducting online classes; even the monetary and banking sector have moved their administrations online. The expanded online movement not only increases the possibilities of digital assaults like phishing against the general population and private division, it also expanded the danger of receiving "fake news."

The internet has permeated every part of our daily lives and is only expected to deepen our connection with one another with the advancements of 5G technology. However, this means we are all exposed to its inherent dangers. This new Cold War will make the internet the digital battle ground for competing interests. Hence, we must always be wary about our digital presence and not be ignorant of our vulnerabilities. As conflicts between the Eastern and Western intensify, 5G will be the new pathway for the troops to travel upon.

SECTION 4: ECONOMIC SANCTIONS AS ACTS OF WAR

"The number of people killed by the sanctions in Iraq is greater than the total number of people killed by all weapons of mass destruction in all of history."

Noam Chomsky, American linguist, philosopher, cognitive scientist, historian, and political activist

"Sanctions are not diplomacy; they are a precursor to war and an embarrassment to a country that pays lip service to free trade."

Ron Paul, American politician, author, and physician

Sanctions have become a political tool for asymmetric warfare to subdue the nations opposing the American hegemony. Governments and multinational bodies impose monetary restrictions or approvals to modify the vital choices of state and non-state actors. Critics stated that sanctions are frequently misguided and only occasionally fruitful in achieving end goals.

At the same time, supporters claimed that they have gotten progressively potent as of late and should stay as an international strategic instrument. Western sanctions are reactions to geopolitical difficulties, like North Korea's atomic program, Russia's relationship with Ukraine, Iranian influence in the Middle East, and Venezuela's choice of government.

The United States has increased aggressive actions against individuals and states who oppose the will of the U.S. According to the U.S. Department of the Treasury, as of May 2020, the U.S. has 32 active sanction programs against numerous counties—some dating back decades Cuba (1958). Furthermore, this does not account the numerous individuals that the U.S. has specifically identified and put under sanction or the countless innocent citizens who bear the brunt of these sanctions.

Jacob G. Hornberger of The Future of Freedom Foundation published a scathing report on September 8, 2017 about the American sanctions where he made an interesting analogy. If the U.S. were to bomb North Korea and kill thousands of North Koreans, it would be considered an act of war. But if the

U.S. targeted North Korea through sanctions that indiscriminately kill thousands of North Koreans through starvation and illness, it would be considered a peaceful diplomatic measure. Either way, sanctions can be just as effective, if not more, as bombs. In most cases, economic sanctions cause everyday citizens to suffer like forcing children to starve to death.

According to him, the theory works twofold:

1. If the North Koreans are dying or watching their children die, they will do what is necessary to oust the North Korean regime and replace it with a regime that is pro-U.S.; or,

2. The North Korean regime, faced with a rising death toll among the North Korean people from starvation and illness, will abdicate in favor of a pro-U.S. regime or simply agree to do the bidding of U.S. officials.

But what happens when neither takes place? Cuba has been under sanctions since 1958. The people have neither rose-up nor has the ruling party abdicated. The country is not suffering from large-scale starvations or illnesses as many have begun to grow their own foods. As reported in Time Magazine by Ciara Nugent on November 30, 2018, Cuba had some of the best healthcare in the world and regularly exported doctors to other countries.

From 1970 to 1973, the U.S. conducted regime-change operations in Chile after they assessed the Chilean people's election of a Marxist president, someone who was a threat to U.S. national security. According to Hornberger, the CIA enacted maximum suffering upon the Chilean people, including starvation by bribing the nation's truckers to go on strike and halt food shipments across the country.

Inevitably, after enough Chileans suffered, including the most vulnerable segments of society, the coup took place in 1973. What followed was a Western-backed military junta, a military dictatorship, which ruled Chile with an iron fist until the return of democracy in 1990. This is a pattern repeated over and over, not only in almost every Latin American, African, and Middle Eastern nation but around the world.

The U.S. cares less about who they back, focused only on preserving their own interests, completely ignoring the desires of the people living in these countries. It was not that long ago that Saddam Hussein and Muammar Gaddafi were American allies, like Mohammed bin Salman bin Abdulaziz Al Saud are today. And this is from a nation that claims to promote democracy around the world. Instead, what we really see is international gangsterism.

Hornberger stated, "One of the fascinating aspects of the Iraqi sanctions was the indifference among U.S. officials to the death toll among children. It just didn't matter to them that they were killing children. In their minds, they were just enforcing sanctions – i.e. rules and regulations. Their mindsets were a perfect demonstration of what Hannah Arendt called 'the banality of evil.' She wrote, 'The essence of totalitarian government, and perhaps the nature of every bureaucracy, is to make functionaries and mere cogs in the administrative machinery out of men, and thus to dehumanize them.'"

Again, what is the purpose of these 11-year-long sanctions? Regime change. The U.S. Ambassador to the UN at the time, Madeline Albright, was asked if the deaths of a half-a-million Iraqi children were worth it. To this she replied, "…yes, the deaths were, in fact, worth it."

In the past, the target of sanctions would be developing nations incapable of, fighting back against Western aggression. However, in recent years, we see the U.S. administration take a more aggressive stance against anyone who opposes them.

On January 22, 2020, CBC News reported that the Trump Administration even threatened tariffs against their allies in the European Union if they would not submit to a trade deal. But like all bullies, if you keep picking fights, eventually, you will meet your match.

On January 14, 2020, Kevin Zeese and Margaret Flowers released an overly critical report of the current policy of imposing sanctions titled *The World Must End the U.S.' Illegal Economic War. Sanctions Imposed on 39 Countries*. In it, they said, "The United States is relying more heavily on illegal unilateral coercive measures (also known as economic sanctions) in place of war or as part of its build-up to war. In fact, economic sanctions are an act of war that kills tens of thousands of people each year through financial strangulation. An economic blockade places a country under siege."

Currently, the Trump Administration has undone the agreements and work by the previous Obama Administration regarding Iran and has taken an increasingly hawkish stance. On January 3, 2020, the Trump Administration took this one step further with the assassination of General Qasem Soleimani near Bagdad International Airport. The Americans have had Iran under sanctions since the 1979 Revolution and the assassination highlights the fact how sanctions can quickly escalate tensions.

On October 26, 2019, the Venezuelan ambassador to the UN, Samuel Moncada, spoke to the XVIII Summit of the Non-Aligned Movement held in Baku, Azerbaijan. Addressing the 120 countries represented, he denounced the imposition of arbitrary "sanctions" by the U.S. as "economic terrorism which affects a third of humanity with more than 8,000 measures in 39 countries." This terrorism, he stated, constituted a "threat to the entire system of international relations and is the greatest violation of human rights in the world."

China and The Group of 77, a UN-based international body representing 134 developing nations, called upon "the international community to condemn and reject the imposition of the use of such measures as a means of political and economic coercion against developing countries."

According to CRG, sanctions were not used by the U.S. to promote freedom but to punish nations that resisted its hegemony. Sanctions have become weapons of war. They attested, "U.S. sanctions are designed to kill by destroying an economy through denial of access to finance, causing hyperinflation and shortages and blocking basic necessities such as food and medicine. For example, sanctions are expected to cause the death of tens of thousands of Iranians by creating a severe shortage of critical medicines and medical equipment everywhere in Iran."

It is ironic that, after years of sanctions, nations often become more radicalized and unstable politically, which contrasts with Washington's narrative. Countries, corporations, and other entities fearful of U.S. sanctions avoid doing any business with nations unless they are approved by the U.S. This leaves the civilian population to look for black market alternatives for every day, lifesaving goods like medicine.

Ironically, while the goal of sanctions is to turn the citizens against their leaders, it often ends up highlighting the American operations that further demonizes them. CRG stated, "Sanctions, which are illegal under the UN, OAS [Organization of American States] and U.S. law[s], have caused mass protests in Venezuela against the U.S."

If sanctions are not sufficient, then why are they promoted as a quick and easy solution? In an age of *Unrestricted Warfare*, the battle takes place on all fronts, with the end goal not being the official narrative of regime change, because it serves instead to retain global hegemony. The concluding results of war are of numerous, individual battles on many fronts. If it is not possible to destroy your enemies, the next best option is to weaken them, thus making yourself stronger. When we view world events with this sort of lens, seemingly irrational events and reasoning can entirely become rational. We have learned numerous things over the years about the causes and effects of sanctions.

Richard N. Hass, American Diplomat, former President of the Council on Foreign Relations, and former Vice President and Director of Foreign Policy Studies of The Brookings Institution, brought us the following evaluations:

1) **Sanctions alone are unlikely to achieve desired results if the aims are large or time is short.** Sanctions—even when comprehensive and enjoying almost universal international backing for nearly six months—failed to get Saddam Hussein to withdraw from Kuwait. In the end, it took Operation Desert Storm.

   Other sanctions have also fallen short. The Iranian regime continues to support terrorism, oppose the Middle East peace process, and press ahead with its nuclear weapons program. Fidel Castro is still in place atop a largely authoritarian political and economic system. India and Pakistan were not deterred from testing nuclear weapons by the threat of draconian penalties. Libya has refused to produce the two individuals accused of the destruction of Pan Am 103. Sanctions could not persuade Haiti's junta to honor the results of an election. Nor could they dissuade Serbia and others to call off their military aggression. And China continues to export sensitive technologies to selected countries and remains a society where human rights are violated.

2) **Nevertheless, sanctions can on occasion achieve (or help to achieve) various foreign policy goals ranging from the modest to the fairly significant.** Sanctions introduced in the aftermath of the Gulf War increased Iraqi compliance with resolutions calling for the complete elimination of its weapons of mass destruction and diminished Iraq's ability to import weapons. In the former Yugoslavia, sanctions were one factor contributing to Serbia's decision to accept the Dayton agreement in August 1995. China appears to have shown some restraint in exporting nuclear and ballistic missile parts or technologies.

3) **Unilateral sanctions are rarely effective.** In a global economy, unilateral sanctions tend to impose greater costs on American firms than on the target, which can usually find substitute sources of supply and financing.

4) **Secondary sanctions can make matters worse.** Trying to compel others to join a sanctions effort by threatening secondary sanctions against third parties unwilling to sanction the target can cause serious harm to a variety of U.S. foreign policy interests. This is what happened when sanctions were introduced against overseas firms who violated the terms of U.S. legislation affecting Cuba, Iran, and Libya. This threat may have had some deterrent effect on the willingness of certain individuals to enter into proscribed business activities, but at the price of increasing anti-American sentiment, stimulating challenges within the World Trade Organization, and drawing attention away from the provocative behavior of the target governments.

5) **Sanctions are blunt instruments that often produce unintended and undesirable consequences.** Sanctions increased the economic

distress on Haiti, triggering a dangerous and expensive exodus of people from Haiti to the United States. In the former Yugoslavia, the arms embargo weakened the Bosnian (Muslim) side given the fact that Bosnia's Serbs and Croats had larger stores of military supplies and greater access to additional supplies from outside sources. Military sanctions against Pakistan increased its reliance on a nuclear option, both because the sanctions cut off Islamabad's access to U.S. weaponry and by weakening Pakistani confidence in American reliability.

6) **Sanctions can be expensive for American business, farmers, and workers.** There is a tendency to overlook or underestimate the direct cost of sanctions, perhaps because their costs do not show up in U.S. government budget tables. Sanctions do, however, affect the economy by reducing revenues of U.S. companies and individuals. Moreover, even this cost is difficult to measure because it needs to reflect not simply lost sales but also forfeited opportunities. Sanctions cost U.S. companies billions of dollars a year in lost sales and returns on investment—and cost many thousands of workers their jobs.

7) **Sanctions tend to be easier to introduce than to lift. It is almost always more difficult to change the status quo than to continue with it.** It is often difficult or impossible to build a consensus for rescinding a sanction, even if there has been some progress on the matter of concern, if the sanction has been shown to be feckless or counterproductive, or if other interests can be shown to suffer as a result.

This is likely to become the case with India and Pakistan, where U.S. sanctions introduced in the wake of the May 1998 nuclear tests will frustrate attempts to influence their behavior in this or other areas. The Bosnia case involves a powerful example of the danger of locking in sanctions, as the inability to amend or lift UN sanctions that blocked military support to all protagonists in the Bosnian war worked to the disadvantage of the weaker Bosnian side.

8) **Sanctions fatigue tends to settle in over time and international compliance tends to diminish.** Inevitably, the issue that led to sanctions being introduced loses its emotional impact. Concerns over the humanitarian impact of sanctions also weaken resolve. At the same time, the target country has time to adjust. Working around sanctions, import substitution, and any improvement of living standards due to adaptation all make sanctions bearable. All of these factors have eroded the impact of sanctions against Iraq, Libya, and Cuba.[42]

Given the overwhelming evidence that sanctions do not produce the desired goals they claim to be, it is safe to say that there is no such thing as "smart sanctions;" only dumb decisions. Instead of accomplishing the stated goals of the U.S. administrations, sanctions only led to the demonization of Western policies, resulting to a growing number of adversaries. Instead of weakening their opponents, they are only harming the civilian population, fueling growing discontent against the Americans. As more and more of the world come under the effect of U.S. sanctions, nations will increasingly look for new ways to evade them.

In recent days, we have witnessed a historic moment, as reported by The New York Times on May 25, 2020, when Iran successfully supplied Venezuela with critical fuel supplies and experts to jump-start their refinery. This move was further bolstered by Russian threats to the U.S. to not interfere with the step. All 3 of these countries are currently under sanction by the U.S. and are acting in clear and open violation as a defiant message to the Trump Administration.

Furthermore, Forbes Magazine published an article on January 29, 2020 detailing how countries such as Iran, Venezuela, and North Korea were turning to cryptocurrencies as viable options to evade U.S. financial sanctions. In fact, Russia had been looking into this option to serve as a new government-backed currency within the country.

The unlawful and shameless utilization of sanctions is a demonstration of the desire for war. Unless the UN approves them, unilateral coercive measures are

---

[42] https://www.brookings.edu/research/economic-sanctions-too-much-of-a-bad-thing/

illegal—and we have seen how sanctions can quickly escalate to military strikes. A fundamental goal of the harmony and equitable development in the U.S., working with partners far and wide, must be to end this fear-based oppression. Economic sanctions are a political manifestation of a schoolyard mentality, not to mention illegal, international gangsterism. The U.S. economy has been structured to feed off constant warfare due to its help in promoting GDP. However, by seeking global chaos, they are increasingly isolating themselves on the world stage, with the nations becoming fed-up with their bullying.

As the economic and financial institutions come under siege within the U.S. markets and global protectionism takes shape, the U.S. will be under pressure to ratchet up conflicts that are already reaching boiling points. The 2020s will bring a conclusion to U.S. hegemony over the world, paving the way for the multipolar world to take shape. The U.S. must adjust to a declining role on the world stage or face more isolation and defiance. They are left with 2 routes: to take the path of Sparta and fall in Thucydides' Trap or seek a new peace.

SECTION 5: TRADE WARS

"The Western world order has – in its post-1945 idiom – placed a high premium on democracy within nation-states while attaching zero importance to democracy at the global level. As a global order, it has been anti-democratic and highly authoritarian. The emergence of China as the globally dominant nation is very unlikely to usher in a new kind of democratic global governance, but the rise of developing nations like India, Brazil and Russia, along with China, will bring, in a rough and ready way, a far more democratic global economy."

(Excerpt from the book *When China Rules the World*)

Martin Jacques, scholar

The Chinese "economic miracle" began in December 1978. Deng Xiaoping had taken office as the Chairman of the CPPCC National Committee in the People's Republic of China. He is credited with a new style of thinking known as "Socialism with Chinese characteristics", a combination of the socialist ideology and the free enterprise.

The move to open China to foreign investments and the global markets would create one of the fastest-growing economies in the world, lasting several generations. Because of this, hundreds of millions of Chinese people had their lifestyles changed and their standard of living revolutionized. For his incredible achievements, Deng was named the Time Magazine Person of the Year in 1978 and in 1985. China's policy reforms had brought the previously closed, economically insignificant country to the forefront of world economies.

When China Rules the World: The End of the Western World and the Birth of a New Global Order is a fascinating book by British Scholar, Martin Jacques. It was first released in 2009 and then updated in 2012. I came across this book at a bookstore in Manila and could hardly put it down until I was finished 3 days later. The way he explains the differences between ideologies and world views by each party were remarkably and professionally researched and engaging to read. Most importantly, it explained the Chinese perspective as a "civilization-state" which helped alter how we perceived their claims.

Whereas, *The Hundred-Year Marathon: China's Secret Strategy to Replace America as the Global Superpower* by Michael Pillsbury explained the conflict from the American point of view. These 2 seemingly incompatible viewpoints will eventually lead to one outcome: increased protectionism in a globalized production chain will lead to further trade wars with devastating effects.

As it stands today, only the U.S. and China are the world's economic and military superpowers. Other nations, such as Russia, may be a military power but not an economic power; whereas the European Union (EU) and Japan can be considered economic forces but not military forces. Experts are already calling the 21st century the "Chinese Century" due to their growing economic might and influence around the world. While the U.S. is wasting resources on fruitless military endeavors to preserve their fledgling alliances and the EU is bailing out its near-bankrupt nations over the last decade, China has been saving and investing in its future.

A recent article in The Conversation by Peter Robertson, Professor at the University of Western Australia on October 1, 2019 stated that while "China's military budget is usually thought of about 40% that of the U.S.—which is often characterized as spending more on its military than the next 10 countries combined. Such an approach, however, dramatically overstates U.S. military capacity—and understates China's. In real terms, China's spending is worth about 75% that of the U.S." This is due to the differences in purchasing power parity between the 2 powers. As a result, China can spend less to get the same or comparable segment as the U.S.

While the U.S. spends a lot more on its military, it increases the costs of everything else. This has been the case for quite a while. It was not until after 40 years of doing business, or about 77 years into their "Hundred-Year Marathon" that the Americans took notice of it during the 2016 election campaign.

Donald Trump was elected on a platform that promised to fight for a fairer deal with China. In the Americans' view, the globalization that their corporations advocated for decades was not designed to be a two-way street. For decades, Western consumers shifted the real costs of manufacturing up the supply chain to developing nations and, surely, they did not think anyone could get rich and powerful off of it. Cheap consumer goods flooded the Western markets, a boon for the corporations that moved their production overseas.

If your manufacturing process involves harmful chemicals, no problem. Find a country with a lax or corrupt legal system. If you need to produce branded products at rock bottom prices, simply look for factories fostering slave labor to do your bidding. If you want to conduct or need products from illegal mining or farming operations, it will not be hard to find a place that would love some "extra help." The environment has been neglected, safety issues ignored, and countless human tragedies created just so large corporations can keep rolling back prices. At the same time, they are concealing the fact that Western consumers are growing poorer.

While this system of injustice keeps profits flowing for corporate America, silently and in the background, the Chinese has been saving as well. Over the years, they managed to monopolize the world production. At first, they were hailed as "the world's workshop." But now, they are being portrayed as the villains. We must remember it was Former President Richard Nixon who flew to China in a bid to beg them to open their economy, not the other way around.

During the 2016 election campaign, Donald Trump made several allegations against China, including stealing American jobs, intellectual property, and technology. He vowed to stop the "unfair transfers of American technology and intellectual property to China." To achieve this, he promised to restrict Chinese access to the U.S. market and impose tariffs on Chinese goods, essentially starting a crusade against China and anything Chinese.

President Trump is doing the bidding of a large camp of U.S. firms complaining how Chinese companies have an unfair advantage and receiving subsidies from the state. But as we have seen earlier, subsidies, bailouts, low to no-interest loans, and more are commonplace in the U.S. financial markets. The Fed has acted as the "bank of mommy and daddy" for many struggling corporations that should have been allowed to fail.

On September 17, 2018, Trump tweeted, "Tariffs have put the U.S. in a very strong bargaining position, with Billions of Dollars, and Jobs, flowing into our

Country - and yet cost increases have thus far been almost unnoticeable. If countries will not make fair deals with us, they will be 'Tariffed!'"

In his next tweet, he added, "When a country (USA) is losing many billions of dollars on trade with virtually every country it does business with, trade wars are good, and easy to win."

While indeed, there have been billions of dollars of money flowing back into the U.S., much of those profits have been used for stock buybacks so CEOs can hit their targets and get massive bonuses. Unless they are buying more homes and renovating them in the U.S., those funds will not trickle down to any everyday American.

As companies shifted towards overseas production, there has been less reliance upon a Western workforce. Hence, we saw many factories close and economies shifted from production to consumption. A consumption-based economy will create a lot of low-paying entry-level jobs, especially in the service and retail sectors, which does not help any Millennial with a bachelor's degree in their desire to buy a house.

The U.S. and China are each other's largest trading partners, and their relationship is believed to be the most consequential in the world. This is according to Dan Steinbock, author of *U.S.-China Trade War and Its Global Impacts*, in *World Century Publishing Corporation and Shanghai Institutes for International Studies China Quarterly of International Strategic Studies, Vol. 4.* According to him:

> "The global importance of the U.S. and Chinese economies, as measured by their nominal gross domestic product (GDP), can be illustrated in two ways that will also illuminate the challenges of the ongoing power transition: one involves the rise of the Chinese economy relative to the U.S. GDP; the other focuses on the concomitant shifts in globalization. In 2000, China's economy was barely a tenth of the U.S. GDP. But after China became a member of the World Trade Organization (WTO) in 2001, its export-led growth soared in the course of the 2000s, when its share of the U.S. economy more than tripled from 12% in 2000 to over 40% in 2010."

Originally, Goldman Sachs famously came out and predicted that China would surpass the U.S. economy in the 2020s[43]. Since then, there have been other projections which follow similar lines of thought. Some even pushing it as far as the 2030s[44]. Regardless, it is not a matter of if but of when China will surpass the U.S. economy, with both projections coming well within the "Hundred-Year Marathon" goal. However, as Steinbock pointed out, we needed to consider the effects of increased protectionism and the impact of COVID-19 on these projections.

According to Steinbock, after a year of back and forth threats, "the Trump Administration initiated a 'tariff war' against China in March 2018." Still, it was not until July 2018 that these measures became effective. What began with complaints from the steel and aluminum sectors quickly transformed into intellectual property rights and technology. While this conflict began with 2 combatants, it had quickly escalated into a global issue. He asserted:

> "Even worse, bilateral frictions with China are spreading to U.S. trade conflicts with other North American Free Trade Agreement (NAFTA) members, Europe, East Asia and practically the rest of the world. If the Trump Administration continues moving away from the post-World War II trading regime, these bilateral frictions will broaden and multilateralize. And if a full-scale trade war cannot be avoided, then the nascent tariff wars have potential to spread across industry sectors and geographic regions."

In fact, since the first half of 2018, the International Monetary Fund (IMF) growth projections had already been revised down for Europe, Japan, the United Kingdom, Brazil, and India, among other major economies. The most important one was how well the Chinese economy would do amid growing trade tensions with the U.S. China accounted for almost 50% of global growth and continued to constitute some 30% of global prospects today. In positive scenarios, such economic spillovers support global growth. In negative scenarios, such spillovers penalize those growth prospects, and the collateral

[43] https://www.worldscientific.com/doi/pdf/10.1142/S2377740018500318
[44] https://www.worldscientific.com/doi/pdf/10.1142/S2377740018500318

damage will most likely be the worst in emerging and developing economies.

As globalization brings countries closer together and increasingly reliant upon one another in the good times, with the trade wars and COVID-19, we are entering a perfect storm of uncertainty, protectionism, political bullying, and a collapse of fragile economic, financial and supply chain systems. In the same ways that nations were dragged into wars they did not want to participate in during WWI, countries today are finding it increasingly difficult to separate themselves or remain neutral in this growing battle of the superpowers.

According to Steinbock, before the Great Recession of 2008, global investment soared to almost $2 trillion USD. But a decade later, this figure had only reached a figure of 20% less. Meanwhile, China and other emerging economies were fueling the growth in the global market, with world merchandise recording its strongest year of growth in 6 years during 2017.

Now, Steinbock asserted that due to COVID-19 measures, coupled with trade war tensions and economic uncertainty, "the WTO warned that global trade growth is losing momentum and that downside risks have grown in the global economy. Following the financial crisis, there has been a dramatic fall in global finance as well. Meanwhile, global debt has continued to swell but has remained stable relative to world GDP (at about 169%) since 2014." With so many negative indicators, no wonder both parties tried their best to put through a quick fix solution in early 2020 with the U.S.-China Phase 1 Trade Deal.

We have seen American -style globalization be replaced with the Chinese model around the world with the emerging economies as its drivers. Steinbock said that the Asian Infrastructure Investment Bank and the BRICS1 New Development Bank (NDB), had been increasingly popular in developing economies. According to the World Bank article posted on March 29, 2018, the China-led Belt and Road Initiative (BRI) involved nearly 70 countries and organizations. Since then, they had expanded with the 21st century Maritime Silk Road to include a string of ports stretching across the old world.

Steinbock said that President Trump labeled these initiatives as "insulting," But these projects are in line with the Chinese proverb, "If you want to prosper, first build roads"—something the Chinese have been doing for thousands of years. While politically, the Americans have pursued a divide and rule strategy of containing China; economically, they have made some minor concessions to developing nations. He further explained:

> "U.S. Secretary of State Mike Pompeo gave a speech on 'America's Indo-Pacific Economic Vision' on July 30, 2018, in which he announced $113 million in new U.S. initiatives to 'support foundational areas of the future' in the regional economy, energy, and infrastructure. But the scale of the 'Indo-Pacific Economic Vision' pales in comparison with the BRI, which involves far greater cumulative investments estimated at around $4 trillion to $8 trillion, dwarfing even the Marshall Plan from 70 years ago (as Pompeo alluded to), whose cumulative aid may have totaled $12 billion, or about $180 billion in today's dollar value."

Given the current situation, if Asia and thus the rest of the world hopes to avoid, or at least limit the effects of, a Global Recession or Depression, further integration, not geopolitical division, is needed. While the American administrations have tried to sow the seeds of division among Asian nations to contain China's influence, we have seen hope in the increasing free trade agreements between countries. As domestic concerns increase, and people search for someone or something to blame, we see Western media shift inwards and deflect blame upon China as a way to cover the mounting inequality, and economic, financial and social unrest.

In a research paper issued by the UN Conference on Trade and Development by Alessandro Nicita in November 2019, we saw the toll the trade war had upon both China and the U.S. According to the paper, in over half a year, tariffed products have seen a 25% reduction in imports. "The analysis finds that China's export losses in the United States have resulted in trade diversion effects to the advantage of Taiwan Province of China, Mexico, the European Union and Viet Nam, among others. The analysis also finds that those effects have increased over time." While Chinese exporters were forced to bear the burden of the tariffs in the form of lower export prices, U.S. consumers were faced with price increases.

In the end, both nations are tied in a lose-lose situation which will only get worse unless restrictions are lifted. The paper further stated, "Economists generally agree that increases in bilateral trade costs such as those resulting from the ongoing trade war between United States and China will result in lower trade, higher prices for consumers, and trade diversion effects."

The empirical evidence produced in the paper showed that this had been the case. While there was a decline in imports from China, companies were forced to outsource to other countries, increasing the costs being passed on to consumers. However, due to the competitive nature of Chinese producers, they managed to retain 75% of their exports.

The Carnegie Endowment for International Peace published a report by Yukon Huang on September 14, 2017. In it, Huang stated:

> "As a former chairman of the Council of Economic Advisors, the Harvard professor Martin Feldstein, has written, 'every student of economics knows or should know that the current account balance of each country is determined within its own borders and not by its trading partners.' Basic accounting principles tell us that the United States' overall trade deficit is the result of a shortage in national savings relative to spending due to excessive government budget deficits and households consuming beyond their means. The countries that show up as being the source of the offsetting trade surpluses are coincidental."

As many economists have stated, the current U.S. trade deficit is the result of low national savings arising from federal budget deficits. The American economy has been centered on a consumer-based economy which created high household debt as more and more people buy what they do not need to impress the people they do not like. The credit-fueled spending spree of the last decade and beyond has been financed by foreign economies, all the while personal savings rates have dropped to record lows.

Economist Joseph Stiglitz published a report on July 30, 2018 in Project Syndicate titled *The U.S. is at Risk of Losing a Trade War with China*. He argued that the trade deficits plaguing the U.S. were because Americans saved too little of their income. To stimulate savings in America and reduce deficits, the Fed should raise interest rates, not cut them.

He added, "…the U.S. has a problem, but it's not with China. It's at home: America has been saving too little. Trump, like so many of his compatriots, is immensely short-sighted. If he had a whit of understanding of economics and a long-term vision, he would have done what he could to increase national savings. That would have reduced the multilateral trade deficit…"

If we look at China, according to the World Bank figures as of May 2020, China's gross domestic savings rate was an astonishing 47% of GDP, whereas the U.S. sat at 17%. Furthermore, Stiglitz attested that if domestic investment continued to exceed savings in the U.S., it would be forced to import capital, further amplifying the trade deficit's effects. Even worse, due to the tax cuts at the end of 2018, compounded by the COVID-19 crisis, U.S. fiscal deficit had reached record highs. This meant that the trade deficit would be forced to increase, regardless of the trade war outcome.

Instead of placing blame on China and placing more trade restrictions which will only make things worse for the Americans, the focus should be on strengthening the productivity of the workforce, infrastructure, and technological investments. The recent decades have seen consumers' purchasing power decrease because wages have not increased by much, so long-term job promotions, not just entry-level positions, should be part of the "America First Policy."

The focus needs to be on the everyday Americans, including small businesses, not on an imaginary outside foe. Millennials are accumulating mountains of debt for degrees they "need" to purchase without any guaranteed job prospects. Yet none of this would happen if unprofitable businesses and industries were disallowed to continue as before. But thanks to a government lifeline, the change needed remains in limbo while masses suffer.

On October 18, 2018, Noma Bar published an article for The Economist titled *The End of Engagement: How the World's Two Superpowers Have Become Rivals*. Here, he discussed the route America should take on the trade war:

"The strategy should leave room for China to rise peacefully—which inevitably also means allowing China to extend its influence. That is partly because a zero-sum attempt at containment is likely to lead to conflict. But it is also because America and China need to co-operate despite their rivalry. The two countries are more commercially intertwined than America and the Soviet Union ever were. And they share responsibilities including—even if Mr. Trump denies it—the environment and security interests, such as the Korean peninsula."

Furthermore, in a report issued by the IMF Asia and Pacific Department on July 26, 2018, they recommended to Chinese policymakers that "[China,] as one of the main beneficiaries of the global trading system, has a strategic interest in playing a leading role in defending it. Doing so also means accelerating China's opening, maintaining progress in reducing the current account surplus, and seeking to resolve trade disputes through established mechanisms (e.g., the World Trade Organization dispute settlement) or negotiation."

While it would be beneficial for both sides to open entirely to foreign investments, it would not be enough to satisfy the underlying problems plaguing the Western nations. As economies start to crumble and policymakers scramble to blame outsiders, a containment approach towards China will only exacerbate them. The U.S. and China need to negotiate an arrangement satisfactory for both sides so that U.S. can focus on the real issues at home. Instead of viewing China as the adversary, the U.S. needs to see them as a partner in this complicated relationship.

Today, the deteriorating relationship between China and the United States is a major geopolitical risk. The relationship's protective insulation has been stripped away, nerves are exposed, and the mechanisms for defusing tensions are defunct. Battles rage between Beijing and Washington over trade, technology, investment, supply chains, journalists, and COVID-19. Diplomats, from the U.S. Secretary of State to China's "wolf warriors," are trading decidedly undiplomatic barbs. Public attitudes toward the other nations have taken a sharp turn for the worse. And China, often a bogeyman in U.S. presidential campaigns, is shaping up as a central issue in the escalating battle between the 2020 candidates.

The often uneasy equilibrium that has marked U.S.-China relations for decades should warn us to the risk that we may now be dangerously close to facing—where even a small action can serve as a catalyst that lets slip the dogs of war. The roar of insults and accusations in the trade war and the COVID-19 blame game should not deafen us to the warnings from either side.

The fact is, no situation is so bad that it cannot be made worse. While there is no reason that chronic problems between Washington and Beijing cannot abruptly become acute, there is abundant reason to worry that the political and diplomatic safeguards against uncontrolled escalation are largely inoperative. Therefore, I leave a caution to both leaders using the adage: "If you can't be good, be careful."

CHAPTER 6: FUTURE TRENDS

SECTION 1: INTRODUCTION

"We are not our own any more than what we possess is our own. We did not make ourselves, we cannot be supreme over ourselves. We are not our own masters."

Aldous Leonard Huxley, English writer and philosopher

"If we don't prepare and act now to secure access, avoid funding shortfalls and disruptions to trade we could be facing multiple famines of biblical proportions within a short few months."

David Beasley, United Nation's World Food Program Executive Director

Globalization, also known as legalized colonialism, has failed to deliver its promised effects. If anything, it created a situation whereby, after decades of exploiting the developing world, the developing world has come knocking on the door of the developed. It has taken over the world's most valuable resources with little consideration for those living there. Often neglected by their governments due to corruption and foreign interference, the advancements in information and technology have allowed the people greater mobility than ever before.

After facing the onslaughts of overpopulation, climate change, food and water scarcity, more and more people have become "climate refugees." However, while being defined, traditional refugees carry legal implications, whereas a climate refugee does not have the same benefits.

Pushed to extreme options often left with little choice, we have witnessed the mass movements of humanity on a scale never seen before. Around the world, we have seen people forced to conduct people smuggling to find a better life. In areas with dramatic climatic events, they have become hot spots for radicalization, leading to even more strains on limited resources, more sectarian violence, and, thus, more migrations.

As if it was not bad enough, we are now facing Mother Earth. The areas of the planet most in need—vast sections ranging from the U.S. to North Africa, across the Middle East to China—are drying up at alarming rates. Much of the developing world is running out of water with the way the population keeps growing, putting stress on ecosystems, agricultural land, and resources.

Not seen since the Great Recession of 2008, many Americans have been food insecure, and the numbers for people worldwide have grown with the increase in populations. As supply chains begin to collapse, we will see food prices go up, increasing the amount of those who are vulnerable. Around the world, the best agricultural lands have been snatched by governments, hedge funds, corporations, and private investors, leaving little leftovers for the locals.

The current inefficient ways of water usage, coupled with the spending practices of developed nations, have led to water being drained through exports from the most vulnerable areas that need it most. Meanwhile, the tropical countries with large amounts of water are seeing erratic weather patterns that cripple local businesses such as tourism and agriculture. As the developed world notices little to no environmental changes and continues business as usual, most of the world is in flux.

Meanwhile, another crisis is brewing among the developed nations—that is, the massive demographic shift currently underway. Never have there been so many older people in one generation, and the number is expected to double by 2050. The Baby Boomers brought with them the "greatest economy ever seen;" but now, they have become its downfall.

While migrants may seem on the surface as the simple solution, it brings its own set of issues to solve. As more foreigners migrate to a country, so does the discrimination from the host population. Nationalism is on the rise and President Donald Trump's "Make America Great Again" campaign can attest to this. The areas facing climate change radicalized and plagued by sectarian violence only add to these issues.

In the end, as the economic, financial, and social fabrics begin to come undone in developed nations, the world will see a rise of new powers from the developing world. After being forced to turn inwards, resources and attention will have to shift to domestic issues amid the growing calls for change.

Regardless of what choices are made, the future will bring tumultuous upheavals in our ways of life as we enter a brave new world.

SECTION 2: CLIMATE CHANGE

"Climate change is, simply, the greatest collective challenge we face as a human family."

Ban Ki-Moon, South Korean politician, diplomat, and former UN Secretary-General

If you turn on the television, we see crisis after crisis sweeping across the world. Swarms of locusts, forest fires, rising sea levels, radiation, oil spills, environmental degradation, and much more fill our airwaves each day. When I was a child, I remembered watching the Matrix, a movie that left a deep impression upon me and is without doubt a cult classic. However, there was one part that has always stuck with me. Agent Smith was about to kill Neo when he said to him:

> "I'd like to share a revelation that I´ve had during my time here. It came to me when I tried to classify your species, and I realized that you're not actually mammals. Every mammal on this planet instinctively develops a natural equilibrium with the surrounding environment, but you humans do not. You move to an area and you multiply and multiply until every natural resource is consumed. The only way can survive is to spread to another area. There is another organism on this planet that follows the same pattern. Do you know what it is? A virus. Human beings are a disease, a cancer of this planet. You're a plague and we… are the cure."

As civilizations have become more complex, we, humans, have become more destructive to our environments. Ask yourself: If we had no clothes, tools, or language—if we were to turn back time—what kind of climate do you think we can survive in year-round? Most of the world would be uninhabitable for us, but we have conquered every corner of this world and others due to our culture. This same culture which is the greatest driving force of our success is also the destructive force that may bring our downfall. The thing we do to the Earth today will have lasting implications for future generations.

There is no doubt that climate change has become a hot button topic in recent years, especially with governments putting pressure on people to start making changes. Hence, it is essential to understand the role that climate change will have in shaping the world to understand our future possibilities better. As humans, we should never forget that everything we have built depends upon the fragility of the environment we inhabit.

These days, the term "climate change" is often synonymous with global warming. But the 2 have entirely different meanings. It would be better to address the topic of climate change, as it shall include the effects of global warming. Global warming is one part of a greater system of occurring and has always happened since the Earth formed.

Personally, I belong to the camp referred to as "Anthropomorphic Climate Change" that believes that climate is being affected by humans. However, I admit that regardless if humans existed or otherwise, no place on Earth has ever escaped the drastic effects of climate change in the past. When we have extreme swings in hot or cold events, we become inundated with changes to which we cannot, along with other animals, adapt. This has been a driving factor in the evolution of life on Earth.

According to an article from The Economist on May 9, 2018 titled *Climate change will affect developing countries more than rich ones*, climate change would have more impact upon developing nations than those already established. Partly due to geography, but also lack of resources. A study by Sebastian Bathiany of Wageningen University and several other scientists found that developing nations would bear the brunt of effects from climate change. These countries would face higher variations in temperatures and rising sea levels, leading to agricultural failures, soil degradation, and mass migrations.

The study found that, as the planet becomes warmer, areas near the equator will dry up. These areas currently act as the "lungs of the world," making up the majority of the world's rainforests. In places like Brazil, there could be monthly changes in the weather of as much as 20%. While those located in tropical environments will see the most drastic changes in weather patterns and temperature, those living further away in northern latitudes will see fewer effects. The study also found that developed countries in northern latitudes, which produce most of the pollution, would see much fewer fluctuations. The *Economist* reported, "In terms of both means and variances, the countries that bear the most historical responsibility for climate change are likely to be the ones least harmed by its consequences."[45]

On July 24, 2019, the Government of Canada issued a report on their website detailing the effects climate change would have on communities and individuals. It stated, "Developing countries are the most impacted by climate change and the least able to afford its consequences."

When I was getting my scuba diving certification in Indonesia, I witnessed firsthand the massive amounts of plastic washed up on the beaches after a storm. The interesting part was that almost all of it originated from other counties, often exceptionally far away. This has led the Philippines government to start mailing the garbage back to their countries and producers of origin.

According to the World Health Organization, climate change can have trickle-down effects such as causing malaria, diarrhea, and heat stroke. They found that in developing countries, women, children, and the elderly are the most vulnerable, with gender inequalities amplifying the effects.

Schroders, an asset management company, recently published a report detailing the environmental effects of climate change on the global economy. Keith Wade and Marcus Jennings stated that the impact of climate change would not be equally distributed across the world and would likely produce winners and losers. They added that because developing countries naturally have warmer climates, they would rely more upon sectors such as forestry, agriculture, and tourism to support their economy. However, all of these sectors are directly affected by climate change.

As the temperature increases, crop yields and exportations decrease, leading to shortage and revenue loss, respectively. The unpredictability of weather patterns will cause severe issues for government budgets, especially with the

---

[45] https://www.economist.com/graphic-detail/20180509/climate-change-will-affect-developing-countries-more-than-rich-ones

infrastructure and healthcare costs.

In the report, the effects of climate change on the developing world are two-fold:

1) As developed countries face an increasing strain on domestic budgets, fewer resources in the form of aid and economic development funds will flow to developing countries.

2) The governments of these nations will be forced to channel resources away from productive and growth-enhancing projects towards countering the costs of extreme weather.

Such effects will damage near-term growth prospects. Furthermore, developing countries are likely to have less capacity to rebuild.

As the length of time will take longer for developing nations to recover, if there are more frequent natural disasters, it could mean that countries will be in a constant state of reconstruction, significantly affecting national budgets. Furthermore, countries that rely heavily upon tourism and selling fishing rights will see reduced traffic which could cause these industries to collapse.

According to the report, Africa and Asia are most at risk from the effects of climate change. Increased flooding, warmer temperatures, and cyclones had threatened major cities in India. The Himalayas' reduction of snowmelt had affected the water flow to the Indus Ganges and Brahmaputra Basins and its energy production. In Vietnam, the Mekong Delta, which accounts for the most substantial portion of the world's rice production, had become vulnerable to rising sea levels. In Sub-Saharan Africa, extreme droughts, heavy rainfall, and infestations had caused food shortages.

"Many developing nations are situated in low latitude countries and it is estimated that 80% of the damage from climate change may be concentrated in these areas. In contrast, northerly regions such as Canada, Russia, and Scandinavia, may enjoy a net benefit from modest levels of warming. Higher agricultural yields, lower heating requirements, and lower winter mortality rates are a handful of economic benefits climate change may bring, although these benefits may diminish as warming continues." While the report recognized that developing countries are hardest hit, it made it clear that these are global issues that need to be solved through clear policy and by working together[46].

The Environmental Justice Foundation (EJF) issued an article detailing the effects of climate change upon developing nations. They stated that climate change had destroyed livelihoods, infrastructure, and communities around the world, forcing many to become climate refugees. "Bangladesh is exceptionally vulnerable to climate change. Its low elevation, high population density and inadequate infrastructure all put the nation in harm's way, along with an economy that is heavily reliant on farming."

In the past, Bangladesh had used migration as a coping strategy for extraordinary climatic events. But these days, they are limited by borders and immigration. EJF stated that two-thirds of Bangladesh was now less than 5 meters below sea level, with 28% of the population living along the coast. In recent years, the salinization process has amplified the effects of climate change, especially in Bangladesh.

With the lack of clean drinking water and the farmland rendered useless due to the encroachment of saltwater, 33 million people in the country are at risk of health problems such as preeclampsia during pregnancy, skin diseases, acute respiratory infections, and the effects from malnutrition and other diseases. As the economy is reliant upon agriculture, the decrease in agricultural yields would be felt across the country. It was expected that Bangladesh would experience a 50-centimeter rise in sea levels by 2050, making them lose about 11% of their land.

Climate change is playing an important role in shaping the world around us. In the past, people migrated to avoid the harmful effects of climate change, whereas these days, that is becoming fraught with difficulties and secondary effects. As the world becomes more interconnected, we are changing the definition of what it means to be modern. In doing so, paying attention to how our actions affect others in not so distant parts of the globe is becoming more

---

[46] https://www.schroders.com/en/sysglobalassets/digital/insights/graphs/climate-change-estimate-of-sovereign-risk.jpg

important with each day. It is becoming harder to deny our reliance upon one another, as we are seeing the problems in the developing world, created by the developed world, come back to haunt them.

As population rises and access to resources scarcer, we will see more climate refugees around the globe. How we deal with these issues will help alleviate some of the tensions which give rise to conflicts, radicalization, and border tensions. Regardless of our stances on these issues, there must be global solutions for these global crises. One of the most important places we can begin to cooperate on is the vital issue of water, the second most precious of all natural resources.

SECTION 3: WATER WARS

"The next war in the Middle East will be fought over water, not politics. Water will be more important than oil this century."

Boutros Boutros Ghali., former UN Secretary General

According to the World Wildlife Foundation's (WWF), about 70% of our planet is covered with water but, as most people know, only 3% is drinkable, of which two-thirds is locked away in glaciers. Whether these figures are accurate or not, there are over one billion people without access to clean drinking water and 2.7 billion having difficulties securing adequate water.

To make things worse, almost half the world's population lacks proper sanitation to prevent diseases such as cholera, typhoid fever, and other water-borne illnesses. Many rivers, lakes, and aquifers have become polluted, dried up, and destroyed, reducing the availability of one of nature's most priceless resources. Agriculture is by far the largest consumer of water, and the WWF estimated that by 2025, two-thirds of the world's population will face water shortage. Nations around the world have been damming rivers to produce electricity for the growing population in a shift towards green energy However, this has caused severe effects for those living downstream, sometimes across borders. If oil became the dominant resource in the 20th century, then it is water for the 21st century.

The Grand Ethiopian Renaissance Dam (GERD) is currently under construction on the Blue Nile—the larger of the 2 tributary rivers, with the other being the White Nile. The Blue Nile originated in Lake Tarna in Ethiopia and is responsible for about 85% of the water flow to the Nile River. Ethiopia is the second most populated African country and, according to the International Monetary Fund (IMF) and World Bank, is one of the fastest-growing world economies for the past decade.

According to the Organization for World Peace article by Julian Rizk on April 26, 2020, the dam, which was currently about 70% complete, had led to an escalation of tension between the countries that share the Nile's waters. The Sudanese ex-negotiator Ahmed al-Mufti said, "I believe in one, two, 10…100

years, this will cause instability in the region. These are the germs of instability, and it will cause a water war. If not under this government then under another, as no population will see itself dying of thirst when they know that there is water very close by. This was my position when I quit, and every day since then I find more evidence that supports this."

However, the reasons for moving forward on the Ethiopian side were very sound. Ethiopia had struggled with low foreign exchange reserves after years of importing more than they export, a lack of electricity, and water scarcity. GERD is the solution to all 3 problems plaguing the nation.

To pay for the project, Ethiopia resorted to starting a lottery, taking the income of all government employees for one month in 2018, and issuing patriotic bonds which were loans from the population. This left one side solidified in their determination to continue with the project while downstream, Egypt would have the most to lose and had even gone as far as threatening to bomb the dam. The Ethiopians responded to the threats with their own to mobilize millions. So far, they have not made good on them. But as the dam nears completion and the reservoir fills, both sides are under increasing pressure as water becomes scarcer.

There are many kinds of water in the world, but have you heard of the terms "virtual water" or "invisible water"? In his book, *Virtual Water: Tackling the Threat to Our Planet's Most Precious Resource*, Tony Allen put forward some insightful terms. He described how regions of the world, mostly developing nations, had been exporting their water through globalization and water-intensive crops with consumers blissfully unaware of their water footprint.

For instance, it takes 140 liters of water to produce a cup of coffee, 168 liters to create a pint of beer, 1,700 liters for a 100g chocolate bar, 10,000 liters for a pair of jeans, and 15,400 liters for one kilogram of beef. Whether you are buying produce or a simple bottle of water, the "real costs" of production have shifted upstream to developing nations that trades fiat for diminishing resources. But how long can the broken system continue?

"He who controls the flow of water controls the flow of life." While water is often undervalued, we do not realize how badly we need it. Without it, there will be no economy, trade, and life. Which is why throughout history, settlements have always been at or near major waterways.

If we cannot manage the water in our own countries, how can we hope to maintain an essential waterway like the Nile River capable of traversing nearly a dozen countries? While most famous for being the end destination of the Nile River, Egypt is just one of many countries sharing this increasingly scarce resource, along with Ethiopia, Sudan, South Sudan, Uganda, Kenya, the Democratic Republic of the Congo, Tanzania, Rwanda and Burundi.

In a piece by Bran Lufkin, published in BBC News titled *Why 'hydro-politics' will shape the 21st Century*, he stated that, "If there was no access to water, there would be no world peace." Lufkin made the argument that as global supplies of freshwater came under threat and the demand for it increased, the strategic value of water as a commodity could cause hyper-nationalism and strain diplomatic relations. In fact, we are already seeing the conflicts due to this arise in several hot spots around the world.

In 2020, India and China saw increased hostilities over their border which happens to straddle the Himalayas Mountains. The hostilities began around an essential glacier in the region. This part of the Tibetan plateau is the watershed and origin of lifeblood waters of India, Pakistan, Bhutan, Bangladesh, Myanmar, Laos, Cambodia, Thailand, Southern China, and Vietnam. Both the Ganges River and the Mekong River Valley, vital lifeblood of the region, source their precious waters from the snowpack of the mountains deep within Chinese territory.

In a report issued by NS Energy, it was stated that, "Asia accounted for about 42% of the world's total installed hydropower capacity of 1,295GW in 2018." Most of these countries had or were planning to develop hydroelectric dams to limit the flow of water and generate electricity. However, for those living downstream, this could result to flooding and restrict vital access to water. If the water you need to survive originates from another country, there is little that can be done to enforce your water rights. Currently, there is no international governance of water resources since water is managed at a local level. This lack of oversight will empower some nations while leaving others at a disadvantage.

The water situation in India and Pakistan has been getting worse each year. According to the World Bank, India is the most dependent nation on water from aquifers globally and accounts for about one-fourth of the global demand for groundwater. 90% of the water is used in agriculture while the rest is for drinking water.

In an assessment from the National Institution for Transforming India (NITI), they found that close to 70% of the country's freshwater was contaminated. The lakes, rivers, and aquifers were more polluted than any other major nation. With water supplies dwindling, many places were forced to dig new, deeper wells which drove the water table lower and were expensive.

Another study from NITI noted that the groundwater level in Bengaluru was a few hundred feet below the ground in 2012; but now, it is more than 1,500 feet, much of which is contaminated. With no alternatives available, many farmers were forced to use raw or slightly treated discharges from sewer pipes and treatment plants.

According to the IMF, Pakistan ranked third in the world when it comes to water insecurity. In May 2018, the Pakistan Council of Research in Water Resources announced that there would be little to no clean drinking water available in the country by 2025.

In a report issued by Development Advocate Pakistan in December 2016, it was found that as households with flush toilets increased, the levels of access to water decreased. While the Indus Valley Basin relied on the rain and snowmelt from the Himalayas Mountains, records showed that the weather events had become drier and more unpredictable. This situation placed more stress upon an already fragile system, leading to diminishing results.

Water also played a vital role in Turkey's conflict with Syria. Since much of Syria's fresh water originated in Turkey, the Turks could limit the flow of water on their territory. They had been using this to their advantage in their conflicts in Syria and Iraq. According to Michael Page, the Deputy Middle East Director at Human Rights Watch, "In the midst of a global pandemic that is overloading sophisticated governance and infrastructure systems, Turkish authorities have been cutting off the water supply to regions most under strain in Syria…Not only is the Turkish authorities' water shut-off to communities in Northeast Syria harmful to civilians, but it could also blowback on Turkey itself." He went on to say, "Rights-respecting public health measures are needed to address the coronavirus; borders alone won't stop a pandemic's spread."

A little further south, in the Jordan River Basin, Israel had been diverting the flow of water for decades, causing unstable water levels of the Jordan River and the Dead Sea. The streams which originated in the Israeli-occupied Golan Heights, and Lebanese Mountains, are crucial lifeblood for those in Jordan, Palestine, and Israel. In an already complex political environment, the Middle East makes up a large portion of environments starting to pass the tipping point of water security.

According to James Famiglietti of the Nasa Grace Study, it is the vast swath of Northern Africa to Mongolia that is expected to experience some of the most challenging fluctuations to water accessibility in the coming years. An ominous prediction given the fact that the rise of ISIS in the Middle East was partly blamed on the worst drought that ripped through the region in the last 1000 years.

The major metropolitan city, Cape Town, recently felt the effects of the water crisis. After years of inefficient water distribution, and using more than could be sustained, the city almost ran out of water entirely in 2018. The situation got so severe, that the BBC reported one of their solutions involved floating icebergs from Antarctica[47].

In the data issued by The World Water Council, we can see the areas that are impacted the most from water security[48]. But this did not mean the tropical countries (shown in blue) were safe from trouble. Unpredictable weather events due to the ever-changing climate would cause havoc on all parts of society. The

---

[47] https://www.bbc.com/future/article/20180918-the-outrageous-plan-to-haul-icebergs-to-africa
[48] https://www.worldwatercouncil.org/sites/default/files/inline-images/1_Water_Stress_indicator2_01.jpg

water stress indicator is based on a ratio of water usage compared to renewable sources.

But even a wealthy nation like the U.S. cannot escape the effects of the water crisis. While many people had heard about the water situation in California, not many have known that there were 6 other states in the same predicament. According to Vero Water, a water processing company, Texas, Arizona, Oklahoma, Kansas, Nevada, and New Mexico were all running out of water.

In an article posted by Tim Radford, of Climate News Network on October 9, 2019 titled *Water stress rises as more wells run dry*, he predicted that within 3 decades, almost 80% of the areas that depend on groundwater would see their wells run dry. As the world deals with increasingly unpredictable weather patterns, climate change is drastically affecting some nations to the point of no return.

Dr. Inge de Graaf, a Hydrologist from the University of Freiburg pointed out, "The effects can be seen already in the Midwest of the United States and in the Indus Valley project between Afghanistan and Pakistan." For thousands of years, communities have relied upon groundwater access, which took millions of years to accumulate. As the human population began to skyrocket, so has our ability to use and destroy these limited supplies. This situation has contributed to the levels of groundwater being depleted around the world in areas that need it the most, whereas other areas are getting too much.

According to computer simulations, Dr. de Graff stated in a report published by the journal Nature:

> "We estimate that, by 2050, environmental flow limits will be reached for approximately 42% to 79% of the watershed in which there is groundwater pumping worldwide, and this will generally occur before substantial losses in groundwater storage are experienced… If we continue to pump as much groundwater in the coming decades as we have done so far, a critical point will be reached also for regions in southern and central Europe – such as Portugal, Spain and Italy – as well as in North African countries… Climate change may even accelerate this process, as we expect less precipitation, which will

further increase the extraction of groundwater and cause dry areas to dry out completely."

Water, Peace, and Security, an organization funded by the Dutch government, has developed an early warning system to locate potential hot spots for water conflicts. The organization considers the environmental variables like rainfall and crop failures, along with social, political, and economic factors, to predict future water-related conflicts.

According to the system, potential conflicts are brewing in Iraq, Iran, Mali, Nigeria, Madagascar, India, and Pakistan. The main areas of concern cover parts of Africa, the Middle East, and Southeast Asia. While the system is interactive and available online, the organization seeks to promote dialogue to avoid conflicts. However, with the growing populations and mass migrations, there is an increasing probability that a number of people will become "environmental refugees."

How we use our precious water resources need to be our central focus moving forward. With the increasing value of water, nations will be forced to make changes to the globalized system of exchange that can possibly put developing countries at a severe disadvantage. If we continue the path of globalization, things will only get worse. Ultimately, conflicts will arise over water, with protectionism and nationalism not far behind.

As countries try to dam and conserve what water they have, it is going to leave less for others. For countries living downstream of other nations and reliant on that water, they are left with limited options to respond. All these factors will heighten tensions in what is already shaping out to be Cold War 2.0, pushing nations further into conflict. A conflict that will become the first true world conflict involving all nations and all segments of societies.

SECTION 4: FOOD SCARCITY

"Clear waters and lush mountains are as valuable as gold and silver."

Xi Jinping, President of the People's Republic of China

Around the world, countries are realizing that instead of the current pandemic, hunger is what is going to annihilate a substantial amount of the world's population. The world has never faced a hunger emergency like this, and the number of people facing acute hunger could double to 265 million by the end of 2020.

The unnerving interruption in agricultural production and supply routes are now leaving millions stressed over the globe. "Logistical problems in planting, harvesting and transporting food will leave poor countries exposed in the coming months, especially those reliant on imports," said Johan Swinnen, Director-General of the International Food Policy Research Institute in Washington.

In places like India, the lockdown is fundamentally a request for workers to starve. There, the health crisis has been called an "equalizer" since it affected both the rich and the poor citizens. However, with regards to food, the commonality ends. It is destitute individuals, including enormous portions of more unfortunate countries, who are presently going hungry and confronting the possibility of starvation.

As the world's population grows and agricultural bases worldwide reach their maximum limit to production, all eyes are turning to Africa for water security, agricultural land, and food security. While colonization in Africa ended in the 20th century, this system of extraction and exploitation was replaced with a new legal system called globalization. Private corporations and investors from other countries are scrambling to purchase extensive sections of its fertile agricultural lands.

African governments had prioritized the sale of the property to foreign investors over the ownership or needs of their people. Billions of dollars had flowed to build infrastructure projects to gain access to the large-scale, modern agricultural zones that serve the needs of foreigners. The locals who had been steamrolled to make room for these projects, at best, were now working on their former land for the new companies, often, in undesirable situations. The land had been and is being leased at bargain-basement rates of $1 USD per hectare per year for as long as 99 years.

This situation had led to incredible opportunities for private foreign corporations, Arab sheiks, foreign governments, Wall Street equity funds, and private investors alike. As Africa struggles to feed its growing population, its most valuable resources for the future are being bought and sold to benefit wealthier nations. With the effects of climate change, water scarcity, food security, and population all on the rise, millions are left with few options for their future: fight or flight.

Grain is an NGO that specializes in helping local farmers in Africa since the 1980s. In a report issued on January 21, 2015, the battles taking place for African land, water, minerals, forests, seeds, oil, and renewable energy sources were all detailed. But it was back on April 13, 2010 that a report was issued, entitled *Turning African farmland over to big business* warning about the massive land transfers that were taking place: namely, the oil-palm plantation in Liberia, the Japanese-Brazilian soya plantations in Mozambique, and the Korean company Daewoo and Indian company Varun in Madagascar. As climate change affects the world and access to clean water comes into question, all eyes are on Africa.

Unfortunately, these were just the tip of the iceberg. Since then, we witnessed Saudi Arabian, U.S., and many more corporations rushing to secure their interests. Under the guise of providing jobs for the communities and investments in the agricultural industries, which would ultimately boost production, African governments are selling land for years. But when the locals are paid practically a slave wage, working 7 days a week with no overtime pay, along with food exportation, what benefits are left for the locals?

In an article from *National Geographic Magazine* by Joel K. Bourne, Jr. on July 7, 2014, we heard the chilling first-hand accounts of globalization in Africa. According to the article, in 2013, Mozambique was the third most impoverished nation in Africa, but only after coal, natural gas, and agricultural deals, Portuguese companies had begun building rails and ports. Meanwhile, Chinese companies invested in a new airport, soccer stadium, and presidential palace. All of which were massive infrastructure projects, financed by massive loans that the local government could probably never repay, done in exchange for their resources.

When Hoyo Hoyo, a Portuguese agricultural company, took over 25,000 acres of farmland, the locals were promised new land, schools, and wells, but none of these materialized. Instead, the local agricultural populations across Africa were pushed off their lands and into crowded cities already strained with resources.

Additionally, Brazil and Japan bought 35 million acres of land in Mozambique, an area the size of North Carolina, for their joint megaproject, ProSavana. A local farmer said, "For us as small farmers, the production of this soy guarantees the family income, even enough for us to send our children to college so they can become engineers or even doctors. Fields are fundamental for us. No fields, no life." Most African farmers have limited access to education, credit, and fertilizer required to boost production on their own. They turn into slaves on their own land.

On December 24, 2019, there was an article in Africa Renewal Magazine by Leon Usigbe titled *Drying Lake Chad Basin, which gives rise to the crisis: Food insecurity, conflicts, terrorism, displacement, and climate change effect compound challenges.* Lake Chad used to be one of Africa's largest freshwater bodies, supporting 30 million people, straddling the North Central African countries of Chad, Nigeria, Niger, and Cameroon. "[T]he Lake Chad 'Basin' that covers almost 8% of the continent, spreads over seven countries: Algeria, Cameroon, Central African Republic, Chad, Libya, Niger and Nigeria." The lake has been drying up due to climate change and protectionist policies of water sources leading into the lake.

Since the 1960s, the lake has shrunk by 90%, mostly due to the booming local population, forcing families to look for other places with water. As the humanitarian situation becomes direr, we have seen the radicalization of the area through militant groups such as Boko Haram. These militants terrorize the remaining locals, forcing even more migrations and atrocities.

What is the driving force behind these acquisitions? Over in the U.S., the situation for farmers has been quite dire for a long time. Battling the complex effects of globalization, climate change, water scarcity, and geopolitics, the "golden age" of farming in the U.S. has come to an end.

On January 28, 2020, the U.S. courts revealed that since 2014, bankruptcies in the U.S. agricultural sector have been rising each year. Even though President Donald Trump had issued $28 billion USD in bailouts for this sector, it failed to buck the trend which resulted to 8-year highs, with a lot of the blame being placed on the trade war[49].

In a report titled *Implications of Water Scarcity for Water Productivity and Farm Labor* published on January 20, 2020 by James F. Booker and W. Scott Trees, we learned how water scarcity in the U.S. was affecting farmers. By analyzing the relationships between water scarcity, water productivity, farm labor, and crop choices, the researchers were able to highlight the key issues faced by the U.S. agricultural sector.

As U.S. agricultural producers face water scarcity across the U.S., this will increase labor demand, leading to increased costs for producers. Globalization led many producers to specialize in crops for export, with many of them having high-water consumption rates that need to be altered if each sector wishes to continue[50].

In a report from Carbon Brief by Robert McSweeney on August 6, 2019, desertification was taking place across the globe and had harsh effects upon the agricultural sector. According to the UN Convention to Combat Desertification (UNCCD), 12 m hectares of productive land that could have been producing 20 metric tons of grains were lost each year due to droughts. Drylands make up 38% of the Earth's landmass and are home to 2.7 billion people, of which 90% live in developing countries. These areas are experiencing

---

[49] https://specials-images.foresimg.com/imageserve/5e4137878b6cf300071e4c02/960x0.jpg?fit=scale
[50] https://www.mdpi.com/2073-4441/12/1/308/htm

soil degradation and water scarcity, leading to vicious dust storms and air quality issues.

Sebastien Malo of the Thomson Reuters Foundation, in conjunction with The World Economic Forum, issued a research showing that the U.S. would have much less water over time and be forced to make changes. The areas most affected were in the Central and Southern Great Plains, the Central Rocky Mountains, the Southwest, California, and the South and Midwest. These areas have been the breadbasket of the U.S., with a significant part of Canadians relying on them for food growth. Currently, 75% of the water in the U.S. goes towards agriculture, but drastic changes are needed to continue.

According to the Fourth National Climate Assessment issued in 2017, different parts of the U.S. would be affected differently. In the North East, it was expected to see the most significant temperature rises and sea level increases, with urban centers being particularly hard hit. In the South East, an additional 100 warmer days and hotter nights per year could be expected thanks to the "heat island effect." In the Midwest, temperatures could rise to 60 days a year above 100 degrees Fahrenheit that could cause its residents to migrate to another place, increasing the number of climate refugees.

The Great Plains, where a large percentage of the nation's meat industries are based, was expected to experience not only drier conditions but also more extreme weather events such as tornadoes. In the Southwest, droughts and megadroughts were expected to become commonplace. The Northwest was expected to see less snow and longer, rainier winters. All these changing weather conditions had drastic impacts on the agricultural sectors, along with food and water security, in the country.

According to an Intergovernmental Panel on Climate Change, nearly 70 of all drylands are currently in Asia and Africa. Depending on the distribution of drylands across the landmasses of the world, some countries will see net gains while other net losses due to climate change[51].

---

[51] https://www.carbonbrief.org/wp-content/uploads/2019/08/The-observed-distribution-of-different-aridity-levels-based-on-data-for-1981-2010-b.jpg

China has taken the initiative to fight climate change head-on in their northern regions, and data from satellites are showing progress in these areas. In recent years, to battle desertification, China began building a new "Green Wall" with much smaller initiatives taking place in Mongolia, Turkey, Algeria, and Iran. Under President Xi Jinping, environmental issues have taken precedence over development. China is leading the world in combatting climate change, planting over 80 billion trees since 1980, according to a report from Generation Progress

Previously, almost one-fourth of China was covered in desert. But their State Forestry Administration claimed that they were able to reduce sandstorms by 20% and desertification by 5,000 miles in recent years. These initiatives, along with the saltwater-grown rice from Yangzhou University, offered hope for the future. But there is a long way to go for most countries if they wish to offset the effects of climate change upon the food and water resources.

Across large swaths of Africa and Asia are pests voraciously ravaging the crops from East Africa to India: desert locusts, a type of grasshopper. Some of the swarms are the size of small cities and can travel upwards of 150 kilometers a day, so thick they block out the sun. When these pests descend upon an area, they can consume the crops in as little as 30 seconds.

According to a report from the UN, a swarm of 40 to 80 million locusts can eat "the same amount of food in a day as three million people." The devastation was so severe that the UN issued a warning of the possible food shortage and famines due to the locust infestation. Pakistan was even forced to declare a state of emergency amid an already tricky agricultural climate due to the wreck this outbreak had cost them. In India, Bhagirath Choudhary, the Director of the New Delhi-based South Asia Biotechnology Centre, said: "We have never, ever seen what we have in the last 6 months in India – never in the history."

Due to the unpredictable weather patterns this 2020, a desirable situation for this phenomenon was created. Desert locusts only lay eggs in moist soil to keep them from drying out. When heavy rains saturate an otherwise arid climate, it causes the locusts to proliferate. When the eggs hatch, they have plenty of vegetation nearby to consume until they are forced to migrate. This migration causes ruin to farmers thousands of kilometers away and will continue to ravage areas from South America, Africa, and the Indian subcontinent to China.

In a shocking report from the UN Secretary-General, Antonio Guterres warned that the world was on the verge of the worst food crisis ever witnessed since WWII. He believed that more than 50 million people could be pushed into instant poverty. "Unless immediate action is taken, it is increasingly clear that there is an impending global food emergency that could have long term impacts on hundreds of millions of children and adults. We need to act now to avoid the worst impact of our efforts to control the pandemic." He also warned that the public health crisis, coupled with a global depression, created the perfect environment for extreme poverty and, in turn, sustained social unrest. Even developed countries were at risk of disruptions. He further explained, "Our food systems are failing, and the COVID-19 pandemic is making things worse."

In the report titled *The Impact of COVID-19 on Food Security and Nutrition* published in June 2020, the UN detailed the unprecedented threats to global supply chains. The UN Secretary-General's Special Envoy for the 2021 Food Systems Summit, Agnes Kalibata pointed out, "It has exposed dangerous deficiencies in our food systems and actively threatens the lives and livelihoods of people around the world, especially the more than 1 billion people who have employment in the various industries in food systems." These experts warned that this food crisis was quite different from anything we had seen before. Its corresponding consequences would be long-lasting and cut across many socio-economic lines.

The European Commission published a report on its website titled the *European Green Deal* which plans to combat climate change and effectively eliminate large scale farming from the continent. As part of the deal, Europe sought to be "climate neutral" by 2050 and included a "Farm to Fork" strategy designed to slash crop productivity by half over the next decade with the aim to reduce the use of fertilizers and pesticides.

Europe is one of the most productive and modernized agricultural regions in the world which helps provide excellent yields for their populations. However, the new initiatives will make large scale production unprofitable while pushing more small-scale operations and, thus, higher prices upon consumers. This decrease in production will put more pressure on importing more of their food products, which could explain why agricultural land was being purchased overseas like it was on sale (and it was). However, these areas employed less advanced agrarian production methods which, in turn, added more significant weight to climate change. Although Europe is making the shift towards a more sustainable local economy, its method of offloading costs does not help other countries.

As a global community, we are all in this together to find solutions that are in line with nature. Eventually, the higher food costs will lead to greater food insecurity in the continent, with counties depending more on imports to fulfill their needs. As we can see with the current crises, any disruption to the supply chain incurs disastrous effects, making the situation even more fragile.

As the world grapples with the immediate consequences of COVID-19, we are only beginning to understand the long-term implications it brought. In some places, we see food shortage materialize, often in areas that need them the most; while in others, supply disruptions left the shelves empty. Countries that sold their more productive agricultural land to the highest bidders would come to regret their decisions. Social upheavals and migrations will become the norm, with the likelihood of spilling over into the political realm.

Corruption in governments has allowed for the takeover of food production in the developing world, and it is all thanks to globalization. Lack of access to resources has led to increased sectarian violence and radicalization in the local communities. This lack of foresight has, in turn, forced those looking for a better life to migrate to where they can gain access to resources, causing the mass movements of people on unprecedented scales.

As unpredictable weather patterns continue to hamper the hard work of farmers, along with the rising demand for agricultural access, conflicts and social unrest are expected to follow. There is a saying that all the money in the world is meaningless without clean air to breathe, freshwater to drink, and fresh food to eat. Food scarcity will come to play a leading role in the coming years as each nation battles to secure their interests, sometimes, at the expense of others. However, regardless of whether these situations are anthropomorphically or naturally caused, they will result in the same effects: fight or flight.

SECTION 5: MASS MIGRATIONS

"No one puts their children in a boat unless the water is safer than the land. No one leaves home unless home is the mouth of a shark."

Warsan Shire, British writer, poet, editor, and teacher

Until the second half of the 20th century, it was uncommon for men, women, and children to cross the Mediterranean Sea from North Africa to arrive in Europe. I am not referring to the raids that took place looking for European slaves, but of migration. However, the Italians, French, Spanish and Greeks, and other Europeans did escape to North Africa to avoid persecution or overpopulation in their respective nations. They looked for their fortunes in new soil, in Maghreb, and the colonies overseas. Looking back on the events of the 19th century, we see how the world went through some incredible transformations. European powers dominated the economies of Africa, their colonization in full swing, and, with it, came waves of settlers. Just before the outbreak of WWI, European colonists numbered one million in Algeria, a nation with a native population of about 9 million at the time.

After the devastations of WWI and WWII that took the lives of millions of men, Europe encouraged North African immigration so it can rehabilitate its shattered economic bases. Shortages in the workforces led to a desire for immigration, to help rebuild the former colonial powers. This was the beginning of what some described as an "invasion", while others consider it the so-called "great replacement theory." This migration of people into Europe began as the result of constructed economic dependence upon exploitation of cheap labor. Now, it has been accelerated by political instability, climate change, lack of access to resources, religious strife, and globalization.

From Asia and Africa to Europe, South and Central America to North America, and even remote islands in the Pacific, millions of people are on the move due to climate change, wars, politics, and more. As human population began to skyrocket about 200 years ago, the strains on natural resources has accelerated, with inequality being exacerbated by climate change. During March 14-15, 2019, a tropical storm, named Tropical Cyclone Idai, ripped through Mozambique. According to a World Vision report on March 5, 2020, it caused flooding and destroyed more than $773 million USD worth of buildings, infrastructure, and crops, as well as 100,000 homes. Incidents like this have become more commonplace in recent years as humans continue to develop and proliferate.

Since humans struggled to find equilibrium with nature, nature began to push back, leaving many with little to no options. In the wake of this and many other crises, in conjunction with a lack of resources, increasing population, and political and social instability, we begin to see massive migrations across the world. The purpose of this section is not to focus on the reasons behind the mass migrations as they are extensive and varied, but more so to explain the movements that are taking place and their impact.

On March 19, 2018, the World Bank Group issued a report estimating that by 2050, more than 143 million people could be forced to migrate to other areas from just 3 regions in the world. Sub-Saharan Africa was expected to see the most refugees, followed by South Asia, and then Latin America. The report highlighted that the areas which would see the least water availability, crop productivity, rising sea levels, and extreme weather patterns would be the most affected. The current trend of migration was expected to continue to increase in the future. Another area expected to be hard hit was East Africa, home to some of the countries with the highest numbers of refugees today. While climate refugees often flee under similar conditions as traditional refugees, the current legal perspectives do not afford them the same rights and protection.

Currently, there are no multilateral strategies or legal frameworks which recognize climate change as a driving factor behind human migration. The UN High Commission for Refugees (UNHCR) has refused to grant refugee status to climate refugees. Instead, they have classified them as "environmental migrants" and are essentially ignored by governments. This lack of clarity regarding the definition of these people has allowed human trafficking and crime networks to thrive in their desperate quest to survive.

In an article from Time Magazine on December 1, 2017, we read about African migrants being sold as slaves for $400 USD in the markets of Libya. Libya, which is on the North Coast of Africa, has become the main transit port for refugees and migrants seeking a better life. Over the past several years, thousands of migrants have drowned trying to make it across to Europe. Some estimates put the number of people being bottled up in Libya between 400,000 and 1 million trying to avoid being robbed, kidnapped, raped, or murdered.

In 2007, the International Organization for Migration (IOC) estimated 4.6 million African migrants were living in Europe, while the Migration Policy Institute claimed it could be as high as 7 or 8 million. Still, since then, these numbers have only increased. According to Lenard Doyle, the Director of Media and Communications for the IOC, "It's a total extortion machine. Fueled by the absolute rush of migrants through Libya thinking they can get out of poverty, following a dream that doesn't exist." Many have sold everything and left everyone they know behind, looking for a better life. In contrast, and in many ways, they escaped certain injustices and climatic events but are unable to integrate into European society.

The Middle East, the cradle of modern civilization, is no stranger to large-scale warfare. Whether due to sectarian violence, lack of jobs, climate change, instability, or more, this region is also seeing widespread migrations. Of the top 10 countries applying for asylum in the European Union (EU), by far, the leading countries were Syria, Afghanistan, and Iraq. Given the Middle East's proximity to Europe, the continent became the obvious choice[52].

As Western culture penetrated deeply into most, if not all, parts of the developing world, specific imaginary images about what life must be like in Western countries come to the forefront. Of the most popular routes taken by refugees and migrants into Europe, the vast majority transition through Turkey. Since then, until now in 2020, Turkey is using the millions of migrants they sheltered as leverage for billions of dollars and political concessions with the EU.[53]

The President of Turkey, Recep Tayyip Erdoğan, even threatened Europe to "open the floodgates of refugees" if the EU dared to be critical of his military adventurism in Syria, Iraq, and Libya. This situation led Eastern European

---

[52] https://ichef.bbci.co.uk/news/660/cpsprodpb/18500/production/_101048599_chart_top10_origins_of_asylum_seekers_2015-nc.png
[53] https://ichef.bbci.co.uk/news/660/cpsprodpb/29BC/production/_101048601_migrant_routes_numbers_v9-nc.png

nations to take strong anti-refugee stances, increasing the popularity for nationalistic politicians across Europe. On the other side, Greece, which shares the border with Turkey and is the most accessible transit country, had been pushed to reinforce border controls with continued heated debates about erecting a wall along their borders.

Europe has been taking in immigrants from the Near East for thousands of years, and even the current countries are no strangers to population shifts and migrations. However, the recent large waves of immigration and religious differences, along with media perceptions, have given Europeans negative opinions about migrants and refugees.

The Pew Research Institute released a data in 2016[54] showing that many Europeans were concerned that taking in more refugees would translate into domestic terrorism. Furthermore, most Europeans polled had negative views of Muslims in general[55]. Regardless of the reasons of migrants coming into Europe, it has become obvious that the opinion of Europeans towards them is overwhelmingly negative.

But Europe is not the first and only choice of the migrants and refugees from the Middle East. According to a report from Info Migrants on December 20, 2019, only 14% of all migrants from the Middle East had reached Europe. In a 2019 UNHCR report titled *Situation Report on International Migration 2019: The Global Compact for Safe, Orderly and Regular Migration in the Context of the Arab Region*, Arab countries had also been experiencing "unprecedented levels as region of origin, transit, and destination" of human migration in recent years.

Since 1990, an estimated 38 million Arab nationals were living outside of their home country within the greater Middle East Region. In 2018, two-fifths of refugees worldwide, about 8.7 million, came from Arab countries; with almost 30% of them deciding to stay in the region. The number one destination for these people was found to be Turkey, with nearly 4 million non-residents estimated to be in the country. Furthermore, non-Arab Asian countries were

---

[54] https://www.pewresearch.org/wp-content/uploads/2016/09/Refugees_1.png
[55] https://www.pewresearch.org/wp-content/uploads/2016/09/FT_16.09.09_refugeesEurope_plot.png?w=310

found to be the origin of 56% of the migrants in Arab countries, mostly coming as migrant workers from Bangladesh, Afghanistan, Pakistan, Malaysia, Philippines, Indonesia, etc.

In Southeast Asia, population transfers date back thousands of years, with new arrivals being incorporated into the older culture. For instance, almost 20 million Chinese descendants are living in the Indo-China region today. However, due to a wide variety of factors, including increasing populations and climate change, these migrations put strains on already limited resources.

Research Gate provided data on the complex importation and exportation of labor across Southeast Asia[56]. According to a November 12, 2018 Inter Sector Coordination Group report, there were so many refugees moving into Bangladesh that it caused a critical humanitarian emergency.

In recent years, the Bay of Bengal witnessed the harmful displacement of people from Rohingya, causing them to flee to neighboring countries. To date, the Association of Southeast Asian Nations (ASEAN) has done little to address the situations concerning Bangladesh and Myanmar.

Across ASEAN countries, labor migration has played an essential role in movements as well. Most of these migrants are low-skilled, often young, and have an equal distribution between males and females. These workers usually make their way to countries with, on average, older population, looking to fill some fundamental roles. They are usually hired to be housekeepers, teachers, construction workers, miners, nurses, farmhands, as well as handling any hazardous jobs.

In a report issued by the Migrations Policy Institute on October 22, 2019, it was found that the demographics of migrants coming to North America was shifting. In the past, most migrants were from Latin American countries. However, in recent years, there was a stark increase of people from Africa, Asia, and the Middle East traveling via Latin American countries to North America. These people were referred to in the report as "extracontinental migrants"

---

[56] https://www.researchgate.net/profile/Karl_Husa/publications/286861741/figure/fig2/AS:669455742939146@1536622095892/The-migration-system-of-Southeast-Asia-at-the-beginning-of-the-21-st-century-Japan-South.png

which means they are not from the Western Hemisphere, and this was not noticed until recently.

Furthermore "the number of extracontinental migrants moving in and through Latin America has increased so dramatically in recent years that it prompted targeted policy responses from some countries, including Panama, Colombia, and Costa Rica." Surprisingly, most extracontinental migrants entered the Western Hemisphere through legal means through visas. In some cases, permits were not even required. This gateway is due to the lax visa requirements of some countries, such as Brazil, Ecuador, and Guyana, which, in turn, make them convenient entry ports for human traffickers.[57]

However, their journey had only begun. The trip to the U.S. or Canada could take months, if not years, often at the mercy of more smugglers and traversing difficult terrain. Some of the common routes happened to cut right through some of the most dangerous drug cartel-held areas, nicknamed "the cocaine express." Given how difficult this journey is, a report found that many decided to abandon their quest and settle in South America instead, either by choice or circumstance[58]. And according to a Center for Immigration Studies report on August 13, 2018, and based on court records, the top 3 origins of Special Interest Aliens coming to the U.S. were from the Middle East, North and East Africa, and South Asia.

For migrants traveling to the U.S. and coming from the Middle East, they often went to Turkey and Greece, then to either European or the Gulf States or took a Southern route through South America, before migrating to the U.S.[59] People from North and East Africa commonly went through the Gulf States, but sometimes passed through Europe. Meanwhile, others preferred to land in Latin American countries like Brazil, Bolivia, Ecuador, Cuba, and Mexico City. On the other hand, those from South Asia often traveled via India, Singapore, Gulf States or South Africa.

---

[57] https://cis.org/sites/default/files/2018-08/bensman-infiltration-m-2.jpg
[58] https://www.migrationpolicy.org/sites/default/files/source_images/Yates-Fig3_updated_T.png
[59] https://cis.org/sites/default/files/2019-11/bensman-infiltration-f3.jpg

For a country like the U.S., which was founded upon immigration, it seemed ironic that they had become so concerned with immigrants as of late. While President Donald Trump was getting considerable criticism for his policies towards immigration, in practice, he did not differ much from Democratic President Barrack Obama. In general, there has been building sentiment with U.S. administrations against immigration, with U.S. sentiment turning inwards.

According to the UN report from 2015, the U.S. already had the highest number of immigrants in the world, with a total of 47 million people or about 14% of the country's population. Meanwhile, the number of undocumented immigrants was estimated to range from 10 to 12 million people or about 3.2% to 3.6% of the country's population. In Europe, according to Eurostat Statistics, an estimated 21.8 million immigrants were living in the Eurozone or about 4.9% of the continent's population as of January 1, 2019. In 2018 alone, an estimated 2.4 million immigrants from non-EU nations entered the EU.

Can the Western world handle more immigrants? Today, the U.S. is looking more like a warzone than a sanctuary. As we have seen earlier in this book, Western nations have long declined in almost every area of ranking. Economically and financially, Western countries are on the verge of the worst depression ever seen, made worse by COVID-19 policies and its repercussions.

As income inequality rises, so has the discontent which had sown the seeds of social unrest we are witnessing today. With each day, the calls for more socialist policies get more robust as those who feel left out want their piece of the pie. We are already witnessing supply chains become disrupted due to the restrictive movements and the protectionist policies of nations. Rising food costs will have a substantial effect on citizens, and this year, 2020, has had a tremendous impact on income.

In the middle of this, the U.S., feeling the threat of its place for world dominance, is seeking to alienate China. They are forcing nations to pick a side in a trade war that can only make things worse for all. All the while, Mother Earth is pushing back against us with diseases and climate change, causing disruptions and misery worldwide.

In a future where access to water and food will become scarcer, it makes sense for whoever can move to make a better life. It is admirable for someone to work hard and make a better life rather than rely on handouts. But as we can see, it will not be the life we once had; it will be a new one we probably do not want.

SECTION 6: DEMOGRAPHIC SHIFTS

"I am very concerned about the millions of baby boomers who are counting on the stock market to deliver them a safe, sound, long retirement. I am afraid the baby boomers who are counting on the stock market are in trouble."

Robert Kiyosaki, American businessman and author

"War is young men dying and old men talking."

Franklin D. Roosevelt, 32nd President of the United States

The year was 1952, and the future was bright. You were driving home in your new Cadillac, past the newly paved roads of the subdivision, with the rows of cookie-cutter houses, and freshly cut grass. It was just about supper time and all the kids were running home to eat. The smell of meatloaf and Jell-O salads filled your nostrils as you pull into your driveway. You sat down in front of the new 13-inch color television in your living room while your wife was preparing a delicious dinner using your new microwave. Later, as your son and daughter sat down next to you, your wife took your coat, casually poured you a drink, and lit you a cigarette. Truly, it was a life to be envied: The American Dream.

Baby Boomers are the generation born between born between 1946 and 1964. They are appropriately named as such after the rise in the birth rate after WWII; when soldiers came home from the war, settled down, and raised families. In the decades since, Baby Boomers had seen it all—from international conflicts and history-making television shows to innovations in communication, technology, and media. Indeed, they have seen massive changes over the course of their lifetime.

According to Pew Research, Baby Boomers in the U.S. peaked in numbers in 1999, reaching a record high of 78.8 million. Now, they have been overtaken by their own kids, the Millennials, who surpassed the Boomers in numbers as of the summer of 2019. But while the Boomers are not the biggest generation out there, they still have a massive influence over the culture and economy today.

Around the world, in most regions and countries, we see a rapid demographic shift. In the last 60 years, the human population nearly doubled and, as we saw with the rise of the Baby Boomers, these kinds of shifts in the community can change the course of nations for decades. Each day, more than 8,000 baby boomers pass the age of 65, and thanks to advancements in medicine and healthcare, they can live longer than ever. However, as the population ages, this puts tremendous strain on the services they require which is costly. It is one of the reasons why the U.S. has yet to implement a universal healthcare system. Increased demands for Medicare, Social Security, and Medicaid will need important innovations to function, but who will be there to pay the bill?

Projections over the next several decades showed us an increasingly divergent world, whereby the developed world would lie stagnate and decline while the developing world would see rapid growth. Fertility rates in the developed world have been falling to levels not able to sustain the current populations. Meanwhile, the developing world is experiencing a boom in younger generations. The developed world is aging, with most of the citizens becoming elderly, while developing countries are getting younger, with most of their citizens in the prime of their lives. In the same way the Baby Boomers shaped "the greatest economy the world has ever seen," their needs have changed, and people are replacing them with entirely different desires. As the U.S. makes a steady march towards conflict with the rise of Asia, demographics will play a key role in understanding who will be the winners and losers.

In a study from John Bongaarts titled *Human population growth and the demographic transition*, he analyzed the demographic trends of the world's population from 1950 to 2050. He estimated that by 2050, the world's population would be 9.2 billion people, a significant rise from the 6.5 billion in 2005. Astonishingly, almost all the growth would occur in what is called the geographic "South," which referred to Africa, Asia (excluding Japan), and Latin America.

On the other hand, the geographic "North," made up of North America, Europe, Japan, Australia, and New Zealand, was expected to stay the same[60]. Surprisingly, this trend did not originate after WWII, but began in the 19th

---

[60] https://www.ncbi.nlm.nih.gov/pmc/articles/PMC2781829/

century, which began with decline in death rates in the North, leading to declining birth rates by the 20th century.

While some European nations were already experiencing declining populations, Africa was expected to double in population. The study found that the communities in Kenya and Uganda were growing at faster rates, doubling their numbers in just 2 decades. Back in 2005, China at 1.31 billion and India at 1.13 billion people, dominated the chart, accounting for almost half of the South's population, followed by 6 Asian countries, one Latin American, and one African. However, the study said that by 2050, "…the ranking is expected to have shifted substantially, with India's population exceeding China's, and with Ethiopia and D.R. Congo rising to the top 10, replacing Japan and the Russian Federation."

As this demographic transition is taking place, declines in fertility and mortality rates play key roles in a population's age composition. Different regions are clearly at different stages of demographic transition, with the North's population becoming older than every other region.[61]

A paper titled *Migration and the Demographic Shift*, published in December 2014 by Anzelika Zaiceva and Klaus F. Zimmermann, analyzed the effects demographic shifts had upon the labor markets and economies. According to the report, migration was being used to offset the impact of an aging population in developed countries. When migrants arrived in their host country, they usually had a much higher birth rate than the hosts, but there were declines after just one generation. Migrants offered a way to share the rising costs of healthcare the older population inevitably required.

However, as we have seen in the previous section, it is not easy to inject a society with large amounts of foreign migrants since it significantly affects the economy. Not to mention, as nations try to seduce the best and brightest from around the world to move, this leaves an effect called "brain drain" on other countries. Just like money, those with skills in demand tend to go where they are treated best.

---

[61] https://www.ncbi.nlm.nih.gov/pmc/articles/PMC2781829/#RSTB20090137C11

The paper found that, globally, the number of people over 60 years old was projected to grow from 810 million in 2012 to more than 2 billion by 2050. This situation was the first in history where the number of adults was expected to be higher than that of children. With this sudden shift in age came changes in spending habits, saving habits, political motivations, etc. and, thus, could possibly upend the current economy.

This situation was found the highest in Europe and Japan, and less so in the U.S., which was offset with higher immigration rates. Out of all the developed nations, the U.S. had the highest immigration rate, followed by Germany, the most popular destination for migrants in the European Union (EU).

While many migrants have turned abroad, looking for a better life, many forces have been at work, leading to what is being referred to as "migration and demographic crises". The migration crisis refers to the varied climatic, social, and economic factors leading to the mass movements of people abroad (given all the factors listed in the sections of this chapter); while the demographic crisis refers to the low fertility rates and aging populations in developed countries. These conditions are only going to continue for the foreseeable future with little being done to solve the issues. When it comes down to it, global migrations and demographic transformations are the effects of the changes in population growth.

In a paper published by Paul Demeny on April 8, 2016 titled *Europe's Two Demographic Crises: The Visible and the Unrecognized*, he said:

> "By most reasonable definitions of the term, the European Union is experiencing a demographic crisis rooted in a shortage of births relative to deaths. In the great majority of the EU's 28 member countries, fertility is far below the level that would be necessary for the reproduction of the population over time. If it were maintained in the coming decades at such a low level, population size in the affected countries would be cut by more than half in the short span of two generations – roughly 60 years. This drastically reduced population would have an age distribution inconsistent with economic sustainability. In contrast, another demographic crisis that confronts

the EU is only too visible and palpable: the crisis of immigration. Like the situation of far-below-replacement fertility, it would call for policy responses that are effective and based on broad public consensus. But despite immigration's dramatic visibility and effects, the responses to it thus far have been confused and ineffective."

Given the current financial, economic, and social situations within the EU, it is not surprising if, like their North American and other developed nations counterparts, they are forced to pursue weakened foreign policies in the future and focus more on internal issues. The striking problems of mass migration are not the problem of any individual nation, nor can they be solved independently. This is a global issue that needs a global solution. Due to the complexity of the vast array of forces at work to produce the crises that we are experiencing today, dramatic changes will need to take place to upend the current establishment.

If these changes are not made or the efforts cannot work together to solve these global issues, then the crises themselves will force changes by sheer force. Whether it is the effects of having a large foreign population or an aging native one, either way, the world we live in will see exciting and tumultuous events. The nations' domestic needs will require more resources and attention, limiting the resources available for foreign endeavors.

The developed countries of the world will be forced to turn inward at a time when the developing world, especially China, is turning outward. All these forces listed in this chapter, along with the economic, financial, and social factors for the developed world, lead me to believe we will witness the rise of new global leaders in the 21st century. While some experts visualize the coming Asian Century, I am seeing longer-term forces at play that will bring the Asian Millennium. Cold War 2.0 is only the first step along the long road of the "new normal."

Our world is experiencing a transformation of historic proportions. Open markets and information technology have broken down barriers, bringing us closer to our international neighbors. Businesses have been transformed by international outsourcing, taking advantage of lower labor cost, high-skilled workers, and global time differences. In America, domestic goods are being edged out by the influx of cheaper goods from China and the Far East as service industries grow to occupy a greater share of the American economy.

Whether our world is getting "flatter" or growing smaller, these global trends have tremendous impacts on our economy, society, and environment. America is experiencing shifting dynamics of its own. By the year 2050, the U.S. population is expected to grow by almost half from its 2000 level, providing tremendous opportunities even as it creates new challenges for communities and regions already reeling from growth-related concerns. But America is growing unevenly, with exacerbating population pressures in some areas while bypassing concentrated poverty in others.

While the southern and western regions of the U.S. are leading the nation's growth, both from immigration and natural births, vast regions like the Midwest, the Great Plains, and the Lower Mississippi Valley will experience flat population growth or decline by 2050. Dense, established regions like the northeast will also add to the growing population, but the constraints of its aging infrastructure systems will limit economic potential. In the southeast, places like Atlanta are booming but are seeing no end to the expansion of outer suburbs. And at the metropolitan scale across the nation, regions continue to experience the problems of concentrated poverty in the inner city and inner suburbs, while new suburban development consumes land at the urban fringe.

By mid-century, more than 70% of the nation's population and economic growths are expected to take place in extended networks of metropolitan regions linked by environmental systems, transportation networks, economies, and culture. These emerging "megaregions" are becoming the new competitive units in the global economy, characterized by the increasing movement of goods, people, and capital among their metropolitan regions.

Just as metropolitan regions grew from cities to become the geographical units of the 20th century global economy, megaregions, the agglomerations of metropolitan regions with integrated labor markets, infrastructure, and land use systems are rapidly taking their place.

Within these megaregions, the problems of the growing highway congestion, overcrowded airports and seaports, loss of open space, and aging infrastructure systems will only be compounded by the growing populations and the rapidly expanding international trade. These constraints limit economic growth and degrade the quality of life, essential parts of attracting and retaining both businesses and knowledge workers in a footloose global playing field.

Meanwhile, the bypassed areas of the nation will continue to suffer from dwindling resource-based economies, population loss, and lack of integration in global markets. A national strategy must address both the pressures of congestion in the growing megaregions and the forces of decline in bypassed places.

The astounding transformation of the global economy we are now experiencing is as significant as the social, economic, and spatial forces that shaped America after WWII. If we are to take advantage of these dynamics of change, the U.S. must make the critical investments necessary to provide capacity for growth and quality of life for the next half century. Increasingly, these investments and interventions must occur at the megaregional scale to provide the necessary breadth of resources to grow and compete globally.

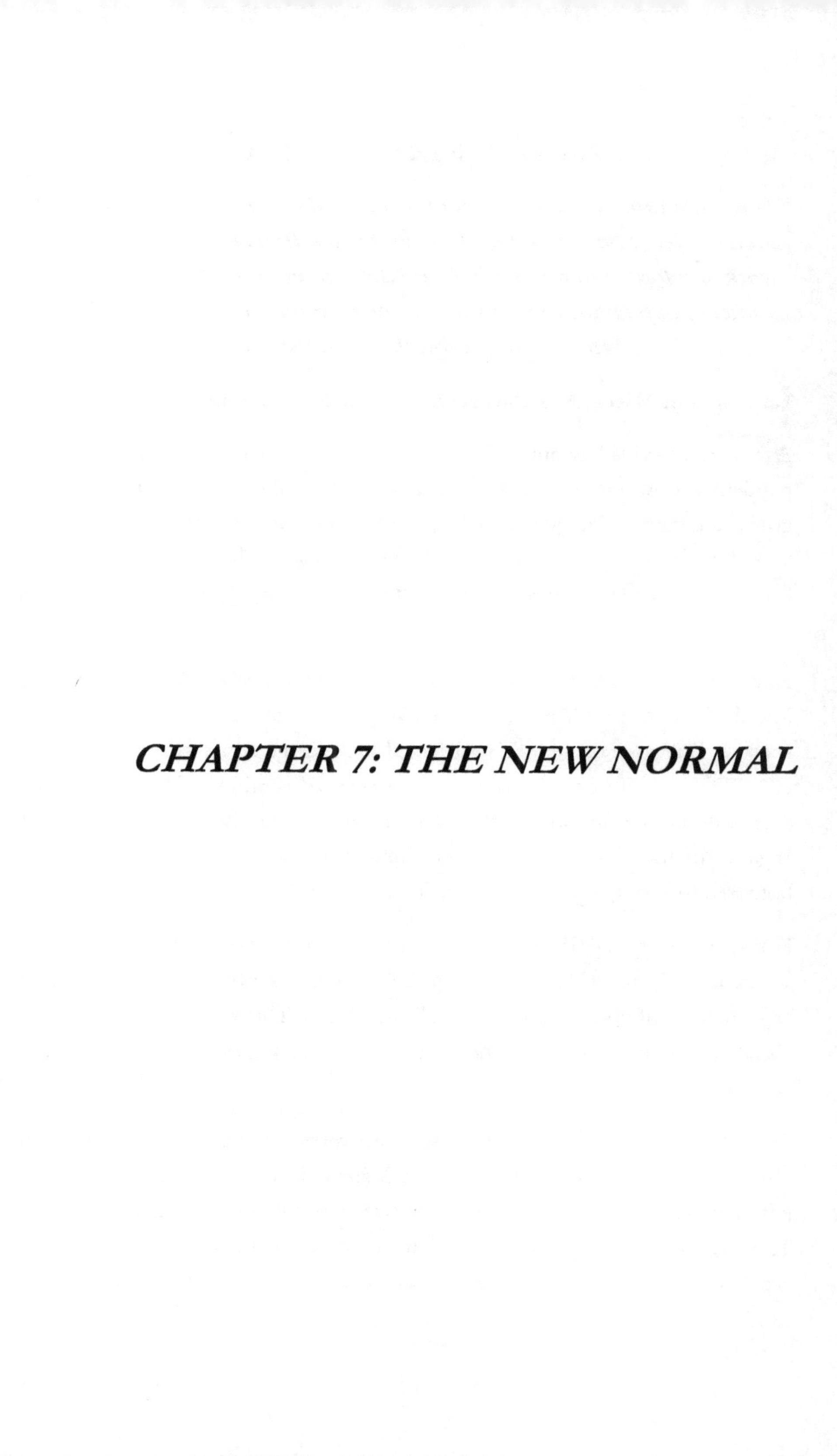

CHAPTER 7: THE NEW NORMAL

SECTION 1: INTRODUCTION

"Permanent mass unemployment destroys the moral foundations of the social order. The young people who, having finished their training for work, are forced to remain idle, are the ferment out of which the most radical political movements are formed. In their ranks the soldiers of the coming revolutions are recruited."

Ludwig von Mises, Austrian economist, historian, and sociologist

As a new world is beginning to take shape in the shadows of the COVID-19 pandemic, nowhere is this more evident than in the U.S. The functions of government are being questioned and vehemently opposed. We are seeing the mass mobilization of people on a scale not seen since the end of the Vietnam War; only, COVID-19 has caused the loss of more life than that decade-long saga.

Since then, the American media has played out the Cold War: wars in the Middle East, War on Terror, War on Drugs, etc.—all of them are prime-time specials. But none of them have affected the average American much. Before COVID-19, each of these events only concerned portions of the population, even with all the division of the 2016 election process where only 55.7% of eligible Americans came out to vote. Almost half of the people could not be bothered to vote for their next president.

However, post-COVID-19, we see for the first time a disruption to all segments of the U.S. population and most countries worldwide. The engagements of communities are at all-time highs. This virus has cut across all social-economic lines, even national boundaries, acting as a precursor of what is to come.

Local businesses are forced to close, with many of them never reopening, affecting our social and spending habits. Many industries are facing layoffs that left millions unemployed, influencing what we do with our savings and income. The housing market is floundering with tenants unwilling or unable to pay rent, landlords unable to meet payments, and creditors restricting lending.

An economy built around a consumer culture faces a shift on the spending habits of people, especially considering their savings accounts and debt payments, and online sales soaring. Never has healthcare been at the forefront of society as it is now, with facemasks and social distancing shaping how we move forward. It is not just our economy, financial systems, and social fabrics that are in flux but also nature and our environments. The culmination of all these powerful forces will shape the future of the world around us, and the only sure thing is that it will be unrecognizable from the past.

With unemployment and inequality at record highs, never-ending lockdowns and quarantines, economic and financial insecurity, and political division across the U.S., it will only take a spark to ignite a revolution. On May 25, 2020, the death of George Floyd under police custody in Minneapolis, Minnesota became that spark. What ensued began with peaceful protests that eventually turned violent. Then, more and more cities across the U.S. and the globe started to take part in the turmoil.

As we have seen earlier, social unrest was already flourishing around the world and this just added more fuel to the fires. Most protests were peaceful, spurred on by additional police violence. However, some areas were exceptionally violent, as the protests were used to cover criminal activities such as lootings and abuse. In the wake of these crimes, it was specifically mentioned that the government and legal authorities in the U.S. had been persecuting people for years, showing that their citizens were acutely aware of the inequalities and injustices taking place. These events unfolded the attempts to level the playing field for those affected.

Nowhere was this more evident than the move by Minneapolis City councilors to disband the police force. For years, visible minority groups claimed it was safer not to call the cops than to call them, showing the rest of the population what they had to deal with all this time. As the government intervenes more, it has only led to increased anger and frustration. The National Guard was mobilized, and the army was called in to try to regain order in U.S. cities: scenes we often were accustomed to taking place only in far-away dictatorships. These protests and series of events helped unmask the totalitarian states that had been building around the world, with the U.S. and its corporations leading the way.

After decades of portraying itself as the model for global societies, the U.S. was finally forced to come to terms with reality: The battles they had sown overseas for so many decades were coming back to haunt them at home.

It is ironic how U.S. authorities, in trying to solve their problems, managed to create new ones. But that is what occurs when a government has grown to humungous proportions. In a free market economy, the economy should be left to its own devices, to adjust as needed. When the government enforced quarantine measures on the population, they also restricted the market from functioning. Consequently, analysts expected that they would experience economic downturn spanning 5 to 10 years, adding another fuel to the already burning flames of inequality and unrest.

Typically, a recession is expected every few years. Still, with authorities having managed to delay the situation by artificially propping up the economy, it only meant that instead of a recession, we will have an economic depression. While a recession may last about a year or two, a depression can last for decades. The bill always gets paid. It does not matter how many items you order and how long you continue to eat because, eventually, you will be full, prompting you to pay and leave the restaurant.

This is exactly the kind of situation we are standing today. The National Bureau of Economic Research released the recent economic figures showing that the U.S. entered a recession in February 2020. The longest economic expansion in history, 128 months long, had finally come to an end due to an "unprecedented magnitude of the decline in employment and production, and its broad reach across the entire economy." This had been a long time coming, so what should the authorities do about this? They should leave it alone and let the market correct itself of all the excesses and bad debts, to ensure a healthy and prosperous economy. However, this is not what they are doing or will do.

To delay the inevitable, making matters worse, the U.S. government announced stimulus plans in line with federal bailouts. Millions of Americans had sought payment deferrals, rent and mortgage freezes or deferrals, and wage subsidies as a quick and easy fix to the complex issues. Instead of people claiming bankruptcy or closing their business today, these actions pushed that date further out. Even so, the waves of delinquencies and closures had already begun and would accelerate since there was no quick way around this.

By trying to provide temporary relief and save what is left of the economy, the authorities have exacerbated the debt situation by printing more debt that has to be eventually repaid. If anything, the last thing the U.S. needs is more debt. So, why are authorities piling on more weight? If they plan to inflate away their debt through endless money printing, the U.S. will face hyperinflation on the levels previously seen in Weimer Germany or Zimbabwe.

While the general population, if they are lucky, had received their chump-change payments, it was the corporations and financial institutions that had prospered and received the bulk of funds. That is right; the authorities are bailing the ones responsible for this mess while leaving the taxpayers to foot the bill. As the result of the government's incessant and incompetent meddling, we are hearing the voices for calls of change get louder by the day.

Unlike with the Great Depression, the Fed is embarking on historic amounts of money printing. When Fed Chair Jay Powell started the New Year in 2020, the Fed's balance sheet was $4 trillion USD. Now it is $7 trillion USD and heading to $10 trillion USD by the end of the year. The ultra-loose monetary policies pursued by the Fed were what led us into this mess. With dollar debasement well underway, various economic distortions are produced. Will we see financial assets increase?

The stock market is booming while the country burns, as analysts cling to rigged figures in the illusion that they translate to the health of an economy. The question now is this: Will "free money" create deflation as people rush to pay off debts or will it cause inflation that drives up prices of everyday goods? Price action in situations like this can be strange and unpredictable, especially when most of it stems on the psychology of the masses. It is unlikely that the stimulus will have the desired effects in forcing people to spend locally, considering that most places are closed, and the people see too much uncertainty around them.

Witnessing people loot a big box shop does not exactly have the same effect as advertisements that make you want to drop $300 USD on shoes. With supply chains being crippled globally, higher prices and different spending choices are a certainty. The U.S. is awash in bad debt and nobody is willing to purchase it other than the Fed. The nation is likely on track for a long and drawn-out depression, like what happened in Japan, as it will increasingly be forced to turn inward to put out the fires after fires that will erupt.

If what we saw on the news happens when the government handed out "free money," what do you think will happen when the money stops? The virus has not and will not go away for some time. Meaning, the "new normal" touted as temporary measures, is likely to hold for the long term. How can businesses remain profitable and where will the jobs come from in this new environment? Likely, those working from home will remain working from home, as companies have been under pressure for some time, to alter traditional business practices.

While Baby Boomers can rely on one job to get them through to retirement, industries have begun to shift to a freelance-gig-style economy which helps reduce the overhead costs. Even office spaces have not been spared from the business revolution that is currently shaping up companies—that is, the online or shared-space solutions. But those companies are the few lucky ones. If job and financial insecurities become commonplace, what does this mean to the auto, house, and travel sectors? Increased economic instability will force market corrections in the auto and house markets, pushing down overbought asset prices. Countries that have built their economies on and companies relating to the travel industry will see massive declines as people generally have less money to spend.

Millennials have long rejected the needs and desires of past generations as innovations in shared ownership and their preferred (unconventional) lifestyles have shown and will continue to show. After years of facing criticisms from the older generation, Millennials are finally getting their time in the sun and have their voices heard. Overwhelmingly, they are avid believers that the old ways are not working anymore, and they want a new deal. And they are coming of age just in time for the next election.

In the past few decades, the U.S. economy has come to represent a stagnant pool of missed opportunities. Entrepreneurship, as estimated by the pace of new-business arrangement, has experienced a steady decline every decade since the 1970s, with the grown-ups under 35 (Millennials) on track to be the least pioneering generation on record.

This decrease in dynamism is harmonized by the ascent of phenomenally huge and productive firms that look discomfortingly like the restraining infrastructures and oligopolies of the 19th century. In almost every sector of the economy, including manufacturing, construction, retail, and the entire service sector, the big companies are getting bigger. For instance, American strip shopping centers and business catalogs used to overflow with new independent ventures. However, today, in the spots where a few mother and-pop shops had once opened, Walmart produced another superstore. The portion of all organizations that are new firms, have fallen by 50% since 1978. As indicated by the Roosevelt Institute, a liberal research organization devoted to propelling the beliefs of Franklin and Eleanor Roosevelt, "Markets are now more concentrated and less competitive than at any point since the Gilded Age."

Derek Thompson of the Atlantic, had given us an interesting thought to ponder:

> "To comprehend the scope of corporate consolidation, imagine a day in the life of a typical American and ask: How long does it take for her to interact with a market that *isn't* nearly monopolized? She wakes up to browse the internet, access to which is sold through a local monopoly. She stocks up on food at a superstore such as Walmart, which owns a quarter of the grocery market. If she gets indigestion, she might go to a pharmacy, likely owned by one of three companies controlling 99% of that market. If she's stressed and wants to relax outside the shadow of an oligopoly, she'll have to stay away from ebooks, music, and beer; two companies control more than half of all sales in each of these markets. There is no escape—literally. She can try boarding an airplane, but four corporations control 80% of the seats on domestic flights."

People have forgotten that the "greatest economy the world has ever seen," was just the product of the free market capitalism. However, the economy has been hijacked by monopolies, pushing out the competition.

As 2020 is an election year, all the topics covered in this book are expected to take the forefront of discussions across America and the world. While they are numerous and varied, it is evident that the U.S. is in trouble and looking for someone to blame, whether it is COVID-19 or China. These topics are expected to be brought to attention, followed by social injustices, immigration, and the economy. In one of the faults of democracy, "he who can promise the most will be the one to take the helm," attempts will have to be made to satisfy and placate the population worldwide. However, realistically, these issues are complex and require multi-level support and, sometimes, international cooperation which is getting scarcer by the day.

Whoever takes over as President of the U.S or the Fed will be left with no good options for moving forward and, thus, is unlikely to make any serious moves. The economic and financial reset required to fix the mistakes of previous administrations will take longer than 4 years of being in office. Which is why, nobody wants to be the bad guy. However, with the way each party tries to offer their version of the best worst-case solution, this will most likely result in further floundering. Furthermore, the methods to resolve the situation is most unpopular, with the calls for more socialism get stronger from disenfranchised youth.

As governments slowly take on more and more socialist policies each day, sending debt levels to ever-increasing highs, with little success, it is only accelerating the demographic and migration crises that are taking place in the developed world. In a vicious tug-of-war between the aging Baby Boomers and the young Millennials, the battle is over access to resources and the direction of the country. Until there is a clear winner, the economy will falter. The needs and desires of these 2 groups are quite different.

It is unlikely we will see a reduction in government. But it is what is needed since it is much easier for governments to gain power and authority than it is to relinquish them. The social experiment in Minneapolis would serve as a test run for changes across the U.S. While some of them, such as diverting funds to low-income education, had positive effects, overall, the policies are sure to be ineffective at adjusting the foundational issues. The system has a corrupt foundation and is in desperate need of rebuilding. Increased tracking methods, censorship, and technology are all hot button issues; but the general trend with younger consumers is to be more interconnected, not less.

Thus, while some may choose to opt-out, it will become more difficult as time goes by. At best, government policies will be able to soften the landing and reduce some of the adverse effects of a prolonged depression. The way they have so far managed to delay things as much as possible is proof of their interest in survival. I expect to see the current recession slowly morph into a more protracted one, which will be looking for distractions to take away from the fact it is the Great Depression 2.0. There will be no segment in the population or sector of the economy that will be left unchanged. But what that vision will look like is driven mainly by the choices we have already made (and less of the ones we have yet to make).

By most definitions, the U.S. is and has been on the verge of a revolution for a long time. But each time, the government has managed to suppress it and distract the people. No wonder gun sales are at record highs across the country as people line up to prepare for what is to come. A recent report published by the Department of Homeland Security Counterterrorism Mission Center in 2020 stated that if the U.S. was subjected to any further restrictions, even in the face of a second wave, it would generate violence and rebellion across the country.

This lockdown has pushed the already fragile economic and financial systems to their breaking limit. There is a massive divide between the Republican and the Democratic states, with the former wanting to open their economies sooner while the latter wanted to ride out the virus, even paying people to stay home. Without bi-partisan agreement and without a concerted nationwide effort like that of China, any steps they plan to take will be ineffective due to the nature of the virus. It only takes one person to start a second wave in one area and, as we have seen with the debacle of government efforts to suppress the virus, they will not be able to stop it.

We have already witnessed the rise of armed militias, sometimes battling in the streets with violence against each other, not unlike 1930s Germany. On one side are those who consider themselves patriots, people who are often conservative and labeled as "Nazis," standing up to uphold the constitution, support gun rights and personal freedoms. On the other side are the "Anti-Fascists or Antifa" who are allied with other Liberals, Leftists, and socialist groups, including the LGBTQ communities and Black Lives Matter. It is shaping up to be an old-fashioned Socialist versus Fascist rivalry where, as history showed us, there can only be one winner left standing.

Of course, these are broad generalizations. But it is fascinating how history tends to repeat itself. Until this rivalry is resolved, I expect to see it increase until a final climactic event occurs, leaving little room for those wishing to walk away mid-battle. Eventually, this divide will pour into the political realm, which we are already beginning to see.

As the famous saying goes, "Never let a good crisis go to waste," for crisis provides excellent opportunities. In what may be a tipping point, President Donald Trump has vowed to label Antifa as a terrorist group that has added fuel to the flames. We will begin to see more on the divide in American society the closer we get to the election and even after the election. However, this is part of a much larger trend that will bleed into the next decade and, possibly, the beyond.

With violence across the country on the rise, so too are calls for socialist policies. People have been calling for rent strikes, mortgage forgiveness, and debt cancellations, all of which are currently being reviewed by Congress. In New York City, a bill is underway as part of the #RentStrike2020 national movement. Congress is considering a Rent and Mortgage Cancellation Act which will cancel all rent and mortgage payments for the duration of the pandemic and possibly even beyond.

In exchange for agreeing to play by the rules dictated by the government for rent and lending practices for at least 5 years, landlords would gain access to funds to cover their losses. Some of the conditions included made it impossible to deny renters based on credit history, criminal records, and not raising rent for 5 years. This law will make any existing contracts between landlords and renters invalid, a move that is already taking place for commercial real estate in California, allowing people to walk away if they wish. Not only will it be impossible to evict tenants, but they also are not required to pay you, so the current levels of unemployment and social inequality would be catastrophic for the market. Who would want to be a landlord under these situations?

With the way that the government is printing money at historic levels, the loss in purchasing power alone in the next 5 years will be dramatic. These are the type of socialist policies that led to the collapse in Venezuela, an event that, until a short while ago, would have been laughed at in the U.S. With the money supply expanding and the number of goods and services shrinking, we all know what the outcome will be for we have seen it happen time and time again. As the U.S. government dictates more totalitarian policies towards the economy, we will inevitably see less prosperity.

It has become almost fashionable for the youth to be socialist. Bernie Sanders, a 78-year-old millionaire and socialist, built most of his foundation with those under 30 years old. It has become an easy sell for any politician. After all, who does not want free stuff?

As always, Scandinavian countries are presented as shining examples of what we can aspire towards. Socialism works great when you have a population of a few million where you can simply sit on massive amounts of high-value natural resources and not sell them to private entities. However, this is not the case for most countries. Many people are angry, rightfully so, but they took the easy way out and placed the blame on capitalism. But is the U.S. even a capitalist country anymore?

While many are quick to point the finger at China for being a communist country, China is in fact more capitalist than the U.S. Communism is not possible at a state level. It is a goal; an idea that works towards and under socialism. Under capitalism, the means of production are in the hands of private individuals who produce goods and/or services based on consumer demand. It has been argued that capitalism only made the elites richer and the average population poorer. However, we cannot refute the fact that it was capitalism that made such a small percentage of the world's population—the U.S. at about 4%—obtain such a high percentage of the world's wealth, equating to about 30%.

However, today, not many countries are adapting "pure capitalism" anymore, and certainly not the U.S. and the European countries. Through an increasing government and interventionist policies born from socialism, most governments have been pressured to limit free market forces through taxes, subsidies, tariffs, laws, and regulations. Whether it is the reforms in healthcare, government bailouts, or economic and financial stimulus, these are not capitalist policies. Free market capitalism does not exist anymore. It has been replaced by a system that is incompatible with its functions. But still, the "anti-capitalistic mentality" persists wherein the haves are being demonized for robbing the have-nots.

It is a well-known fact that governments are inefficient at anything they do. The more the government gets involved in any matter, the more inefficient it is. Just look at how much is wasted through the military-industrial complex. We have seen scandals arise in recent years, showing how the government gets billed tens of thousands of dollars for something that costs pennies to produce—or spending $2 million USD on building a bathroom in a park.

This is not how capitalism works. It should promote economic prosperity through competition between producers to provide the best value to consumers. The market will find the best price on their own, the market equilibrium, based on what people are willing to sell for and what people will buy it at. As socialist policies become more popular, it will only exacerbate the current social-economic disparities that we are trying to solve. Adding fuel to the fire, to put out the fire, as socialism takes root across the country, it will only add to the divides taking place.

As Winston Churchill once said, "If a man is not a socialist by the time he is 20, he has no heart. If he is not a conservative by the time he is 40, he has no brain." Indeed, everyone loves free stuff. But, as they say, "There is no such thing as a free lunch." Costs are involved in everything we do and do not do. Just because you are not the one paying it now does not mean you won't later.

SECTION 2: AMERICAN CIVIL WAR 2.0

"None are more hopelessly enslaved than those who falsely believe they are free."

Johann Wolfgang von Goethe, German writer and statesman

"Democracy is the road to Socialism… Socialism is the road to Communism."

Karl Marx, German philosopher, economist, historian, sociologist, political theorist, journalist, and socialist revolutionary

"If liberty means anything at all, it means the right to tell people what they do not want to hear."

Eric Arthur Blair (a.k.a. George Orwell), English novelist

In Ancient Rome, the ruling class began with the foundation of the city itself. According to the Roman historian Livy, after killing his brother, Romulus created 100 senators from the most powerful families in Rome. These leaders were called the "padres," which is Latin for "father," and it is from this word that we have the term, Patricians. The Patricians were not so much a single race or ethnicity. They were an economic and political force that shaped the direction of the republic and, later, the empire.

As the Roman Empire grew, they were not opposed through marriage and other means, to include outsiders into their fold as things evolved. And with this growth came opposition from most of the population and they were referred to as the Plebeians. Numerous times, often through revolts, the Patricians were forced to the negotiating table, pushed to relinquish more and more of their power as time went on.

The tug-of-war for power lasted from 494 BCE to 287 BCE and was known as the "Struggle of the Orders," an event which resulted in the passing of the Canuleian Law. Eventually, the Plebeians were afforded their own Council of the Plebs, a legislative assembly for the Plebeians.

After hundreds of years of reforms, the conflict ended with the passing of the Lex Hortensia, the Constitution of the Roman Republic, which was to be applied to all citizens equally. However, since the Patricians had spent generations solidifying the best resources and amassing unknown amounts of slaves, they managed to cling to power and influence well past the decline of the Roman Empire.

While their influence waned over the years, the term Patrician became more of an honorary title that allowed new families to rise in prominence. *The Social History of Rome* by Dr. Geza Alfoldy gave a more detailed description of Roman society's life and times, and from which I have taken the story above.

In the same way that Ancient Rome was ruled by a handful of elites, most developed nations today have become plutocracies, ruling over the disenfranchised and trivialized citizenry. We only need to look as deep as the words used by the control structure to refer to those under their authority to know their views of us: terms like undesirables, basket of deplorables, herd-immunity, masses, etc. Such insulting terms as if we are slaves or animals for them to step on.

History has shown us that civilizations and nations come to an end more so at the hands of internal forces rather than external. The first American Civil War was from 1861 to 1865, and the second one is currently underway. For the first time since the last civil war, the control structures put in place were becoming fragmented and slowly eroding. Never had there been so much animosity and hatred towards the police, who have even faced death for the sole reason of doing their jobs. Police officers had become victims of targeted attacks, with some getting shot at and run over by vehicles, simply out of the raw disdain for their profession. Also, we witnessed law enforcement agencies being held accountable for their members' actions in ways never seen before.

In the face of massive backlash, countless officers had decided to quit or retire. For the first time since the last civil war, cities were unable to control their streets and armed gangs roaming with impunity within some places. The lawlessness had led numerous citizens to arm themselves and set up roadblocks in communities to protect their homes and stores from violence.

For anyone who watched the news these days, parts of the U.S. now closely resembled the U.S. interventionist policies in foreign countries than the U.S. we had all come to know through Hollywood or travels. Much like the last civil war, American Civil War 2.0 was not an overnight creation. It had taken years to build up (and it is still building), it. As each community fights for their definition of what it means to be American or what America should be, the battle lines have been drawn, with not much room left on the sidelines.

The battles taking place in the streets have become part of a global coordinated effort spanning across many different nations. Still, the effects of these protests are only beginning to be felt. According to a report from Tim Ellis of Redfin, a property management company, on April 2, 2020, *Interest in Rural Areas and Small Towns Spikes During the Coronavirus Outbreak*, Americans are showing interest in moving away from major cities like never before. In the past, major cities became a massive draw for those looking for a better income and lifestyle. But thanks to the coronavirus, depreciating economic situations, and social unrest, people are rethinking this strategy.

According to Glenn Kelman, the CEO of Redfin, "We're also preparing for a seismic demographic shift toward smaller cities. Before this pandemic, the housing affordability crisis was already driving people from large cities to small. Now more permissive policies around remote work and a rising wariness about close quarters will likely accelerate that trend." As the worst civil unrest seen in decades grips the nation, more and more people are likely to consider making a move.

The Harris Poll conducted a survey on Americans. They found that 3 in 10 people wanted to move to a rural area while 1 in 4 wanted to move from a major city to the suburbs. In another poll they conducted, they found that nearly 40% of people living in cities were considering moving due to the pandemic. In an economic climate where almost 50 million Americans lost their jobs and counting, with more people working remotely than ever before, there was no better time to make the switch. In the past, the bright, new, modern cities of America were the envy of the world. But with retail stores boarded up, office buildings abandoned, and surging homelessness, the recent coronavirus and rioting were more than enough to tip the scales.

Gregory R. Copley is a historian, author, and strategic analyst who wrote *What Would A U.S. Civil War Look Like* on August 19, 2017. In his views, the growing polarization we were seeing in the U.S. and U.K. began long before the election of President Donald Trump or the Brexit vote. These events simply signaled the discontent festering beneath the surface with the status quo, representing the reactions to what he described as "urban super-oligarchies." These "urban super-oligarchies" had sought the erosion of state sovereignty and nationalism through globalization policies.

In the U.S., the famous phrase "drain the swamp" refers to entities engaged in ultra-leftist, if not outright, communist policies. He pointed out that the term "urban super-oligarchies" has become a 21st century Marxist term for these groups seeking to dominate the means of communication. With the mass media firmly under their control, they could disseminate any narrative they wish to further their agendas.

While this is often most prominently pointed out in the U.S., he noted that these policies were pursued in other countries as well, like the U.K., Europe, Canada, Australia, etc. For instance, one of the most famous comments made by President Donald Trump were his allegations against "fake news." As a result, this highlighted the bias apparent in media conglomerates with each side claiming the other was pushing a fake narrative. Nowhere was this more evident than in President Donald Trump's allegations against CNN, which were later verified by inside sources through Project Veritas.

Recently, there have been calls to fund more conservative news outlets as they are claimed to be unfairly censored, while liberal narratives could proliferate. This has brought attention to the censorship role of large-scale platforms like YouTube, Twitter, and Facebook into the limelight. As the battle for the hearts and minds across the globe heats up, Copley saw the U.S.'s descent into civil war as a slow acceleration into chaos, not unlike the breakup of Yugoslavia. Instead of being led by the desires of the constituent states, American Civil War 2.0 would happen through the gradual breakdown of law and order. As segments of society decayed further, each side would have to draw more support for their respective causes, portrayed as separate and independent events. But the existence of Antifa proved that there are organized forces at play.

Antifa had made headlines recently, with President Donald Trump vowing to label them as a domestic terrorist organization. Still, they have been in and out of attention for much of the last decade. Antifa is a loose ideology with numerous chapters and allied organizations, including anarchists, communists, liberals, BLM, and the LGBTQ communities to name a few.

Broadly, Antifa embodies many communist ideologies; namely, support for the working class, no government or police forces, and the abolition of all forms of authorities, borders, and ultra-liberalism. The ones found dressed in black and seen on the front lines consider themselves as "armed revolutionaries," fighting against fascism, racism, and discrimination. They do not seek a reform of the system; instead, they seek its destruction. They have numerous subchapters, including the Redneck Revolt or John Brown Gun Club, self-described as an "above ground military formation."

Antifa is the tip of the spear against "white supremacy" and at the forefront of anti-Trump demonstrations. They adamantly oppose capitalism, calling for socialist policies and speaking against wealth creation. They have been known to recruit members at gun shows, according to former members. Furthermore, they created the anarchist website with an alluding title "It's Going Down" to promote "armed struggles," as well as offering a 36-page *Mini-Manual of the Urban Guerrilla* that details guerilla warfare tactics such as sabotage, kidnapping, executions, armed propaganda and terrorism.

Project Veritas had released 4 installments from insiders of the organization that showed hidden camera videos on their ideology and training methods. These clips showed how a well-funded and well-organized group went to great lengths to keep their meetings and training activities secret, operating more like a paramilitary wing than most people had realized, including arming and training recruits.

The death of George Floyd was a tragic moment in American history. Usually, tragedies bring nations together, but this event tore apart the U.S. In some parts of the country, the protests were being used by highly organized groups to stoke violence on a nationwide scale.

According to the top terrorism cop, Deputy Commissioner for Intelligence and Counterterrorism John Miller, "…before the protests began, organizers of certain anarchist groups set out to raise bail money and people who would be responsible to be raising bail money, they set out to recruit medics and medical teams with gear to deploy in anticipation of violent interactions with police."

Miller further added, "And they developed a complex network of bicycle scouts to move ahead of demonstrators in different directions of where police were and where police were not for purposes of being able to direct groups from the larger group to places where they could commit acts of vandalism including the torching of police vehicles and Molotov cocktails where they thought officers would not be." In other words, highly coordinated and targeted criminal actions were done under the guise of angry mobs.

Even Chicago Mayor Lori Lightfoot had spoken out, "There is no doubt. This was an organized effort last night. There were clearly efforts to subvert the peaceful process and make it into something violent."

In Minnesota, law enforcement had discovered "several caches of flammable materials." John Harrington, the State Public Safety Commissioner, stated that these were found both in neighborhoods with fires and "in cars we've stopped as recently as this morning." Some of the vehicles used to transport the flammable materials have been reported to be stolen, with looted goods and weapons also found in the vehicles. In a particularly disturbing trend across the nation, law enforcement authorities have located pallets of bricks at or near protesting locations.

In a tweet from the Kansas City Police Department, they said: "We have learned of & discovered stashes of bricks and rocks in & around the Plaza and Westport to be used during a riot." In Baltimore, authorities rushed to dismantle mounds of bricks and bottles before major demonstrations occurred on that day. In New York City, bricks appeared between St. Marks Place and Seventh Street, with no construction site nearby. And in Texas, outside of the Dallas Courthouse, "a large pile of bricks" were stacked up along the path of protestors. All of these "coincidences" and "isolated events" are slowly building-up to what will become the final showdown.

While many people will shrug these events off, we are undoubtedly witnessing more lawlessness in America than ever before. In a report from the Washington Times on June 1, 2020, David Sherfinski detailed some alarming figures for May about how average Americans would respond to the unfolding events. He stated that the month would see surging gun sales across the nation, with many shops struggling to keep up with the demand.

His claims were proven true when Small Arms Analytics & Forecasting, a private research firm, recorded more than 1.7 million guns sold in May, an 80% sales increase compared to that of May 2019. If these figures were even remotely accurate, this demonstrated that a large segment of the U.S. population was gravely concerned and getting prepared. Other than protecting their families and property, what else could they possibly be preparing for?

On June 10, 2020, the Antifa and BLM members, along with their supporters, rushed Seattle City Hall, demanding that in lieu of the events in Minneapolis, the Mayor defund the police. Furthermore, the local police station was forced to be abandoned as armed members set up a barricade around it with armed patrols. They labeled the area an "autonomous zone" and as such, not subject to the U.S.'s rules and laws. Spurred on by recent successes, leftist groups continued to push the boundaries (of what is acceptable), demanding further concessions until their ultimate goals are met.

As we have seen, they are seeking the destruction of the state. If these groups are not dealt with severely and allowed to behave as they please, they will become further emboldened with each passing day. The U.S. will start to resemble the images shown by the media—of foreign regimes who dared to stand up against American hegemony. In the end, it is the media that would benefit from this situation as never before have Americans been so divided, and look to media to choose their camp, thus affecting the final winners and losers. As we watch civilization's thin illusion shatter, exposing us for what we indeed are, people are beginning to wake up to the fact that this war is only getting started.

Honestly, are U.S. administrations no strangers to overthrowing governments? They are the world's leading heavyweight that they literally wrote a book about it: the *U.S. Special Forces Unconventional Warfare Manual*. Here is an excerpt from the book:

> "The intent of U.S. UW [Unconventional Warfare] efforts is to exploit a hostile power's political, military, economic, and psychological vulnerabilities by developing and sustaining resistance forces to accomplish U.S. strategic objectives. Historically, the military concept for the employment of UW was primarily in support of resistance movements during general-war scenarios. While this concept remains valid, the operational environment since the end of World War II has increasingly required U.S. forces to conduct UW in scenarios short of general war (limited war)."

Enabling a resistance movement or insurgency entails the development of an underground and guerrilla forces, as well as supporting auxiliaries for each of these elements. And these always have an underground element. The armed component of these groups is the guerrilla force and is only present if the resistance transitions to conflict. The combined effects of 2 interrelated lines of effort largely generate the result of a UW campaign. The efforts are armed conflict and subversion. Forces conduct armed conflict, normally in the form of guerrilla warfare, against the security apparatus of the host nation (HN) or occupying military.

Conflict also includes operations that attack and degrade enemy morale, organizational cohesion, and operational effectiveness and separate the enemy from the population. Over time, these attacks degrade the ability of the HN or occupying military to project military power and exert control over the population. Subversion undermines the power of the government or occupying element by portraying it as incapable of effective governance to the population.

It appears that the very playbook the U.S. created for use against other countries has been employed against their creators. The question is, who is organizing and funding this all? After all, a pyramid structure of insurgency and resistance movements exists and what is alarming is that about three-fourths of the steps have already been taken or are well underway within the U.S.[62] We appear to be at the stage of "Overt and Covert Pressures Against Government (Strikes, Riots, and Disorder)."

The rage and social disruptions are boiling across the nation, with calls to defund the police, break white privilege, and take down the system. In a 1983 interview in Los Angeles, according to the former KGB informant who defected to Canada, Yuri Alexandrovich Bezmenov, when conducting an insurgency, "useful idiots" could be valuable to furthering the organization's objectives. This term has come to refer to celebrities, politicians, or other famous people who use their public recognition to (virtually) hop on the bandwagon.

The massive opposition from many U.S. celebrities against President Donald Trump just proved this. But these subversive tactics were employed by the Soviet Union to reverse Western public opinion in sympathizing with their cause. These tactics were included in a training program on Psychological Operations used against Americans. In the interview, Bezmenov stated:

> "You see, the useful idiots, the leftists who are idealistically believing in the beauty of Soviet socialist or Communist or whatever system, when they get disillusioned, they become the worst enemies. That is why my KGB instructors specifically made the point: never bother with leftists. Forget about these political prostitutes. Aim higher.

> "This was my instruction: try to get into large-circulation, established conservative media; really filthy-rich movie makers; intellectuals, so-called 'academic' circles; cynical, egocentric people who can look into your eyes with angelic expression and tell you a lie. These are the most recruitable people: people who lack moral principles, who are either too greedy or too suffer from self-importance. They feel that they matter a lot. These are the people who KGB wanted very much to recruit.

---

[62] https://publicintelligence.net/wp-content/uploads/2011/03/unconventional-warfare.png

"They serve purpose only at the stage of destabilization of a nation. For example, your leftists in United States: all these professors and all these beautiful civil rights defenders. They are instrumental in the process of the subversion only to destabilize a nation. When their job is completed, they are not needed anymore. They know too much. Some of them, when they get disillusioned, when they see that Marxist-Leninists come to power—obviously, they get offended—they think that *they* will come to power. That will never happen, of course.

"They will be lined up against the wall and shot."

In an article for the Havok Journal, Dr. Alice Atlanta, Ph.D. wrote *We Are The Useful Idiots: How Our Nation Divided is Playing Straight Into the Hands of our Greatest Enemies* on June 2, 2020. She gave a detailed analysis of Bezmenov's interview about the "useful idiots" portrayed in the media today. She stated:

"Embedded in his rhetoric, one notable phrase repeats: 'useful idiot.' It occurs 14 times throughout the nearly 3-hour interview. Celebrities, professors, politicians; none are spared the indignity of this dismissive moniker… To Bezmenov, 'useful idiots' are the American citizens who are unwittingly manipulated and mobilized to carry out a foreign power's bidding—while thinking it's their own idea.

"For proof that these tactics are still alive and well today, one need look no further than the cacophony of celebrity voices that have banded together to self-congratulate for the donations they are making to protesters' bailout funds. While their giving may be, at best, a genuine effort to assist peaceful protestors, and at worst, a tastelessly virtue signaling attention-grab, either way, it fulfills the 1983 prophecy of the KGB defector.

"Chrissy Teigen, Seth Rogen, Mark Ruffalo, Steve Carell, Harry Styles… in them is embodied the crux of the paradoxical challenge that the American people are facing. Ruffalo thinks he's 'combatting the harms of incarceration by paying bail for low-income individuals who cannot otherwise afford it.' Styles is giving, he says, because 'BLACK LIVES MATTER.' Noble causes, all, but the problem is that these noble celebrities are playing straight into the hands of the ones who most want to see this country destabilized by failing to recognize that their unbridled support of the rioters fails to draw any distinction between the black Americans and allies attempting to conduct peaceful protests, and the radical insurgents from both the left and right ends of the spectrum who are seizing this as an opportunity to wreak havoc for their own objectives."

While Dr. Atlanta pointed out that these celebrities likely had no idea of the implications they had on events, it did not dismiss them from their social roles.

There are those who unknowingly assist in creating more division and strife in the U.S. and there are those who benefit from it. Other than the media organizations that are greatly benefited from the stoking of flames, politicians are also not keen on letting a good crisis go to waste.

In an article posted in *Politico* on November 13, 2015 by Kenneth P. Vogel and Sarah Wheaton, it was reported that some of the biggest donors to leftist organizations and politicians were meeting with the BLM leaders behind closed doors. These meetings included the annual winter gathering of Democracy Alliance (DA), a liberal donor's club that includes Tom Steyer and Paul Egerman.

On August 16, 2016, Valerie Richardson of the Washington Times reported that BLM had received over $100 million USD in funding from Democratic supporters, on top of around $33 million USD in grants from top Democratic Party donor George Soros through his Open Society Foundations and the Center for American Progress. They also received financial support from the Ford Foundation and Borealis Philanthropy.

BLM had released a statement that their goals are "for defunding police departments, race-based reparations, breaking, voting rights for illegal immigrants, fossil-fuel divestment, and end to private education and charter schools, a 'universal basic income,' and free college for blacks."

The DA had reportedly wanted to increase their support, according to Vogel and Wheaton, for "scrappier local groups that have utilized confrontational tactics to inject their grievances into the political debate." Fundamentally, groups like BLM and Antifa are simply pawns to further division, which can be relayed through the media to portray a narrative, for a party like the Democrats to take office. But why are the elites utilizing social justice groups to suit their agendas?

When it comes to Liberals, they seem to be in a tough position with African American voters. Going back to the 1960s, African Americans, which make up around 13% of the U.S. population, have overwhelmingly voted for the Democrats, often at 90% and above. Given that the turnout of voters is around 60%, this equated to 25 million votes. If the Republicans can secure 20% of the African American vote, it is enough to swing the election in their favor, which makes sense that Republicans do not want more immigration.

In contrast, Democrats push to give even illegals the right to vote because minorities and newcomers traditionally vote left. Not only do they need a high percentage, over 85% of the African American vote, they also need high turnouts plus pretty much any of the other votes they can get. This conflict between the 2 parties could explain some of their motives for stoking the flames and dwelling upon the division existing in the U.S. It is essential to consider who really benefits from all of this.

Indeed, there are numerous African Americans dissatisfied with the status quo. Still, according to official figures, under Donald Trump's Administration, African Americans had the lowest rates of unemployment and government assistance in U.S. history. People are furious and fed up with the government but that does not mean the government is going anywhere. More than likely, this will settle down before the next "crisis" arises. The degradation of U.S. society is not going to be a sudden revolution that will unite the disenfranchised against their oppressors. It will be a slow and gradual decay and is basically what which has been occurring in the U.S. for decades.

While American Civil War 2.0 is well underway, it needs time to build, as with all great things. Indeed, civil war is inevitable and is something every nation has or will face in the future. Fortunately, the Americans are too well-armed to go out without a fight. However, this will not happen until the social, economic, and financial decline fully. At this time, things are bad, and they will only get a lot worse in the near future.

Currently, the U.S. administration and the Federal Reserve have many options they can use to delay the inevitable, but they cannot stop it from happening. With each day, more and more Americans see their hopes of returning to normal fade away and will have to shift to life after COVID-19. While Antifa and BLM offer their versions of what that future looks like, the reality is that they do not have enough popular support.

However, the more things deteriorate, the more polarization and division become evident, which makes it a natural weapon for the media. What we are witnessing today is more of a generational shift as each generation seeks to define itself against the rest. Trends shift towards the Left and Left-leaning policies, which are aided by institutions; while those who might be otherwise considered "center" are being corralled to the Right. The more extreme this dichotomy becomes, the quicker it will have to be resolved to one side or the other.

Right now, the media is transfixed upon President Donald Trump. No politician has been so polarizing and attractive to the media than him. Looking back, President George W. Bush and President Ronald Reagan were also no strangers to controversies either. But never has the media been so fixated on every action or lack of action taken by a president. In fact, due to social media, it is no longer a matter as to who will come after Trump and what the U.S. will look like then. It is now about the drama happening in the political arena and how it is turning into some kind of farce. This is not surprising considering we are a culture dominated by reality TV.

Stephen Kotkin is a professor of history at Princeton University, a Senior Fellow at the Hoover Institution at Stanford University, and considered an expert on the Soviet Union. According to him, when the Russian Revolution began, the Bolsheviks made numerous promises not unlike today's Leftists. They promised peace by ending WWI, food for all, taking properties from the rich to distribute to the poor, minimum wages to ensure a livable wage, a limit on working hours, and a system by the people for the people. However, by the end of the civil war, with around 12 million dead, the promises made were largely forgotten.

He then went into detail on the life of Stalin and the power he held in his book *Stalin: Paradoxes of Power, 1878-1928*. What is evident is that, while all dictators start from the right place, eventually, absolute power corrupts absolutely, and human greed takes over. Today, as always, these idyllic concepts promised to us sound good on the surface but implementing them is another issue. Indeed, it is the people who carry the power in any system of government, or lack thereof, but how they are mobilized will translate into wealth creation or destruction. The media plays off the current political events while those seeking power provide funding, organization, water, medical supplies, pre-staged bricks, and other destructive materials, all to achieve the goal of access to additional power.

As a Canadian, I do not have a "dog in the fight", but the events in the U.S. will reverberate around the world. The situation today is not so much a revolution but a battle for power, and the citizenry, just like in the Soviet Union, will be left in the middle to shoulder the brunt of the destruction.

How much of what we see in the streets today is organic and how much has been bought and paid for to achieve political gain? While it is true that there are injustices in the U.S. and abroad, is the sole cause of this race-based or is it the slew of factors described in this book? It should be quite clear now that the American economy, financial system, and society have all been on a downward trajectory for some time now. As income inequality rises, so are the calls for socialist policies. If the U.S. spent as much time worrying about their people as they do about the Middle East, it would be prosperous. Instead of investing in infrastructure to create jobs within the U.S., they have been building airbases in other countries. There are probably more U.S. bases in Iraq and Afghanistan alone than there are states and territories administered in the U.S.

The U.S. was once the leader when it came to healthcare and education but, according to recent figures from The Lancet, it had fallen to the 27th spot in the world. The growing disparities had become evident for most Americans, leading to the popularity of slogans like "Make America Great Again" which portrayed the awareness that things were not getting better.

If the underlying issues causing inequality within America are not addressed, and it is unlikely they will be, then the next time people riot, it will be much worse. Much like how the Plebeians required several negotiations with the Patricians in Ancient Rome to get their fair share of access to resources took hundreds of years, it may take as long, (if ever), before the U.S. can regain its former glory.

Throughout history, it is much easier for a government to gain powers through crisis than to relinquish them. When analyzing the events unfolding across the globe, with social unrest becoming the norm, it is essential to consider who benefits from all this. Is it possible that the architects of such unrest themselves be the very ones who reap the benefits of this outcry? Indeed, whenever most of the population speaks up and is passionate about an issue, changes are made but these changes rarely bring the desired effect.

Have the calls for safety ever been heeded in the U.S.? Instead, we have seen the militarization of the police force, increased delays, and security checks sacrifice personal freedom and information all in the name of safety but without receiving more protection. Did the War on Drugs ever stem the flow of narcotics in the U.S? Did the War on Terror even bring peace to the Middle East?

If anything, we are more at risk today than ever with how governments never ceased their relentless onslaught for totalitarian controls. With each passing day, the U.S. slips more into the dystopian vision of the world portrayed in George Orwell's *1984*.

Author Jim Keith explained his views on the topic saying, "Create violence through economic pressure, the media, mind control, agent provocateurs: thesis. Counter it with totalitarian measures, more mind control, police crackdowns, surveillance, drugging the population: antithesis. What ensues is Orwell's vision of 1984, a society of control: synthesis." Sound familiar?

Regardless of who comes to power, one thing is for sure: expect to relinquish more of your freedoms for a false sense of security. As violence and lawlessness take hold across parts of the U.S., the worse the situation becomes, the more freedom people will be willing to part with to bring it to an end. The U.S. has been slowly transitioning into a police state for the past decade. While most police officers are fine people, the powers wielded by the bad ones have only increased. Profit-driven militarism, coupled with endless foreign wars and the highly trained soldiers coming back with post-traumatic stress disorder, has created a militarized police culture that treats the U.S. as a foreign battleground. All of this has been made possible in light of the 9/11 attacks, under the guise to make the nation safer for its citizens.

Essentially, the U.S. citizens have been funding their oppression, turning the streets into the battlefield, while police officers have become a standing army. Those who drafted the U.S. Constitution and Bill of Rights envisioned a civilian police force, made up of members of the community, to serve and protect their communities; they were not designed to be a branch of the military. However, after years of increased funding, the vast array of weapons and uniforms at their disposal now closely resembles a paramilitary wing than a community police.

A retired Philadelphia Police Captain, Ray Lewis, warned that "corporate America is using police forces as their mercenaries" and that they had become "an oppressive organization now controlled by the one-percent of corporate America." He claimed that the system had become "corrupt to the bone" and stated that every recruit was put through a battery of tests, including the Minnesota Multiphasic Personality Inventory test that assesses physiological fitness. This test was supposed to assess the degrees of sensitivity and compassion but, according to him, "Unfortunately, they do not hire those people that score high on sensitivity. They reject them believing those people will quit because they can't handle the blood and guts in the street. They view that as wasted money." However, if an officer is involved in legal troubles, it can cost the taxpayers more than what is "wasted."

According to Human Rights Watch, taxpayers paid for officers 3 times when they committed offenses: "Once to cover their salaries while they commit abuses; next to pay settlements or civil jury awards against officer; and a third time through payments into police 'defense' funds provided by the cities." If the justice system was not reformed, these costs might seem minuscule compared to the long-term social and economic impacts we are witnessing today.

As domestic issues take higher precedence for the lives of Americans, we can expect to see more riots, each pushing the boundary a little further. While some regions within the U.S. are and will inevitably be bankrupt, the new migrants to hit the media will be the economic migrants within the U.S. Politicians will pander to the groups that will give them the most votes, and we will see more socialism and communism on one side.

In contrast, on the other side, we will see nostalgia, focus on traditional markets, and business. In the end, neither will be able to solve the decay which is beginning to form around us as both cases will be too long for the terms of elected officials to handle. The types of austerity, cutbacks, and coordination on a national scale needed to overhaul the system will only be approved after it gets much worse.

The First New Deal proposed by Franklin D. Roosevelt came only after 4 years of anguish and the Second New Deal 2 years later. Still, it was not until WWII, which created a massive demand for goods, that America was able to lift itself out of the Great Depression. Today, Roosevelt would be considered a conservative, but back then, he was a liberal and socialist since his programs focused on the "3 Rs": (1) relief for those who are unemployed and poor, (2) recovery of the economy, and (3) reforms of the financial system. The militarization of America's police forces represents an alarming trend that coincides with our gradual loss of liberties.

Governments have always sought to take advantage of crises to extract greater controls over their people, often under the guise of safety. It is not surprising that record levels of Americans are renouncing their citizenship, with a number of them deciding to move abroad. The current social unrest gripping the U.S. is the result of and has highlighted the progression of the police state and totalitarian rule. Areas of the U.S. that can afford it will likely turn to private security forces if security cannot be attained.

As Americans sleepwalk themselves into the Great Depression 2.0 and the American Civil War 2.0, expect politicians to make the same mistakes of the past in their quest to extract more control over their populations. However, while it was Japan and Germany pushed the U.S. into war last time, expect the powers that be to push themselves into a great battle, escape their numerous troubles, and divert the blame to a foreign power.

SECTION 3: COLD WAR 2.0

"If I must choose between a policy of blood and iron and one of milk and water… why I am for the policy of blood and iron. It is better not only for the nation but in the long run for the world."

President Franklin Roosevelt and published in the book *Diplomacy* by Henry Kissinger

"When goods do not cross borders, soldiers will."

Frederic Bastiat, 19th century French liberal economist

If politics is nothing more than a show, then all the world is a stage. And there is no place that the spotlight shines brighter than on America. If America were to be personified as a family, it would be the Kardashian clan, living its life in the open glare of public life—its flaws, and contradictions there for all to see. In contrast, China has benefitted from a silk veil, protected by cultural and linguistic incomprehension. Looking in from the outside, it seems that this extraordinarily successful yet dysfunctional family we grew up watching is falling apart.

The immense cultural dominance of the U.S. has been both a strength and a weakness. While it has managed to pull the best the minds the world has to offer to study, emulate, and work with it, this has only fed its own fallacies. The world can see everything the U.S. does but when Americans look at the world, they cannot see past the blinding lights. The world has always been acutely aware of the U.S., but the U.S. has been blissfully ignorant of the world.

Since the end of WWII in 1945, the U.S. has been the world's prevalent economic power and funded organizations such as the World Bank, International Monetary Fund (IMF), and World Trade Organization. These and other organizations have worked to promote the U.S.'s political and economic goals around the world. Thought to be a model for world economies, they have sought democratization, free trade, globalization in other countries and punished those who refused to play by their rules.

The Washington Consensus was created to help developing countries with economic crises become "more American." This agenda has structural reforms that promote free market forces but are often criticized as being unhelpful and exploitive for developing nations. Apparently, in American English, the "free market" translates to "Western markets." One of the problems facing the U.S. is their pervasive beliefs in being a "Shining City on the Hill" and an "Exceptional Nation."

American exceptionalism can be broken down into 3 main tenants: (1) the U.S.'s history is different than in other nations, (2) the U.S. has a mission to transform the world, and (3) the U.S. is culturally and morally superior to all other countries. Most Americans believed they are the leading power because they are destined to be the best and it is incomprehensible for them not to be Number One in anything they do or attempt to do. The reasoning behind such logic falls upon the freedom, democracy, capitalist free market, and military power that make them the best in the world. These concepts are reinforced in the education system, television shows, and Hollywood productions portraying the U.S. as the world's leader.

These ideas were rooted from Eurocentric and colonial concepts like "Manifest Destiny" which has been married to certain sects of Christianity. Europeans and their religion were considered superior to the world's and thus had a duty to conform the world to their image. However, today we are witnessing a shift in world power, inevitably upending these long-held beliefs. Generations of Americans have grown up and lived under the guise that, on the surface, these notions are as solid as the forces of nature.

In recent years, the rise of China and other powers will challenge these beliefs on every level and, so far, they are winning. As the U.S. struggles to reinvent itself and its place in the world, it will find itself cornered into conflict for a New World Order. While many people foolishly think the Cold War ended with the collapse of the Soviet Union, it has continued on and we are part of it: Cold War 2.0, an event with the ability to spark World War III.

As the trade war heats up, so has the demonization of China. While it is no secret that China's government is one of "Socialism with Chinese characteristics," it was never much concern for Washington that their largest trading partner had a communist government until they became a perceived threat. All the most prosperous nations of the world shared the same key characteristics: small, democratic, resource-rich, or a mix of these. Even though China is the opposite of these 3 characteristics, it is essential to remember that all the wealthy nations of today built their economic foundations when they were authoritarian and relatively poor.

Not a single country got rich from having more freedom and, if anything, democracy hampers economic development. Even the American allies South Korea and Taiwan were ruled until quite recently by brutal dictatorships. The U.S. has a long history of aligning with dictatorships, so the role of the Chinese political system is irrelevant. In truth, the rise of China has coincided with the rise of anti-American exceptionalism whereby China has offered an alternative to the demanding and exploitive ways of American hegemony.

If the U.S.'s claims to the superiority of their nation are true, how can they explain China's rise? This creates a dilemma for those seeking to further the American agenda and leading more and more nations into China's side.

China has become the world leader in foreign loans, supplanting the U.S. for which the latter has criticized as "debt-trap diplomacy." Whenever and wherever China seeks to invest and develop overseas, it comes under the harsh scrutiny of the U.S. since it takes away their opportunities. Militarily, even some of the U.S.'s closest allies have rejected U.S. aggression, which runs the risk of alienating China.

This was the case with the Japanese Governor of Okinawa, Denny Tamaki, who refused to host U.S. missiles which could be used to threaten Chinese expansion in the region. Tamaki reported to the LA Times, "I firmly oppose the idea," as nations and leaders worldwide have shifted away from the U.S. and towards China.

China's rapid economic growth and development happened at a speed that has left those in Washington stunned, and they are only beginning to realize the gravity of the situation. After 40 years of opening its economy to the world, China is set to overtake the U.S. as the world's largest economy. This helped to manifest the rise of President Donald Trump, who campaigned on a tough stance against China and immigration.

During the 2016 presidential campaign, Trump vowed to seek a new deal with China in response to the illegal transfers of, according to Calvin Miao of the Center for Global Business, "American technology, American jobs, and played a dirty game when it comes to restricting access to the Chinese market for U.S. firms.".

In the U.S., a coalition of business and politicians have claimed that China has deliberately pushed back against the U.S.'s will abroad, and that America needs a more robust response. This response materialized on March 22, 2018 when President Trump signed the first memorandum putting tariffs on Chinese products.

President Trump claimed that China has an unfair trade advantage, costing the U.S. billions in dollars and jobs. President Trump's "America First" strategy involves the rise of nationalism and protectionism in the face of declining economic prosperity. He had since placed tariffs on steel, European autos, and Chinese imports to give domestic industries a comparative advantage. This method is based on the Mercantilist trade policies that were popularized in Europe from the 16th - 18th Centuries.

According to the Nobel Prize-winning economist Paul Krugman, "Trump is really a Tariff Man. Some naïve souls may still have been hoping that he would learn something from the failure of his trade policy so far… But no: it's pretty clear now that he refuses to give up on his belief that trade wars are good, and easy to win; his plan is to continue…" This is ironic because President Trump received a Bachelor of Economics Degree from Wharton School of the University of Pennsylvania in 1968, and he "should know better" than to compete against those with a competitive advantage. Instead, the U.S. should focus on the areas where they do well, such as research and development, to stay ahead of the global curve in technology, which is decreasing by the day due to inefficiencies.[63]

As the economic woes around the world worsen, the next major global military conflict is much closer than people think. We are currently witnessing the economic and financial decline of the U.S., coupled with significant social unrest. A rise in nationalism has led to polarization, and xenophobic tendencies to blame anyone except who is responsible for their woes.

According to Benjamin Friedman, a political economist and professor at Harvard University, nations who experienced prolonged periods of economic distress had been characterized by public antipathy towards minorities and foreign countries, attitudes which helped to fuel social unrest, terrorism, and war. While WWI and WWII began because of a variety of factors, and there was no set road to war, they were both founded during economic recessions and heightened periods of nationalism and discrimination.

During the Great Depression, U.S. President Herbert Hoover signed the 1930 Smoot-Hawley Tariff Act, a form of protectionism for American workers and farmers. As more and more protectionist policies took shape, global trade declined by two-thirds, and the U.S. would not exit the Depression until WWII. In *Capital in the Twenty-First Century*, Thomas Piketty, a French economist, analyzed a unique collection of data from 20 countries, going as far back as the 18th century, to uncover key economic and social patterns. According to his research, a rise in income inequality was often followed by a great crisis, which helped to lower-income inequality for a period, before rising again and leading to the next crisis. This analysis is especially alarming since income inequality is at record highs in the U.S.

While China is a relatively young nation by modern terms, the U.S., as the global superpower struggling to keep the reins of power, suffers from numerous socio-economic disruptions. If infrastructure and militaries are good indicators for the health of a nation, China would be healthy and modern, whereas the

---

[63] https://www.bbc.com/news/business-48196495

U.S. is outdated and falling apart. When it comes to integrating technology within the society at large, China has the U.S. beat hands down.

China is a relatively homogenous nation, whereas the U.S. suffers from polarization and an immigration crisis. China has been leading the world in anti-climate change measures, whereas the U.S.'s agricultural sector is going bankrupt and facing water and food scarcity due to climate change. The recent events regarding the handling of COVID-19 showed that while the Chinese people acted in a single concerted force to stamp out the virus, Americans could not even agree on what to do. This led to the U.S. becoming the most abundant host to the virus in the world.

As tensions increase in the U.S., China becomes the easy target of the American population's anger. While U.S. citizens have good reasons to be upset with the status quo, emotionally charged pandering by politicians will only lead to ill-conceived policies that exacerbate the situation and further escalations in conflicts. How the U.S. deals with their issues will affect their role in shaping the 21st century.

According to the political scientist Samuel Huntington, in the book *The Clash of Civilizations and the Remaking of World Order*, it is essential to consider that, unless we think carefully about our steps moving forward, we cannot help but avoid mistakes. He advocated respectful dialogue to crucial issues instead of the finger-pointing and blaming, which we have seen so far.

One of the book's core tenants is that culture and cultural identities shape the patterns of cohesion, disintegration, and conflicts in the modern world. For the first time since the collapse of the Soviet Union, global politics are shaped by a multipolar climate instead of a unipolar one. Modern society has neither become uniformly Westernized, nor is there a sense of Westernization in the developing world. These discrepancies are coming to shape new and exciting world views. Thus, the balance of power is shifting from the West, which has been an aberration in world history, back to the East, where it has been for much of history.

In addition, new powers are rising in Africa, South America, and the Middle East with world views arising from the oppressed and the legacy of colonization. Huntington asserted that civilization-based world order was emerging, with nations growing closer due to shared identities, religions, and cultures. As these rising powers grow more confident, they are coming into conflict with the persisting American exceptionalism, increasing the risks of hostilities.

Developing nations have come to reject the Western identities and ways forced upon them and started to create their own ways of doing things. This has been especially evident with the shift towards China for preference in doing business, leaving the U.S. scrambling to drum up business as they are forcefully being expelled from Africa as a whole.

After the U.S. tried to isolate Russia from the Group of 8 for their legal annexation of Crimea, China and the BRIC nations welcomed Russia with open arms. In Southeast Asia, China has effectively muscled the U.S. out of most significant organizations and taken their lead on issues facing the region. If the U.S. wishes to avoid conflicts and retain any level of respect in global affairs, it needs to reflect and reassess their position in an increasingly multipolar world. If they wish to oppose this through military means as they have done in the past or currently doing in the South China Sea, they will be alienated and left out of the New World Order.

In the past, civilization centers were separate and often disconnected, but the rise in technology has allowed for an interconnected, globalized world. During most of human history, contact was difficult and relied on vast networks which led to many significant conflicts. In the modern era, as European nations colonized much of the world, western influence spread to the world, creating the first global society.

Today, we have become more interdependent and interconnected than ever before. On the world stage, nation-states make up the principal actors in world affairs, leading to the formation of alliances of countries over the last century.

Before WWI, it was precisely the complex web of partnerships that forced the hands of empires to wage a war they did not desire. During WWII, we again saw these alliances solidify through the Axis and the Allied forces, but these were broken down to generally the post-war setup we see today. During the

Cold War, Communist revolutions became real threats when it spread to other countries.

Following the collapse of the Soviet Union, a decrease in popularity and support for Communism worldwide came. While governments opened their economies to make more business and trade, this often did not translate into more freedom. Totalitarianism thrived and still thrives today as dictators have come to represent some of the U.S.'s longtime partners. However, as nations outside the Western Bloc prosper, they are starting to represent new ideas and new voices on the world stage. These nations have enhanced their economies, their military and political influences, and, regionally, have begun to oppose the traditional systems of extraction and business.

According to Henry Kissinger, the "international system of the twenty-first century …will contain at least 6 major powers – the United States, Europe, China, Japan, Russia, and probably India- as well as a multiplicity of medium-sized and smaller countries." These 6 nations are part of 5 entirely different civilization groups, made more complicated by Islamic states and oil-producing countries with a significant influence on world affairs. In this new world, regional politics are based on ethnicity while global politics are founded in civilizations. The rivalries of past political doctrines and national powers have and will continue to become a clash of civilizations.

The European Union (EU) and the U.S. could trace their history back to the legacies of Greece and Rome. If you were to open any high school or university textbook or watch the History Channel, it always begins with the Greeks and Romans. It is as if the U.S. is the last in a long line of successors to the throne of world civilization. But in China, they do not have to base their culture on some distant land they have little to no connection with. In fact, the nations around them have based their civilizations on the Chinese.

The Chinese civilization is one that stretches back as far 5,000 years and has been a unified empire since Emperor Qin, in 220 BCE. The Chinese civilization had contact with and watched the mighty Greek and Roman civilizations rise, become corrupted, and then fall. The birth of Rome out of their waging war with the Etruscans even resembled the founding of America in their conflict with the much more powerful British Empire.

In the same way that the Romans sought to create a new Rome wherever they went, the U.S. also wants to Americanize and democratize the world in its image. While the Romans fought perpetual warfare, a doctrine admired and advocated for by President Franklin Roosevelt, the Chinese fought wars to protect their lands from invaders. The Romans pursued similar policies as the U.S., incorporating what they described as the "barbarians" under their empire and made them Roman. Whereas China built the Great Wall to fend off the "barbarians" and protect China. As a result, 91.95% of China is comprised of the single ethnic group, the Han.

Traditionally, China saw its lands and culture as self-sufficient and only desired foreign lands to acknowledge Chinese apparent cultural, economic, and natural position as the center of the world through tribute. If Western civilizations were founded on the premise of rites of passage through conquering, then Chinese culture is based upon inward reflection and defense. While China is a true civilization-state, the U.S. is a fledgling nation, trying to find its own identity. Chinese people have a rich history to draw from, whereas the U.S. is still making its history. The viewpoints of these 2 cultures could not differ more than they do, and this very difference will bring them into eventual conflict. China seeks to be the regional leader, a position it held for most of its history (except for the last hundred years).

In contrast, the U.S. seeks global hegemony and cannot tolerate differences. Any nation that dares challenge American exceptionalism faces rhetoric, sanctions, tariffs, cyberattacks, international gangsterism, and eventually war. But while the 20th century belonged to the U.S., the 21st century will be China's.

So, what is being done on a political level towards China? In a letter to the House and Senate leadership, Republican Study Committee (RSC) Chairman Mike Johnson and National Security & Foreign Affairs Task Force Chairman Joe Wilson outlined 10 conservative policy recommendations designed to hold the Chinese government accountable for the COVID-19 pandemic. The Task Force had brought up numerous concerns and claimed China influences international organizations like the World Health Organization. Furthermore, they sought to end all visas for Chinese government officials and their families and prohibit Chinese state-run media organizations within the U.S.

According to the letter, "The American people will not tolerate the CCP's lies any longer. The time has come to be tough on China and push back against its campaign of lies and disinformation. The RSC Foreign Affairs and National Security Task Force hope that Congress can move this collection of common-sense policies to hold China accountable for its direct role in this pandemic."

Also, the Senate Armed Services Committee passed a $740.5 billion USD annual defense policy bill, which included a Pacific Deterrence Initiative aimed to counter China. On June 11, 2020, U.S. Senators Ted Cruz, Kelly Loeffler, and Joni Ernst introduced the "Bring Entrepreneurial Advancements to Consumer Here in North America (BEAT CHINA) Act" which specified the relocation of medical devices and supplies to the U.S. from China. It was also part of a concerted effort to pull Western companies from China.

Senator Loeffler said, "For too long, our manufacturing has moved overseas, taking American jobs, jeopardizing our supply chains and forcing us to depend on competitors." These Senators called the COVID-19 pandemic a "great awakening" and sought to disrupt foreign investment in China while decreasing reliance. The Senate Foreign Relations Committee outlined some key features of focus regarding China-U.S. relations: (1) end U.S. dependence on China, (2) hold China accountable, (3) combat China's propaganda campaign in the U.S., and (4) counter Chinese espionage. These areas carried an overly hawkish tone which sought to confront China in numerous areas while risking diplomatic relations.

A ban on Chinese diplomats is essentially an act of war and pressuring nations not to invest in China does not make it better. If the stance on China is not renegotiated soon, some of these political consequences can spill over into military consequences, as we are just beginning to see.

According to an article in the Economist from June 9, 2020, the North Atlantic Treaty Organization's (NATO) Secretary-General Jens Stoltenberg had noticed China was "coming closer to us." China, which is the second-largest military spender in the world, was accused of confronting NATO from Africa to the Arctic and from cyberspace to infrastructure investments. It was mentioned that if NATO did not take a more aggressive stance on China, the alliance might face a lack of interest from its biggest member, the U.S.

Ian Brzezinski of the Atlantic Council, a Washington based think-tank, advocated for a NATO-China Council to be formed with more robust military exercises in the Pacific, a move that would not please Beijing. He would also like to see the creation of a "center of excellence" in the region, a military headquarters to keep an eye on the area. While Stoltenberg was not ready to move NATO into the South China Sea just yet, he would like to increase collaborations with allies in the region, including Australia, Japan, New Zealand, and South Korea.

While NATO and the U.S. look towards containing Chinese influence in the region, the EU's Foreign Policy High Representative Josep Borrell had been in talks with Chinese Foreign Minister Wang Yi, "I told him: 'Don't worry, Europe is not going to embark on any kind of Cold War with China.'" With the rift between the U.S. and its allies growing each day, countries are forced to pick a side, but hopefully, enough will choose China's side, forcing the U.S. to back down from its aggressive stance.

In 2019, President Xi Jinping, in response to hostilities from the U.S., requested Chinese diplomats to show more "fighting spirit." As the U.S. stepped up its pressure on countries not to do business with China, a new form of diplomacy dubbed as the "wolf-warrior diplomacy" had arisen from China. This new approach gained popular support among its domestic audiences and pursued a proactive and high-profile approach to critical issues. For example, *Wolf Warrior* and *Wolf Warrior II* are famous Chinese action movies that feature the roles of Chinese Special Forces in overseas missions and increased national pride in foreign affairs. But this new doctrine has seen itself in the military realm as well, especially in the South China Sea.

On April 19, 2020, China moved ahead with naming 80 islands, reefs, seamounts, shoals, and ridges in the South China Sea to assert its historical claims. This has come as they have reinforced their positions and are increasingly confronting American aggression in the region. The last time that China named islands and other features in the region was back in 1983. With the rise of China's economic growth, comes new confidence within itself and its foreign policies.

The Chinese Communist Party (CCP) follows and promotes a policy of "four confidences:" (1) the chosen path, (2) the political system, (3) guiding theories, and (4) their culture. As certain nations fear or try to disrupt the rise of China to its natural place in the world; the "wolf-warrior diplomacy" seeks to tell things from a Chinese perspective. For a long time, the world has been dominated by a significant number of countries speaking with a single voice, but now other voices are rising. The former Vice-Foreign Minister Fu Ying said in a report to People's Daily, "A country's power in international discourse relates not just to its right to speak up on the global stage, but more to the effectiveness and influence of the discourse."

One of the critical areas of friction between the U.S. and China lies in technology. According to an article from Forbes Magazine by Rebecca Fannin on December 9, 2019, Western companies and governments became concerned about their reliance on Chinese technology. In the face of pushback from the U.S., China had sought to decouple its reliance upon Western technology, opting to promote domestic development. Beijing ordered all government offices and public institutions to remove any foreign software and computer equipment, intending to replace it with local suppliers over the next 3 years. This was the result of U.S.'s pressure on Western companies to refuse the sale of products that could be used in artificial intelligence (AI) and telecom networking.

Under President Xi Jinping, China seeks to become self-reliant in vital technological areas, perhaps in preparation for a future conflict. While China was reliant upon the U.S. for core technologies in the past, it strengthened its efforts to compete on the global stage instead. One of the most controversial areas was China's development of 5G networks, which the U.S. has been pressuring its allies not to let China deliver. The threats made by Washington have forced countries to choose sides in this ongoing economic war.

When it comes to AI, the U.S. is the world's leader. Still, China has been taking the research and development in the field a step further by incorporating it into healthcare, economic, transportation, finance, and education. As the tech race picks up speed, it will leave the rest of the world with less efficient technologies and higher prices, with both sides competing for the world's markets. As one of the knock-on effects in the technology realm, Twitter had taken to removing 170,000 accounts it claimed had ties with China and was spreading false information.

In a report from the Associated Press on June 12, 2020, a battle for narratives was taking place, with free speech being the victim of an ongoing censorship battle. Twitter in the past had deleted 20,000 "fake" accounts, claiming to have government ties around the world and were a "targeted attempt to undermine the public conversation."

According to a report from the IMF, the escalating U.S.-China trade war was one of the factors that contributed to a "significantly weakened global expansion" late last year, cutting its projection for growth in 2019. Many countries were expected to be significantly impacted, a situation that was only exacerbated by COVID-19 restrictions, collapsing economic and financial conditions, and increased regulations. As countries get forced to pick sides and tariffs increased on both sides of the fence, the U.S. might find itself increasingly isolated by forcibly trying to isolate China.

According to the 2019 World Investment Report, published by The UN Conference on Trade and Development, China ranked second in foreign direct investments. However, this came under threat when U.S. placed pressures to try and drive these investments back to the U.S. or, at the very least, away from China. This received lukewarm responses from allies, at best, that found the costs of relocation prohibitive before the current crises.

Again, President Donald Trump is trying to compete in areas where the U.S. does not have a competitive advantage and is only worsened by current economic situations. However, if a conflict is brewing, and it most likely is, then it is essential to create the necessary industrial base for domestic production. It is impossible to wage war against an enemy you rely upon for crucial products, so the cracks are only likely to grow into a rift.

Since the January 13, 2020 "Phase 1 Deal," diplomatic relations between U.S. and China had only taken a turn for the worse. This began in March with both sides blaming each other for their handling of the virus. Then, the economic and financial conditions had pushed both sides to more independence from each other.

In the U.S., legislation is underway to use grants and tax breaks to persuade foreign businesses to relocate from China, a costly and logistically tricky task. The special status of Hong Kong has been removed to limit trading further and increase the costs of doing business in U.S. dollars. Also, U.S. companies have been banned from using products from Chinese telecom giant Huawei. A China distraction has become a valuable tool and is being popularized through the media, as the cause of the slew of issues facing the U.S. The Anti-China rhetoric had coincided with the president's declining popularity in the polls as he struggled to deal with a worsened economic situation and social unrest.

In what is quickly shaping up to be a repeat of past failed protectionist measures, President Donald Trump had placed tariffs on imports from Mexico, Canada, and the EU to promote domestic products. However, all these countries retaliated by placing equivalent tariffs on U.S. products which, during the current economic conditions, only worsened the situation for the U.S. Large areas of the globe being hit with a wide range of trade restrictions. Although some countries have gained temporary exemptions, do not expect this to last indefinitely.[64]

During election season in the U.S., increased blame has been put on China since it provided President Trump success in the past. By taking a hard stance on China, President Trump is able to portray himself as the strong leader needed to handle the insurmountable issues plaguing the U.S. and, thus, belittle

---

[64] https://www.bbc.com/news/business-48196495

his opponent Joe Biden. No matter who wins, there will not be much of a different approach towards China moving forward.

In the meantime, China has been preparing for both outcomes. It has expelled several American journalists and state-run food companies (Cofco and Sinograin), have been instructed to purchase fewer U.S. products, a move that throws the trade deal out the window. It is unrealistic that the "Phase 1 Deal" was anything more than a publicity stunt, as neither side has shown much interest in upholding it and was only designed to get by until the next election.

As we move forward, several unresolved issues can make the current situation from bad to worse. Will there simply be a second wave of COVID-19 or, will this turn into a never-ending saga? The economic toll alone had already done dramatic effects which we are only beginning to feel. The economic crisis is quickly morphing into a financial one that will come to head over the next few months to a year. Zombie companies are on the rise, putting the viability of recovery any time soon into question. Finally, social unrest is at all-time highs across the globe and there are no quick solutions for these complex issues.

Many revolutions and wars had been the result of people being motivated due to depressed economic conditions, suffering, poverty, and starvation. Trade wars caused depressions and depressions caused shooting wars. Most civil wars had been the product of civil unrest that grew to become battles in the streets.

Many of the reasons behind the protests, riots, and looting in the U.S. were because of income inequality and poor economic conditions. Desperate regimes have often been forced to resort to drastic measures such as warfare as a fruitless attempt to revolve their situations. What once was a rhetoric war has now become an economic war and signs of escalating to a military conflict are appearing.

As the U.S. seeks to distract its citizens from the domestic crises plaguing the nation, they have pursued an increasingly aggressive stance towards China. This is manifesting itself in legislation, which only drives the 2 world powers further apart. Technology and trade have become the central issues in this battle, forcing the rest of the world to reevaluate their relationships with each power.

While China seeks to unite the world in a collective effort towards greater prosperity, American exceptionalism sought to undermine these efforts, reversing to the disastrous Mercantile economic policies t. As Cold War 2.0 begins to unfold, as the divide grows deeper, each power grows closer to a confrontation, which will inevitably result in WWIII.

SECTION 4: THE ASIAN MILLENNIUM

"Heaven is above, earth is below, and that in between heaven and earth is called China. Those on the peripheries are the foreign. The foreign belong to the outer, while China belongs to the inner."

Shi Jie, *On the Middle Kingdom*, 1040 CE

"China is a sleeping giant. Let her sleep, for when she wakes, she will move the world."

Napoleon Bonaparte, French Emperor, statesman, and military leader

Our world has become a new, fast-paced, and exciting place. Smart cities have risen from the ashes of the old ones, and are managed by artificial intelligence and powered by green technologies. Each one is a sparkling diamond, encrusted in a solid gold necklace known as a "mega-region cluster." Data and people move at lightning speeds through these regions, interconnected in every part of their lives. Humans have become the resource that each region competes to attract. As national borders fade away, new regional identities take shape.

The transformation process that has taken place in China, and is continuing to take place, is nothing less than spectacular. Even at the height of U.S. economic power, they've never come close to the speed or sheer scale of development like that of China's. China is undergoing urbanization with numbers never seen before. Even when it comes to investments overseas, the Chinese have been buying and investing in everything—from hydroelectric dams, roads, bridges, ports, mines, houses, businesses, and every other kind of asset.

Over the past decade, world growth has been carried on the back of the Chinese economy—an economy that managed to maintain its levels of fantastic growth when the developed world barely skimmed by. If China is not already the world's most significant power, they soon will be and it does not matter how the figures are broken down. It feels like traveling to the future when visiting or living in any of the first-tier cities in China such as Beijing, Shanghai, or Shenzhen. The levels of technological integration within the culture and the proficiency and speed of adopting new technology are unmatched in the world.

In many ways, China is the same bright-eyed teenager that the U.S. was back in the early part of the 20th century, trying to find its place in the world and with a bright future. But there are other ways in which China differs from the U.S. China is a civilization-state with thousands of years of cultural practices to draw upon, whereas the U.S. is a new nation which sees itself as the descendant of Europe's powers. For much of recorded history, the power structures of the world were generally laid in Asia, a great power with flowing wealth of distant lands. It is only the past few hundred years, thanks to advancements in technology, that Europe and North America have taken a lead role in the world affairs.

If we look back over the past 2000 years, we can see that the centers of economic power have been firmly within Asia and have only recently moved along the spectrum towards Europe but have recently shifted back. The coming century is often dubbed as the "Asian Century," with Asia retaking its global position in this new and exciting multipolar world. Through integration and cooperation, China laid the foundations for a new multi-civilizational approach to global governance which will outmaneuver and outclass the U.S. at every step.

In the words of the famous Chinese general and military strategist Sun Tzu, "是故百戰百勝，非善之善者也；不戰而屈人之兵，善之善者也" which means "The best victory is one where you submit your enemy without fighting." This philosophy runs contrarian to the barbarous concept of continual warfare.

Over the past 200 years, Western nations have dictated the world what it means to be modern. A small percentage of the world's population has ruled over the majority, trying to shape the world in its image. Today, we see the real democratization of global politics which will bring the voices of the oppressed to the forefront. It is these voices that will shape our future.

Parag Khanna is a bestselling author and a Ph.D. holder from the London School of Economics. In his recent book: *THE FUTURE IS ASIAN: Commerce, Conflict, and Culture in the 21st Century*, he details his vision for the future. He sees the "Asian Century" going well beyond just China and India; it will be extending to multi-civilizational world order that spans from the Middle East to Japan, from Russia to Australia. This vast expanse, not even in the periphery of Westerners, makes up 5 billion people and is becoming interconnected through trade, finance, and infrastructure networks that will total to about 40% of the current global GDP.

Drawing from the historical lessons of their past, China is paving the way through the new Silk Roads that stretch from Europe and Africa, all the way to East Asia. If the Romans built roads that all led to Rome, China is building roads that will transform key areas into vibrant economic hubs of the future. Asia is returning to the stable multipolar world order that existed before European and American colonialism through these economic and strategic hubs. These hubs link the isolated but significant populations of people, stretching from Iran to Indonesia and Saudi Arabia to Vietnam, incorporating them into a real global network.

This shift will come to impact all areas of life, from investment portfolios to how and where people take their holidays, as the effects of "Asianization" continue to take shape. Khanna asked, "What happens when Asia no longer produces for the West, but the West produces for Asia? And when Asians don't aspire to live like the West, but rather Western societies wish they had Asians' stability and far-sighted leadership? Get ready to see the world, and the future, from the Asian point-of-view."

In a report from McKinsey & Company on June 1, 2012, it detailed their analysis and projections of the world's geographic centers of economic activity from Year 1 to 2025. The report found that over the last 2000 years, the centers of economic activity were slowly moving westwards and, until recently, were making a shift back towards Asia.[65]

Daniel Velkov, a Silicon Valley and Wall Street engineer, had issues with this representation, as the figure places the centers of global economic activity over Scandinavia, misrepresenting the data. Since China and the U.S. were on

---

[65] https://www.mckinsey.com/featured-insights/urbanization/urban-world-cities-and-the-rise-of-the-consuming-class#

opposite sides of the world, and the data was being plotted on a sphere, it skewed the results towards the North Pole. Instead, he moved forward with his modeling of the data to provide a more accurate representation[66]. The 2D representation was easier to understand and it clearly showed that the past economic centers of the world were in China, India, Anatolia, and the Middle East.

According to the original data, Asia's historical total economic output was 5 times larger than that of Europe's. However, as the economies of Europe began to develop, the center shifted towards Europe more and reaching its peak with the U.S.'s economic output, until around 1950 when this trend reversed. The rise of Asian economies started to push the center back towards Asia to the point wherein the year 2000s erased all the gains accumulated in year 1900s.

In the original projection[67], the center shifted even further towards China and India, leaving Europe in the dust. What do these models tell us? The trend is your friend until the end. For much of human history, the great civilizations that inhabited the Eurasian landmass have been the economic powerhouses of the global economy; and from the distant lands of their peripheries, to them flow the world's wealth.

This may come as a surprise for most Westerners who have been raised to believe that world civilization began in Greece and Rome, and then flowed to the great powers of Europe, which civilized the world before coming to its final resting place in the U.S. But Western dominance in this world represents more of an aberration in history than the norm. Like all economies, civilization moves in cycles; and now it is that time in the cycle for Asia to rise again and take its rightful place in the world. In the past, this might not have much bearing on the distant lands of the world other than small amounts of trade. However, in the interconnected world of the future, this will send shockwaves which will be felt around the globe. It is no wonder the Americans are working so hard to disrupt and delay the inevitable, but they will not be successful.

---

[66] https://danielvelkov.blogspot.com/2014/07/finding-worlds-economic-center-of.html
[67] https://www.mckinsey.com/featured-insights/urbanization/urban-world-cities-and-the-rise-of-the-consuming-class#

According to a report from Bruno Macaes of the World Economic Forum on February 18, 2020 titled: *Eurasia, the supercontinent that will define our century*, the rising powers in Eurasia would come to shape the 21st century. With China leading the way with the Belt and Road Initiatives (BRI), which spans nearly 70 countries, a new geographic superpower and the importance of Eurasia is rising.[68]

Currently, 4 out of the 5 largest economies are in this geographic area, but Eurasia is becoming more than just geography. It is becoming an identity. Macaes reported that the statements coming out of China spoke of new confidence for the future. This nation has mastered modern technology and built a modern society, all without adopting the political, economic, and social models laid out by the West. But didn't Americans always say that nations must be democratic to become successful?

For the first time in a long time, this has created a contradiction about what it means to be modern and rewrote the notions about the stages of development a society must take. Nations are free to choose the systems that suit their needs the best, rather than submit to the will of a foreign power. Containing some of the most varied cultures and communities, Eurasia is a region formed through integration. Democracies are linked with dictatorships, authoritarians are doing business with liberals, and the definition of what it means to be modern is broken down and redefined. Technology is now able to span the vast distances that, in the past, acted as barriers. New high-speed railways can cut the travel time for people and goods between Europe and China from 2 months to 2 days.

Greater integration will inevitably dissolve borders and lead to greater prosperity which will culminate into what Macaes called the "Eurasian Age." As time goes on, the pull upon Europe towards Asia and, thus, away from the U.S. will only increase. Europe is helpless to stop the gradual march towards Asia; and if the Europeans wish to remain relevant in the world, they need to accelerate it.

---

[68] https://www.nytimes.com/interactive/2018/11/18/world/asia/world-built-by-china.html

China is leading the world when it comes to trade, investment, and infrastructure, and these moves seek to reshape the region's financial and geopolitical realm. An article published by the New York Times on November 18, 2018 titled *The World, Built by China*, it detailed the sheer scale of what was being dubbed as China's modern-day "Marshall Plan." The article listed 41 pipelines and other oil and gas infrastructure projects, 203 bridges, roads, and railways to move goods, and 199 power plants for nuclear, natural gas, coal, and renewable energy. Over the last decade, China had helped finance nearly 600 significant projects overseas, with billions of dollars in grants, loans, and investments.

All of these are parts of a much grander strategy known as the BRI[69]. The article detailed some of the more notable projects, including the strategic deep-water port in Sri Lanka, one which China leased for the next 99 years. The 7 dams built in Cambodia generated almost half of the nation's electricity requirements. In South Africa, a coal-fired plant was financed by China, while in Zambia, China built a $94 million USD soccer stadium.

While Western governments avoided the countries that do not deem agreeable with their policies, China embraced them with open arms. China had no problems lending to nations like Venezuela, Nigeria, and Zimbabwe without the strings of Western institutions. Through these valuable infrastructure investments, China is developing a good reputation and build long-lasting friendships where Western countries fail to establish and thereby harming their global image.

According to Koshy Mathai and in regards to the International Monetary Fund's (IMF) latest regional outlook, "The west's two-century epoch as a global powerhouse is at an end." What this would mean for the world, we are only beginning to find out. Andrea Colli, a professor of economic history at Bocconi University in Italy, stated: "Around the end of the 17th century, Europe was looking with admiration and envy at a region of the globe which

---

[69] https://www.onthemosway.eu/wp-content/uploads/2018/07/china-silkroad-security.jpg

concentrated… more than two-thirds of the world's gross domestic product, and three-quarters of the world's population."

According to Indian politician and author Shashi Tharoor, during the 18th century, India's economy was as large as all of Europe's combined. Then, as Europeans experienced a hyper leap in technology, the rest of the world stagnated. Western economies experienced the Scientific Revolution, the Enlightenment Period, and the Industrial Revolution, which led to their time in the sun[70]. By the 1950s, the whole continent of Asia accounted for only approximately 20% of the world's GDP but had about half of the population.

The recent rise of the Asian Tigers and China led to a trend reversal, using a mix of integration with the world's economy through trade and foreign direct investment, high personal savings rates, significant investment infrastructure, and far-sighted macroeconomic policies. Hundreds of millions of people had been lifted out of poverty and watched the world around them transform in just a single lifetime. The recent surge in Asia could be traced to Japan's post-war economy, representing the historical norm.

However, while there is much focus placed upon China as the sole leader in Asia, it is the growth experiences in small to mid-sized economies that are making the growth lasting and impactful. According to the IMF, Indonesia is on track to becoming the 7th largest economy by purchasing power parity (PPP) and will soon surpass Russia sometime in 2020, which is currently at 6th pace. Meanwhile, Vietnam is one of the fastest-growing economies in Asia. Currently, the Philippines has a much larger economy than the Netherlands, and Bangladesh has also shown a lot of growth over the past 20 years.

The rise of Asia happened so quickly that it had barely given the Western societies and analysts the ability to catch up. Many people have outdated images in their heads of what Asia looks like on the ground today. At the same time, analysts are often dismissive of the growth potential, relying too heavily on indicators such as per capita income which can possibly give a skewed result. Still, according to the data provided by the IMF[71], the nominal GDP of Asia in

---

70 https://www.ft.com/content/520cb6f6-2958-11e9-a5ab-ff8ef2b976c7
71 https://www.ft.com/content/520cb6f6-2958-11e9-a5ab-ff8ef2b976c7

PPP per capita is expected to overtake the rest of the world by the end of the 2030s.

One of the driving factors of record-breaking growth in Asia is how the energy sector is shaping geopolitics between nations. In a report by Miyeon Oh published in the World Economic Forum on November 2, 2018, we learned the relationship between large scale projects and long-term relationships. According to the report, building a pipeline or an infrastructure project went beyond business aspirations and joined states in security, political, and geopolitical relationships. China had developed energy projects across Asia, bringing countries together and improving China's geopolitical influence in the region.

Within the framework of the BRI, the Asian economies are set to become more significant than the rest of the world combined. The century ahead, often referred to as the Asian Century, will be built by Asians working closely together on their continent and overseas. In the past, these diverse cultures were kept separated by challenging geography and even more complicated history. However, the mutual benefits of cooperation have shown to be more significant with the increasing momentum of their regional integration.

The reboots in relations between China, India, South Korea, and Japan, along with local cooperation organizations such as the ASEAN, APEC, and the Shanghai Cooperation Organization have attested to this. As the Western world shows cracks in division and fragmentation, Asia is becoming more integrated, especially in trade, tourism, and investment. After the U.S. abandoned the Trans-Pacific Partnership (TPP), Asia took the helm for multilateral trade liberalization. Through joint infrastructure initiatives, Asian partners are looking to fuel a cycle of mutual gain through connectivity and trade liberalization.

The rise of China as a regional and global power happened at such a speed that it would be impressive to understand the incredible statistics. In an article from the New York Times on November 18, 2018, *The Land That Failed to Fail*, it provided details on these fantastic accomplishments and their consequences. While the debate over the global leader continues, China has quietly taken the lead in the number of homeowners, internet users, college graduates, and even billionaires. China has become less concerned about catching up to the U.S. than it is about how to overtake it.

While the past 8 American presidents assumed that China would become more like the U.S. with time, we see China becoming more confident in its own identity. The Chinese leadership has continued to defy expectations, presiding over 40 years of uninterrupted growth. One of the critical areas outside of economic growth is in the educational field where China produces more science and engineering graduates than Japan, South Korea, the U.S., and Taiwan combined. Many younger leaders in China's government have pursued education abroad and brought their skills and expertise back to China. These new minds are part of a system of reforms that have sought to improve bureaucratic mechanisms, making the government function more efficiently.

According to Yuen Yuen Ang, a political scientist from the University of Michigan, "China created a unique hybrid, an autocracy with democratic characteristics." This system has led to some of the most qualified party members being elected to positions where they can make real improvements in the lives of people. The Chinese Communist Party (CCP) has a membership of over 91 million people, which is the highest number of representations in the world.

Chinese officials are part of a system of meritocracy that dated back 2,000 years ago, pioneered and perfected in China, where promoting officials are based on merit rather than hereditary clans. Only those highly educated and the most efficient at doing their jobs can rise through the ranks. To understand how the system works, you only need to review the life of Xi Jinping to see that the Chinese values the abilities of their leaders and how there are no separation between the CCP and the people they govern.

As the American dream begin to fade away in the U.S., it is alive and well in China. Prosperity has led to increased expectations from the people that go beyond economic growth. Cleaner air, safer food and medicine, better health care and schools, less corruption, and greater equality are all part of the social responsibility of Chinese officials. The CCP is enjoying broad public support and levels of popularity that are not often found in Western-style democracies. Even as economic growth slows worldwide, China is exceptionally well situated to continue to see amazing improvements in the near future. If you are Chinese, you know that your future is bright.

Chinese officials have been looking to reinvent urban lifestyle for the future as Western nations decay from a lack of resources to maintain their crumbling cities. In an article from The World Economic Forum on September 3, 2018 by Andrew Sheng of the Fung Global Institute and Xia Geng, a professor at the University of Hong Kong, they detailed China's plans to build 19 "supercity clusters."

According to the article, Beijing policymakers pursued a "BREEP methodology"—browse, research, experiment, evaluate, and push forward what works—while refining and adapting any tools and tactics. This type of strategy is flexible, allows for community feedback, and is far from the image of the CCP the media is portraying. While the West has sought to export their system to the world through violence and intimidation, China seeks to be an example in allowing others to choose their own paths. Through the introduction of smart cities and the integration of urban clusters, China seeks to provide an efficient urban lifestyle for its educated consumers in a sustainable manner.

In 2010, 3 major urban clusters were identified by China's State Council for smart urbanization: the Yangtze River Delta (YRD), the Beijing-Tianjin-Hebei cluster (BTH), and the Pearl River Delta (PRD). According to a report from HSBC, these 3 clusters would account for 45% of China's total GDP by 2025. GBA has a population of 70 million people, BTH has 112 million, and YRD has 120 million. By 2030, HSBC expected that these clusters would account for 80% of the country's GDP when China was midway through their mass urbanization project. To plan, China's National Development and Reform Commission has been working with the World Bank, McKinsey, and others on how to provide smart urbanization.

These organizations created their approach using close coordination with local officials, investors, and foreign experts. This had led to the establishment of the Shanghai Free-Trade Zone, Qianhai-Shekou Pilot Free-Trade Zone, an ambitious plan to create a green model city in the BTH cluster. As China continues to move forward and redevelop itself, it will continue to seek a better way of life.[72][73]

As the Asian community begins to form an identity based on diversity and inclusion of various economic systems, the gravity of the mass will start to pull in outliers who do not want to be left on the sidelines. As the largest economy in Asia, China will play a central role in shaping this identity in what will become a multipolar century.

If the U.S. decides to stand up to China, they will find themselves picking a fight by themselves and, thus, destined to lose. The U.S. will find itself increasingly outclassed and outmaneuvered throughout the Asian Century and beyond. Unable to dictate to the world and facing domestic issues at home, the U.S. will be forced to take a secondary role in global affairs as reality slowly but surely catches up to it.

Currently, U.S. Secretary of State Pompeo is demanding that other countries comply with the U.S. decision to activate "snapback sanctions" pursuant to the Joint Comprehensive Plan of Action (JCPOA), an international agreement that the U.S. unilaterally pulled out of in May 2018.

Exactly one year after the US abandoned the nuclear deal, Iran started gradually scaling down its compliance with the commitments made under the pact, including those concerning its stockpile of enriched uranium. Even so, Iran had been subjected to the most comprehensive international inspections regime out of any country in the world with respect to its nuclear program and continued to grant access to the International Atomic Energy Agency. This consistently confirmed that it found no evidence that Iran was pursuing a nuclear weapons program.

Of the 15 UN Security Council members, 13 said that the U.S.'s request to activate the "snapback sanctions" provisions was illegal since it was withdrawn

---

[72]https://www.mckinsey.com/~/media/McKinsey/Industries/Capital%20Projects%20and%20Infrastructure/Our%20Insights/Smart%20cities%20Digital%20solutions%20for%20a%20more%20livable%20futures/SVGZ-Smart-cities-digital-solutions_ex1_expanded.svgz

[73] https://www.mckinsey.com/industries/capital-projects-and-infrastructure/our-insights/smart-cities-digital-solutions-for-a-more-livable-future

from the JCPOA and was therefore no longer a party to the agreement, which was signed by the U.S., France, Germany, the U.K., Russia, China, Iran and the EU in 2015. Washington argued that as 1 of the 5 permanent Security Council members, they had the right to call for the snapback sanctions. Eleven council members abstained in the vote to extend the arms embargo pursuant to the JCPOA, with Russia and China opposing the measure. Only the U.S. and the Dominican Republic supported the resolution.

In a letter to the Security Council, the European signatories to the deal – the U.K., France and Germany – stated that the winding down of the UN sanctions against Iran would continue, adding any decision or action by the U.S. to reimpose them "would be incapable of legal effect." The U.S. was witnessing unprecedented isolation in their desperate attempt to try to cling on to their remaining power.

In contrast, China's comprehensive strategy is firmly anchored in the realities of geopolitical situations. Instead of seeking to become a hegemon, China's role will be part of a multi-civilizational order, providing cooperation in global governance and trying more actions rather than reactions. Repeatedly, China has shown how they are taking a long-term perspective with international relations, even allowing Japan to shelve their disagreements for at least a decade in favor for their current cooperation.

As China continues to reimagine itself and what it wants for the future, it will continue to seek a better way of life for those involved. China has already given the world the confidence to reinvent itself, seeking new alternatives than those of the past. Instead of forcing others to become a copy of themselves, they encourage nations to choose their own systems that suit them. This unique approach can be summed up by the simple yet meaningful foreign policy of the Chinese government to seek a "win-win" approach. With the groundwork being laid throughout the Asian Century, it will allow for the fruits to come to bear during the next segment of history: the Asian Millennium.

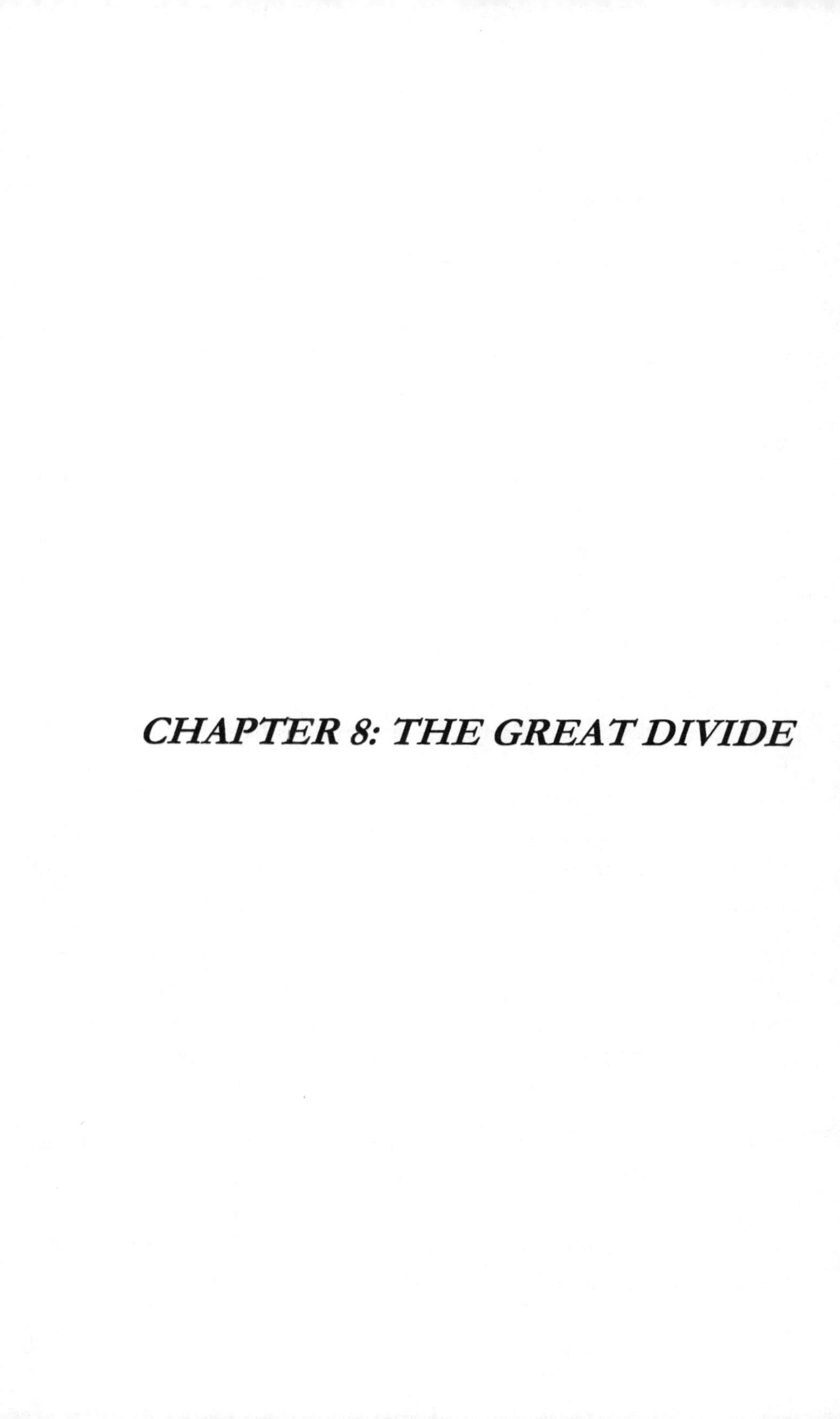

CHAPTER 8: THE GREAT DIVIDE

THE GREAT DIVIDE

INTRODUCTION

The drums of war are beating stronger with each passing day. Social unrest and terrorism have swept across the globe and risks engulfing the world in chaos, warfare, and atrocities. The events unfolding around the world have been a nonstop progression of calamities and crises. For instance, environmental crises are pushing many nations with swelling populations to the brink.

While many people are hopeful that a return to normalcy is just around the corner, we have only witnessed the opening act. Slowly, in the background, the world that we have grown to know has eroded. We have entered a period in history where dynamic flux will be the new normal. The global systems in place for generations will be questioned as new ones replace the old ways of business and thought. The U.S. has enjoyed its role in a unipolar world as the de facto dictator and model for the rest of the world to emulate.

The U.S. is the world's most powerful country. This superpower dominates and exerts its power and influence across the world. Russia comes in second, followed by China. China has had a turbulent history, but has risen to become a major force in the global community. Leading multinational banks reckon that Asian economies are going to grow significantly between 2020 and 2030. We will be seeing these countries take top spots on the list of the world's biggest economies.

There are books available on China's future economic strength, and these books tell us how this Asian country is set to change the political and cultural landscape of the world as we know it. The question that worries Western pundits is this: Will China's historic rise contribute to a better world or just make a more powerful country?

As U.S. hegemony retreats from many parts of the world, it is being replaced with a new world order. The historical role of Asia as the center of economic activity, culture, and development was usurped for the last 200 years, but we see a return to the norm. A few decades ago, it would have seemed unthinkable that U.S.'s power and influence would be challenged by what was at those times, relatively insignificant regions of the globe. However, thanks to developments in technology and investments spearheaded by China, these same regions are becoming the powerhouses of the future.

While Europe and Western powers may have enjoyed a comfortable lead in technology and innovation, they are being challenged in the factories, marketplaces, and military. China represents a rising civilizational power regaining its rightful place as the center of the world. With rapid development comes rising confidence as well as the ability to confront the U.S.'s encroaching aggression.

We have found ourselves the hapless bystanders in the battle of worldviews which encompassed every facet of our lives. Indeed, the outcome of this battle will shape our future. No longer can we afford to stand idly by, ignorant of our surroundings, for this battle has and will come to our doorsteps and into our homes.

The threat of losing our civil rights has never been higher in recent memory than today. How we earn our livelihoods and how we spend those earnings will all be affected by this war of attrition, which can only delay the inevitable. The developing world has grown tired of having its voice ignored; finally, we need to start listening. There are several key issues in important areas that will need to be solved or they will come to shape the next century.

POLITICAL

Mahatma Gandhi was once asked what he thought of Western civilization, to which he famously replied, "I think that would be a good idea." The U.S. and China each face key decisions. The U.S. must conclude whether to see China's ascent as an existential danger and attempt to keep China down through every accessible means, or to acknowledge China as a significant force in its own right.

On the off chance that it picks the second option, the U.S. must create a way to deal with China in a way that will cultivate participation and sound rivalry at every possible opportunity, and not permit contention to harm the relationship. Preferably, this competition will happen inside a concurred multilateral system of rules and standards, of the sort that oversee the UN and the World Trade Organization.

The U.S. is likely to find this a painful adjustment, particularly with the developing agreement in Washington that drawing in Beijing has failed to subdue it, and that a more aggressive approach is important to save U.S.'s interests. In any case, however difficult this will be for the U.S., it is well worth putting forth a genuine attempt to oblige China's yearnings inside the current arrangement of worldwide guidelines and standards. This framework forces duties and limitations on all nations, fortifies trust, oversees clashes, and makes a more secure and more stable condition for both participation and rivalry.

If the U.S. chooses instead to try to contain China's rise, it will risk provoking a reaction that could set the 2 countries on a path to decades of confrontation. The U.S. has extraordinary versatility and qualities, one of which is its capacity to attract talent from around the globe. For instance, of the 9 individuals of Chinese ethnicity who have been granted Nobel Prizes in technical studies, 8 were U.S. residents or became U.S. residents. On the opposite side, the Chinese economy has enormous dynamism and progressively cutting-edge innovation not unlike that of the Soviet Union in the past. It also cannot be defined as merely another communist state for it is a civilization that has endured countless enemies rise and fall. Any showdown between these 2 incredible forces is probably not going to end as the Cold War did: in one nation's serene breakdown.

Whether or not China becomes a friend or foe is solely reliant upon how it is treated by the West. Western nations have been working hard to demonize China with limited success outside of the Western world. On the one hand the U.S. encourages China to take on more responsibility as it is a major power while, on the other hand, it chastises China for more engagement. The demonization of China will not solve the deep intractable issues faced by the Western liberal democracies today.

The Western camp is confused about what to do with China and how to interpret it. However, there are only 2 real options: either the U.S. seeks more integration with China and its markets, effectively making China more competitive on the global stage; or it can try to lock out and isolate China which will inevitably force the world into hostilities. Until today, the Americans are undecided on what to do, with both these options clearly on the table and battling it out in different sectors. While Europe has been distancing itself from the U.S., it is also equally confused on which path to take in regard to China.

Throughout the rest of 2020 and beyond, the U.S. will be forced to pursue a continuation of isolationist policies as its global credibility and influence begin to wane. From trade to foreign policy, traditional allies have slowly drifted away and forged their paths and perspectives to cater to their respective nation's needs. The global economic slowdown is accelerating this process, leading each country to protect its interests, shifting some alliances, and forging new ones.

In the wake of the power vacuum left behind, new players such as China, Russia, Europe, and others, will rise to play a more significant role in global affairs, expanding their spheres of influence. We witness Turkey trying to rekindle the Ottoman Empire today, under the leadership of their dictatorship. In the face of new realities, global leaders will be forced to choose between competing political, economic, and technological systems, with the vast majority forced to make realistic choices as to what is best for their respective nations. The global political environment is intertwined with the economic uncertainties occurring, along with the financial, environmental, and social concerns of its citizens.

The U.S.-style democracy has already reached its peak, and we are witnessing the rise in totalitarian policies as a new global order takes shape. Even in Ancient Greece, democracy was only valuable during times of peace and when war came, it flew out the window. The multipolar and multi-system world order is taking shape. As trade wars continue to spread across traditional U.S. allies, the EU may face the most significant increase in tensions. EU member states are fragmented at the best of times but with different competing interests, they may face its most pressing challenges. The COVID-19 pandemic forces nations across the globe to make tough choices to preserve what little economic activity remains.

Since the driving factors behind the social unrest and income inequality are unlikely to be resolved, many governments will be pressured into more socialist policies, exacerbating the situation. As disruptions to supply chains continue, sovereign nations will be forced to hoard critical commodities as the flows of business continue to be disrupted and the health crisis continues. The increase in protectionism over access to precious resources will continue, leading to conflicts to certain areas.

As the U.S. retreats from the Middle East, leaving it to its allies to manage, there will be more focus on the South China Sea. To confront and contain China, the U.S. will make its last-ditch attempts to preserve its sovereignty in this critical region. However, China already laid the groundwork to mitigate economic damages from a worsening trade war and will continue to pursue less reliance upon the U.S. As trade war tensions increase with the U.S., China will continue to seek alternative markets and diversify its trading partners.

With the Belt and Road Initiative (BRI) and its continuing unabated expansion, China will see greater assertiveness in Asia and set global norms that suit its preferences. The critical areas of technology and infrastructure will play vital roles in China's ability to reshape global affairs to reflect its rising power.

ECONOMIC

While the U.S. still has the U.S. dollar as the world's global reserve currency, China has a plan to realize its global economic drive. Its "One Belt One Road" infrastructure plan is designed to strengthen China's connectivity with the world. This is a network of roads, pipelines and ports that will link the economies of more than 60 countries across Europe, Asia, and Africa. This BRI project is designed to increase trade, investment, and connectivity between China and these countries, making them all more dependent on the Chinese economy and increasing China's economic leverage over them.

Some financial experts believed that because the demand for dollars made it more expensive, this has contributed to U.S. trade deficits. As China's economy grows, the U.S. will not be able to deal with the capital inflows that are necessary to remain as the world's reserve currency. China will then shoulder some of the burden of being the global reserve currency. This could be seen in the recent development of the digital yuan.

Global economies will continue to decline for short to medium-terms due to loose monetary policies, with the declines in trade and tourism making matters worse. However, China is in a much better trading position with a broader range of countries to rebound faster from the global slump. More nations in the world are doing business with China than that of the U.S. While developed nations will find themselves in a depression, the developing world is poised to lead towards growth.

When the U.S.-China trade war shifts to technology and investments, especially now with the upcoming U.S. Presidential Election, this will be the start of the decoupling of economies that will harm both countries, more so on the side of the U.S. that leaves them in a much more vulnerable state than China. The economic situations of the developed world will continue to deteriorate as high levels of debt and lack of quality jobs continue to hamper their economies.

Over the next year or two, delinquencies will continue to rise despite the governments' efforts in delaying the inevitable. Real estate prices usually move the slowest of all and will take the longest to see the pressures placed by lack of qualified buyers and the growing waves of sellers. The auto market requires a major downsizing and remodeling to suit the requirements of the changing economic climate. The airline and tourism sectors may never recover from the travel restrictions, and will undoubtedly be forced to raise prices, further leading to less demand as safety concerns continue to prevail indefinitely.

The forced economic decoupling from China will have hostile political consequences and dangerous economic effects. The gradual retreat from globalization will result to the relocation of low-end jobs and higher costs for the consumer. The lack of diversity in the business market is already translating to higher prices at the store in a time when most of the population is income insecure.

By the end of 2020, it will become clear that there is no corner of the globe safe from the economic realities. The economic consequences of geopolitical oil wars and COVID-19 will send shockwaves that will reverberate around the world for years. Nations who have built their economies around commodities and tourism will face the most considerable stagnation with the slow and delayed lifting of mobility restrictions. This also resulted in increased transportation, freight, and logistics costs, along with new regulations that hamper business development.

In the wake of these existential crises, China is uniquely positioned to take the lead role in the global economy. It is already the leading driver of economic growth, accounting for 50%. But it will be the development of major infrastructure projects with its neighbors and beyond that will bring light at the end of the tunnel. The BRI is just one in a series of works in progress that will deepen economic ties between China and the global community. With its prudent overseas investments, China is poised to rebound much quicker than the U.S. from the current economic situation.

ENVIRONMENTAL

Climate change is playing an important role in shaping the world around us. In the past, people migrated to avoid the harmful effects of climate change; whereas, these days, that is becoming fraught with difficulties and secondary effects. As the world becomes more interconnected, we are changing the definition of what it means to be modern. In doing so, paying attention to how our actions affect others in the not so distant parts of the globe is becoming more important with each day that passes by. It is becoming harder to deny our reliance upon one another, especially now that we are seeing the problems created by the developed world in the developing world come back to haunt them.

Climate change is threatening our lifestyles and is affecting each nation differently. Extreme weather events are becoming more common and devastating, leading to a slew of knock-on effects. The areas of the globe that will be the hardest hit by climate change are also the ones facing the greatest increases in population and food and water scarcity.

As access to precious resources becomes more critical for nations, certain areas will act as hot spots for conflicts. It is no coincidence that these regions have become hotbeds for radicalization and sources for mass migrations of people.

As populations rise and access to resources become scarcer, we will see more climate refugees around the globe. How we deal with these issues will help to alleviate some of the tensions that give rise to conflicts, radicalization, and border tensions. Regardless of our stances on these issues, there must be global solutions, for these global crises. One of the most important places we can begin to cooperate in on is the vital issue of water, the second most precious of all resources after air.

SOCIAL

Across the globe, social unrest will continue to flourish as the economic and financial situations worsen. Governments will take more drastic measures, something that would have been unthinkable just a year ago. The underlying issues, arising from colonization and globalization, have created such well-entrenched inequality and lack of access to resources, making it impossible for Western liberal democracies to solve. Instead, what we are witnessing is a social revolution from the developing world fighting to right the wrongs of the past.

Plagued by Western intervention and corporate exploitation, the developing world suffers from corruption, inequality, lack of access to resources, and unfortunate economic situations. The social injustices of the lower-income classes are being felt by the shrinking middle classes across the globe. However, China has led the way with investments and developments, allowing nations a path out of the current cycle of poverty.

Across the old world, a new society is created with new identities that facilitate the flow of people, ideas, investment, and trade. As these policies become more attractive, more countries that were otherwise opposed will become further integrated within this network.

China has been changing the world for a long time now and for the better. But the changes to come will overshadow anything we have seen so far. While the world is generally ignorant of China, especially on to how it is being demonized in the media, the time has come to recognize that China will reshape our world. Western analysts have always assumed that every other country wants to be like the U.S—that somehow, if we trade enough with China, it will become just like America. This blindness, arrogance, and ignorance to modernity can only be defined by American exceptionalism. However, modernity is not defined by markets, politics or the will of outside nations but is shaped by the unique culture, history, and values of each nation state instead.

The definition of what it means to be modern in the 21ˢᵗ century will be shaped by those living and working in this new region. The developed world will face more threats of social unrest and instability, along with more migrations, leading to more radicalized policies. These draconian policies will only further fuel the social unrest and authoritarianism that are already taking place. By the end of the Asian Century, the world's nations will be drawn into this new network and will signal the start of the Asian Millennium.

TECHNOLOGY

Donald Trump has promised to "Make America Great Again," but China's president Xi Jinping has been busy "realizing the great renewal of the Chinese nation." The Chinese president is determined to see China become one of the most innovative countries by 2020 and a leading technological power by 2049. China is a well-connected nation, with more than 500 million Internet users compared to the U.S.'s 245 million users. The Chinese are determined to keep up with technology and be part of the global brain, contributing massively to the culture of the global consumer.

A country is not the most powerful because of its technology and its military forces, there are other factors that come into play. It also lies on intelligence and how a country puts these other factors to use that contributes to its power. America is a superpower because of its innovative, scientific research which ensures they have a technological and economic lead over many other countries. However, when it comes to intelligence, China is not far behind. They placed heavy importance and focus on improving their quality of education and this have resulted to them having the largest university population in the world, ensuring that their younger generation can step into any job anywhere.

China also launched its social credit system. They will have access to their citizen's financial data, their consumption habits, and their social connections to assess their trustworthiness and their ability to access certain sought-after services. The system has already been implemented and the Chinese will have sanctions and rewards as the country steers its nation to less privacy but to better behavior.

From social media and AI technology, to 5G and big data, the role of technology plays in our life will only increase and be at the heart of any geopolitical or domestic tensions. This technological trend will proliferate into our lifestyles, but the duality of use between civilians and the military will keep the topic at the forefront of debates. Technology is both the great liberator and an ideal tool for oppression, and this is a fact faced by every nation on Earth. These essential systems drive economic growth and competitiveness and are critical for national security. While the West has enjoyed a monopoly in most fields of technology, the rise of Asian powerhouses has started to challenge those long-held notions.

In the coming years, the battle for innovation will shape the global order as these technologies become more important to our daily lives. In Western nations, privacy concerns have delayed technological progression; whereas, in Asia, they have been allowed to develop. Major tech companies in the West have come under scrutiny about data collection, privacy, and anti-competition practices which risks further impeding the U.S.'s technological interests.

In Asia, technology-based smart cities seek more significant integration of tech giants into all aspects of daily life. These companies have been exporting their influence overseas to create a better-connected global community. As with the last cold war, Cold War 2.0, which we are now a part of, will see technology come to the forefront. This will force the tech giants of today to be caught up in the crossfire and, just like the other nations, be forced to choose a side.

THE GREAT DIVIDE

China is busy expanding and increasing its might. The country is ahead in the conventional missile arms race, while the U.S. is trying to come up with alternative strategies. Senior intelligence officers in the U.S. agreed that China has the means to overwhelm the defensive systems they are pursuing. Many Western experts said that Chinese armed forces and weaponry suffer from technological lags, but you must look at the sheer power of numbers. China has the largest armed forces in the world and is Asia's leading missile power. China is also committed to modernizing its military to equal those of other advanced military powers. The rise of China's military will have a multi-dimensional impact on other Asia-Pacific states.

Some other things that contribute to a country like China being powerful is the size of the country in terms of population and being able to defend itself. China is certainly the biggest state in the world in terms of population, perhaps, apart from India. Furthermore, rapid modernization is busily transforming this country into a powerful one based on geographical elements, location, climate, borders, etc. China may share its borders with 14 other countries, but because of mountains, swamps, and deserts, it has been like an island that cannot easily be accessed. Its western border is made up of impassable mountains and its eastern border is the Pacific Ocean which has access to major trade routes. Geographically, China has several advantages as well as natural resources to make it a major world player.

This year's list of Fortune Global 500 Companies had 119 Chinese companies, 2 companies lesser than the U.S., which had 121. Export certainly sets China apart. After all, everybody has bought something that is "Made in China." No wonder that the West wants a piece of this lucrative market. China's economic growth has outdone most other countries and they also have massive buying power. American companies such as Google must come up with new ideas and products to get into the Chinese game.

There are some political experts who said that China's economic growth and naval investment could topple the U.S. off its pedestal of power as soon as 2020. China is economically, technologically, and politically expanding, which is important to the rest of the world. Certainly, the U.S. needs to understand what China's direction is going, and what will come in the place of the current global order. The political order, make no mistake, is going to be authoritarian, but that is not a bad thing.

China is poised to dominate the world, and the world is waiting to see just what China will do with this power. During the Cold War, the U.S. was a beacon for governments to embrace certain values. But in the 21st century, it is China who is now offering authoritarian values. The difference is, Beijing will not be negotiating but demanding that other governments accept China as it is, as it was, and as it will always be. Additionally, China does not seek to force its system on other countries for it acknowledges that the Chinese system is designed for the Chinese people where it works best. Instead, China allows other nations and civilizations to find their own balance and what suits them best.

Anyone who knows anything about China, or its culture would know that its society could not be more different than the U.S. For decades, experts such as Gordon Chang had been preaching about the collapse of China socially, economically, and even politically, but this never happened. Instead, despite the coercive attempts from the Western media, patriotism, economic prosperity, military strength, and unity have only increased through this period. In contrast, we have seen the U.S. slowly decline by all measures despite its strong propaganda, looking worse by the day.

While many Western analysts misread China as an aggressive external threat, this is contrary to Chinese culture. Asian culture is vastly different than Westerners. Westerners are taught to be individualistic, but Asians are collective. East Asians see themselves as part of a larger community, with 91% of China coming from a single ethnicity called the Han. Meanwhile, Westerners value freedom and individual rights, and are made of many ethnicities with a loose cohesion.

In China, their family unit and values go as far back to Confucianism, where children are taught filial piety and respect for elders and the reason why they are against the law to abandon your parents. Grandparents will often move in with children to raise their grandchildren and cook. In Western culture, the child is taught through the education system to "resist conformity," "create a new sense of identity," and to "be an individual." Some Westerners are being mocked for living with their parents for it is a sign of being unsuccessful. Good luck getting your average 3 generations to live in one house in the West. But 3, 4, or even 5 generations are not uncommon for the Chinese.

To truly begin to understand China, you need to realize it is not a mere nation state. It has only used this distinction for the past 100 years or so, but it is not accurate. Chinese people know they are not a mere 100-year old country, and they will be quick to inform you that they are one of the most ancient living cultures in the world. Chinese people have existed in roughly the same geographical location since ancient times in the Eastern part of the continent where most people live. China is a civilization-state which has derived its identity not from the last 100 years, but from its thousands of years of history, and its singular identity from using a single language script and practically the same fundamental culture we see today that slowly evolved over time.

In contrast to this, the U.S. had formed its identity from the formation of a nation-state, occurring over the past few hundred years. Much of the people today who are proud to be American, their ancestors or cultures were not even a part in the creation of the identity they adopted. The American culture is an identity which is based on taking the best elements that other much older cultures of Europe and Asia created and then wrapping it in a bow calling it "proud to be American." By historical terms of measure, the U.S. has not even begun to form a concise identity. Different parts of the U.S. have vastly different definitions of an American identity and quite different ways of life. These differences only grow when you engage members of different ethnicities. The reason the U.S. is called a "melting pot" is because when you move there, you are supposed to forget your culture and history and adapt to theirs. The American identity is a culture with amnesia.

The great Chinese civilization-state is the modern embodiment of thousands of years of development. In just 30 years, China went from being one of the poorest agricultural countries in the world to the second-largest economy. 650,000,000 people were lifted out of poverty, more than all the other democracies combined, while having a 1-party state and no official voting system.

There are 3 main fallacies made by Westerners when thinking of China: operationally rigid, politically closed, and morally illegitimate. However, these assumptions are wrong. China's system is based on adaptability, meritocracy, and legitimacy. While the Western narrative always tries to claim that elections are the only way to bring freedoms, prosperity, and legitimacy to the people, China has continually proven them wrong.

Every aspect of Chinese society, of how the nation is governed, has adapted to meet the needs of the people. Since the foundation of the CCP, there has been a wide range of powerful and insightful political philosophies being made, something that elections cannot hope to produce to such effects. It began with the radical land collectivization, to the Great Leap Forward, then privatization of farmland, the Cultural Revolution, Deng Xiaoping's market reforms, to Jiang Zemin's political steps of opening up the economy, to opening party membership to private businessmen. Institutionally, the introduction of term limits for political leaders, who used to retain positions for life, and mandatory retirement ages have been dramatic. Political reforms have never stopped occurring, changing every facet of itself in the process.

The CCP happens to be one of the most meritocratic political institutions in the world, with a membership of 91 million people. At the top is the Politburo, of which the vast majority of the members came from humble backgrounds, and the same is true for the larger Central Committee. This political structure works like a rotating pyramid of upward mobility and is made up of 3 components: civil service, state-owned enterprises, and social organizations. Together, they form separate but fully integrated career paths for Chinese officials. It all begins by recruiting the best college graduates to entry-level positions of all 3 sections, referred to as "keyuan" (clerk). Then, as they get promoted, they will progressively rise to 4 elite ranks: "fuke" (deputy section manager), "ke" (section manager), "fuchu" (deputy division manager), and "chu" (division manager).

Once a year, the department reviews their performance, including conducting public opinion surveys and interviewing their superiors and subordinates. The best will get promoted further to the positions of "fuju" (deputy bureau chief), and "ju" (bureau chief). At these levels, they are responsible for managing a district with millions in population and hundreds of millions in revenues. This system is so competitive that it took Xi Jinping 30 years to go from being a village manager to a member of the Politburo.

When Westerners talk about political legitimacy, they think the only source is through multi-party elections and universal suffrage, but how about competency? The CCP has steered the Chinese civilization from a Century of Humiliation to a century of domination, while liberal democracies have done the exact opposite. The COVID-19 pandemic has only cemented the inefficiencies of these broken systems. While China does not hold elections, they do more polling than any other country. Every law, every decree, every official is constantly being polled to get feedback.

There is a great divide between the mindsets of those in the West and those in China. It is the main barrier in how each side approaches the issues listed in this chapter, and more. While the world has become uncomfortably familiar with the ways of the West, being under its subversive dominance, this has made the West become increasingly ignorant to the rest of the world. However, the coming years will see the West for the first time be forced to listen to new voices with vastly different opinions than that of its own.

Since the CCP is an ideal representation of the Chinese people and their civilization, then we can look to the Chinese people to understand the role China will play in the coming age. Wherever Chinese people go in the world, they are all hard-working, industrious, and successful. They have created the largest and most successful diasporas in the world, often in the face of institutionalized racism and discrimination. Hence, wherever Chinese people go, wealth and prosperity follow.

It is only natural for a part of human nature to fear what we do not understand, but this is nothing more than an excuse for our own ignorance in the modern age. The Asian Millennium will usher in a new epoch of civilization that will shatter all known existing models. Therefore, you are presented with a choice: either embrace the future or be left behind. The future has never been brighter, so which one will you choose?

REFERENCES

Adams, V. (2020March26) disaster-capitalism-covid19. http://somatosphere.net/author/vincanne-adams/

Agence France-Presse. (2020 June 10) Not Going To Launch "Cold War" With China: EU. https://www.ndtv.com/world-news/coronavirus-european-union-eu-says-not-going-to-launch-cold-war-with-china-2244011

Alessandro, Nicita. (2019) Trade and trade diversion effects of United States tariffs on China. https://unctad.org/en/PublicationsLibrary/ser-rp-2019d9_en.pdf

Allison G. (2017 JUNE 9) The Thucydides Trap. https://foreignpolicy.com/2017/06/09/the-thucydides-trap/

America's struggle against poverty in the twentieth century. ISBN 0-674-00434-5 https://books.google.com.ph/books?id=2b3ZesIFQ0oC&pg=PA173&lpg=PA173&dq=facts+about+explosive+growth+of+poverty+in+america&source=bl&ots=ymNX997pRO&sig=ACfU3U3Lo3-a26D3ymRRiyD_Hbv4ypkN0w&hl=en&sa=X&ved=2ahUKEwjC686Qm7rqAhVB62EKHcI_DzAQ6AEwCnoECBIQAQ#v=onepage&q=facts%20about%20explosive%20growth%20of%20poverty%20in%20america&f=false

Arezki, R.; Deininger, K.; and Selod, H. (2012 March) Global Land The Rush. https://www.imf.org/external/pubs/ft/fandd/2012/03/pdf/arezki.pdf

Atalanta, A. (2020 June 2) We Are The Useful Idiots: How Our Nation Divided is Playing Straight Into The Hands of Our Greatest Enemies. https://havokjournal.com/world/we-are-the-useful-idiots-how-our-nation-divided-is-playing-straight-into-the-hands-of-our-greatest-enemies/

Average Age of Cars, Light Trucks Rises (2019 June 27) https://www.ratchetandwrench.com/articles/8281-average-age-of-cars-light-trucks-rises

Backman, M. (2020 February 7) Millennials' savings habits might actually be pretty good, report shows. The Motley Fool.

https://www.greenbaypressgazette.com/story/money/2020/02/07/millennials-savings-habits-might-shock-you-in-a-good-way/41142261/

Baijie, A. (2017 August 3) New rules fit with Xi's ecology push. https://www.chinadaily.com.cn/china/2017-08/03/content_30336869.htm

Bank of Canada. Real Estate Market. https://www.bankofcanada.ca/rates/indicators/capacity-and-inflation-pressures/real-estate-market-definitions/

Bahri, Yilmaz (2019) The US-China "Trade War": The War Nobody Can Win. https://ideas.repec.org/p/koc/wpaper/1911.html

Bar Nova (2018 October 18) The end of engagement.

https://www.economist.com/leaders/2018/10/18/the-end-of-engagement

Barkham, R. Ph.D., and Levy S. Mellot D. (2020 May 8) U.S. Economic Watch: As Expected, COVID-19 Lockdowns Decimate Jobs Market in April. https://www.cbre.us/research-and-reports/US-MarketFlash-US-Economic-Watch-COVID-19-Lockdowns-Decimate-Jobs-Market-in-April

Bishop, T. (2020 April 25) Anatomy of the Crash – The Financial Crisis of 2020. https://www.getfreeebooks.com/anatomy-of-the-crash-the-financial-crisis-of-2020/\

Bivens, J. (2005) Social Security's Fixable Financing Issues: Shortfall in Funds Is Not Inevitable. Economic Policy Institute, Issue Brief No. 207. http://www.epi.org/publication/ib207/

Bivens, J. (2011) Failure By Design: A Story behind America's Broken Economy. An Economic Policy Institute book. Ithaca, N.Y.: Cornell University Press.

Bivens, J. (2013) America the Unequal: Origins and Impacts of a Policy Revolution. Demos, New Economic Paradigms, and Rockefeller Foundation (text accompanying the New Economic Paradigms conference) http://www.demos.org/sites/default/files/ publications/Bivens.pdf

Bivens, J. (2019 January 30) The economic cost and benefits of Airbnb. https://www.epi.org/publication/the-economic-costs-and-benefits-of-airbnb-no-reason-for-local-policymakers-to-let-airbnb-bypass-tax-or-regulatory-obligations/

Blanchet, T.; Chancel, L.; and Gethin, A. (2019 April 22) Forty years of inequality in Europe: Evidence from distributional national accounts. https://voxeu.org/article/forty-years-inequality-europe

Boaz, S. (2018 July 24) A most destructive milkshake. https://www.capitalandconflict.com/investing-in-gold/a-most-destructive-milkshake/

Booker James, Scott Trees W. (2020 January 20) Implications of Water Scarcity for Water Productivity and Farm Labor. https://www.mdpi.com/2073-4441/12/1/308/htm

Bordo, M. D.; Simard, D.; White, E. France and the Bretton Woods International Monetary System: 1960-1968 NBER Working Paper No. 4642 (Also Reprint No. r2057) https://www.nber.org/papers/w4642

Bordoff, J. (2020 May 5) The 2020 Oil Crash's Unlikely Winner: Saudi Arabia. https://foreignpolicy.com/2020/05/05/2020-oil-crash-winner-saudi-arabia/

Bourne, J. JR. The Next Breadbasket. https://www.nationalgeographic.com/foodfeatures/land-grab/

Bowen, D. (2020 May 20) OVER HALF OF SMALL CANADIANS BUSINESSES CAN'T AFFORD TO REOPEN IN JUNE. https://604now.com/half-small-canadians-businesses-cant-afford-reopen/

Buchanan, P. J (2020 May 12) Coexistence with China or Cold War II?. https://buchanan.org/blog/coexistence-with-china-or-cold-war-ii-138549

Campbell, C.J. (August 2006) The Rimini Protocol an oil depletion protocol: Heading off economic chaos and political conflict during the second half of the age of oil. Publication: Energy Policy. https://doi.org/10.1016/j.enpol.2006.02.005

Campbell, C. and Laherrère, J. (1998 March) The End of Cheap Oil. JOURNAL ARTICLE. https://www.jstor.org/stable/2605770

Carvon Brief (2020 April 19) Analysis: Corona virus has temporarily reduced China's co2 emission by a quarter.one only natural energy. https://www.only-natural-energy.com/analysis-coronavirus-has-temporarily-reduced-China's-co2-emission-by-a-quarterDuskcn20|18V

Central Bank Gold Reserve Survey. (2020 May 18) https://www.gold.org/goldhub/data/2020-central-bank-gold-reserve-survey

Chamley, S. (2016 November 11) Corporate capture of African agriculture. https://newafricanmagazine.com/12585/

Clark, J. (2020 May 8) The Setup For a Long and Deep Crisis is In Place—Here's How I'm Preparing Financially. https://goldsilver.com/blog/the-setup-for-a-long-and-deep-crisis-is-in-placeheres-how-im-preparing-financially/

Clark, W. R. (2005) Petrodollar warfare: Oil, Iraq and the future of the dollar. Gabriola Island, B.C: New Society Publishers. https://newsociety.com/books/p/petrodollar-warfare-pdf

Constantino H., Pablo A.N. (2020 April 21) A perfect storm: COVID-19 in emerging Economies. https://voxeu.org/article/perfect-storm-covid-19-emerging-economies

Coppes, C.H. OFASFR DAY - IDP Consulting Group Special… (2007) chuckcoppes.com

CORESIGHT RESEARCH. (2020 July 3) Weekly US and UK Store Openings and Closures Tracker 2020, Week 27: Microsoft To Close All US Stores. https://coresight.com/research/weekly-us-and-uk-store-openings-and-closures-tracker-2020-week-27-microsoft-to-close-all-us-stores/

Dalio, R. (2020 March 29) THE CHANGING WORLD ORDER. https://www.principles.com/the-changing-world-order/#

Damodaran, A. and Thakkar, Shamta and Aiyer, Neerja, Syriana Once Again: Speculations on the Future of OPEC (2020 March 13) IIM Bangalore Research Paper No. 606.

Debt Consolidation Team (2018 May 23) The $22 Trillion U.S. Debt: Which President Contributed the Most. https://www.debtconsolidation.com/us-debt-presidents/

Dehghan, S. K. (2020 January 8) Water wars: early warning tool uses climate data to predict conflict hot spots. https://www.theguardian.com/global-development/2020/jan/08/water-wars-early-warning-tool-uses-climate-data-to-predict-conflict-hotspots

Deffeyes, K. (2005) Beyond oil: The view from Hubbert's Peak. (New York: Farrar, Straus and Giroux)

Delmendo, L. (2020 March 29) Canada: Slowdown before a new boom? https://www.globalpropertyguide.com/North-America/Canada/Price-History

Desilver, D. (2018 August 7) For most U.S. workers, real wages have barely budged in decades. Pew Research Center. https://www.pewresearch.org/fact-tank/2018/08/07/for-most-us-workers-real-wages-have-barely-budged-for-decades/

Desta, M.G. (2003) Organization and Regional Trade of Petroleum Exporting Countries, the World Trade Organization and World Trade Agreements. Journal of world trade. https://heinonline.org/ho2/landing page

DiChristopher, T. (2019 March 11) U.S. will soon threaten to topple Saudi Arabia as the world's top oil exporter. CNBC. https://www.cnbc.com/2019/03/11/us-threatens-to-topple-saudi-arabia-as-worlds-top-oil-exporter-iea.html

DiGruttolo, M, and Siegel P. (2020 April 27) 2020 Geopolitical Forecast. https://ankura.com/insights/2020-geopolitical-forecast/

Dobbs R., Remes J., Manyika J., Roxburgh C., S.Smit, and Schaer, F. (2012 June 1) Urban world: Cities and the rise of the consuming class. https://www.mckinsey.com/featuredinsights/urbanization/urban-world-cities-and-the-rise-of-the-consuming-class#

Dooley, M.; Folkerts, D.; Landaur; and Garber, P. (2005) "An essay on the revived Bretton Woods system," Proceedings, Federal Reserve Bank of San Francisco, issue Feb. https://www.nber.org/papers/w9971

Durden, T. (2020 June 12) "We Need To Act Now" - UN Warns World Faces Worst Food Crisis in 50 Years. https://www.zerohedge.com/commodities/we-need-act-now-un-warns-world-faces-worst-food-crisis-50-years

Durden, T. (2020 June 11) "Not On My Island": More Allies Reject Hosting US Missiles In Pacific Aimed At China. https://www.zerohedge.com/geopolitical/not-my-island-more-allies-reject-housing-us-missiles-pacific-aimed-china

Durden, T. (2020 June 10) Seattle Protesters Storm City Hall After Running Cops Out Of Precinct, Establishing "Autonomous Zone". https://www.zerohedge.com/political/seattle-protesters-establish-autonomous-zone-after-police-national-guard-pull-out

Durden, T. (2020 June 9) Antifa Militia Wing Wants 'Complete Abolition' Of System; Coached Undercover Veritas Journo To Deny Affiliation. https://www.zerohedge.com/political/antifa-militia-wing-wants-complete-abolition-system-coached-undercover-veritas-journo

Durden, T. (2020 June 8) "Break The Glass" – Guggenheim's Minerd Warns Fed May Start Buying Gold To Support Dollar Hegemony. https://www.zerohedge.com/markets/break-glass-guggenheims-minerd-warns-fed-may-start-buying-gold-support-dollar-hegemony

Durden, T. (2020 June 8) The Longest Expansion in History Is Officially Over: The US Entered Recession in February, NBER Finds. https://www.zerohedge.com/economics/united-states-economy-officially-recession-nber

Durden T. (2020 June 7) A Quarter of Americans Skipped Meals or Relied on Food Banks during Virus Lockdowns. https://www.zerohedge.com/health/quarter-americans-are-skipping-meals-or-relying-food-banks-during-virus-lockdowns

Durden T. (2020 June 5) The Price Of Half The World's Staple Food Is Up 70% In 2020.https://www.zerohedge.com/markets/price-half-worlds-staple-food-70-2020

Durden, T. (2020 June 4) Project Veritas Infiltrates Violent Antifa Cell. https://www.zerohedge.com/political/project-veritas-infiltrates-clandestine-meeting-violent-antifa-cell

Durden, T. (2020 May 4) Greek Brothels To Reopen But Hookers And Clients Required Wearing Masks And Gloves. https://www.zerohedge.com/markets/greek-brothels-reopen-hookers-and-clients-required-wear-masks-and-gloves

Durden, T. (2020 May31) Citi Warns "Markets Are Way Ahead Of Reality", Urges Clients To Raise As Much Money As They Can Before The Next Crash. https://www.zerohedge.com/markets/citi-warns-markets-are-way-ahead-reality-urges-clients-raise-much-money-they-can-next-crash

Durden, T. (2020 May 30) Watch Live: Riots Erupt from Coast to Coast; Curfews Imposed; Stores Looted; D.C. Activates National Guard. https://www.zerohedge.com/political/america-descends-chaos-nationwide-unrest-erupts

Durden, T. (2020 May 26) Anti-Lockdown Protesters Could Become Violent If US Revives Quarantine Measures, DHS Warns. https://www.zerohedge.com/political/anti-quarantine-protesters-could-become-violent-if-second-lockdowns-seen-dhs-warns

Durden, T. (2020 April 1) Is America Preparing For Civil War?

https://www.zerohedge.com/political/america-preparing-civil-war

Durden, T. (2020 March 25) 47,000 Stores Shutter Across The US As Virtually All Retailers Stop Paying Rent. https://www.zerohedge.com/economics/total-halt-47000-stores-shutter-across-us-virtually-all-retailers-stop-paying-rent

Durden, T. (2016 October 14) Is The US on the Verge of Mass Race Riots. https://www.zerohedge.com/news/2016-10-14/us-verge-mass-race-riots

Economy (2020 March 26) Unemployment caused by Corona virus will leave deep scars in US.
https://www.theguardian.com/business/2020/mar/26/unemployment-caused-by-coronavirus-will-leave-deep-scars-in-us

Eldred, C. (2010 August 10) China Plants More Than 40 Billion Trees Since 1981. https://genprogress.org/china-plants-more-than-40-billion-trees-since-1981/

Environmental Justice Foundation Charitable Trust (EJF) (2020) Displacement In Bangladesh. https://ejfoundation.org/reports/climate-displacement-in-bangladesh

Ermatinger, James William. *The decline and fall of the Roman Empire*. Greenwood Press (2004) Page 58.

Fannin, R. (2019 December 9) Stakes Rise In U.S.-China Tech Cold War With Latest Block.
https://www.forbes.com/sites/rebeccafannin/2019/12/09/stakes-rise-in-us-china-tech-cold-war-with-latest-block/#19dc33291833

Farhad, Taghizadeh-Hesary. (2020 May 18) Economic impacts of the COVID-19 pandemic and oil price collapse. ECONOMICS, HEALTH. https://www.asiapathways-adbi.org/2020/05/economic-impacts-covid-19-pandemic-and-oil-price-collapse/

Farrell, S. (2020 May 11) Hold on for inflation equities trade, JP Morgan says. https://www.sharecast.com/news/broker-recommendations/hold-on-for-inflation-equities-trade-jp-morgan-says--7480627.html

FDIC Quarterly Banking Profile. (2020 June 16) https://www.fdic.gov/bank/analytical/qbp/

Flounders, S. (2019 December 3) U.S. war on the defenseless / Sanctions harm one-third of world's people.
https://www.workers.org/2019/12/44711/

Friedman, B. (2006 January/February) THE MORAL CONSEQUENCES OF ECONOMIC GROWTH.

https://scholar.harvard.edu/files/bfriedman/files/the_moral_consequences_of_economic_growth_0.pdf

Glubb, S.J. The Fate Of Empires And Search For Survival. http://www.thegreatstory.org/glubb.pdf

Gold, J. (2018 June 1) Cyber warfare is the new reality. Canada's allies are offering help. We should take it. https://eestielu.com/et/arvamus/teised-arvamuslood/8137-cyber-warfare-is-the-new-reality-canada-s-allies-are-offering-help-we-should-take-it

Golubova, A. (2017 October 17) China owns more gold than data shows - Wells Fargo. https://www.kitco.com/news/2019-10-17/China-owns-more-gold-than-data-shows-Wells-Fargo.html

Gordon, MN (2020 May 29) This is a Full Societal Breakdown. https://economicprism.com/this-is-a-full-societal-breakdown/

Government of Canada (2020 June 23) Climate change in developing countries. https://www.international.gc.ca/world-monde/issues_development-enjeux_developpement/environmental_protection-protection_environnement/climate-climatiques.aspx?lang=eng#immigration

Graham, P. (2020 March 25) How will Covid-19 impact the real estate market in Canada. Mysense. https://www.moneysense.ca/spend/real state/how-will-covid-19-impact-the-real-state-market-in-canada

Grain (2012 February 23) GRAIN releases data set with over 400 global land grabs. https://www.grain.org/article/entries/4479-grain-releases-data-set-with-over-400-global-land-grabs

Grain (2010 April 3) Turning African farmland over to big business. https://www.grain.org/article/entries/4062-turning-african-farmland-over-to-big-business

Gross, J.A and Staff, T. (2018 February 10) Iranian UAV that entered Israeli airspace seems to be American stealth knock-off. https://www.timesofisrael.com/iranian-uav-that-entered-israeli-airspace-seems-to-be-american-stealth-knock-off/

Guerrieri, V.; G. Lorenzoni; L. Straub; and I. Werning (2020), "Macroeconomic Implications of COVID-19: Can Negative Supply Shocks Cause Demand Shortages?", NBER Working Paper No. 26918. (DOI): 10.3386/w26918

Hall, R. (2011 June 21) Land grabbing in Southern Africa: the many faces of the investor rush. https://doi.org/10.1080/03056244.2011.582753

Heinberg, R. (2006) The Oil Depletion Protocol A Plan to avert Oil Wars Terrorism and Economic Collapse. https://books.google.com.ph/books?hl=en&lr=&id=_U87TSxpd_4C&oi=fnd&pg=PR1&dq=oil+depletion+protocol+economic+collapse&ots=vzocjwqIR-&sig=Yt2M3Hzu1WOjOT-DhplSsr_SeFM&redir_esc=y#v=onepage&q=oil%20depletion%20protocol%20economic%20collapse&f=false

Harvey, F. (2018 June 18) Are we running out of water. https://www.theguardian.com/news/2018/jun/18/are-we-running-out-of-water

Hirch, R. (2005 October) The Inevitable Peaking of World Oil Production. The Atlantic Council of the United States. https://www.files.ethz/isn/13958/Peaking of the World Oil Production.pdf

Hogue, R. (2020 June 25) Recent housing affordability loss may prove temporary. Royal Bank of Canada. https://thoughtleadership.rbc.com/recent-housing-affordability-loss-may-prove-temporary/?utm_medium=referral&utm_source=economics&utm_campaign=housing

Holmes, F. (2019 September 19) Pierre Lassonde Says Gold Could Hit $25,000 in 30 Years. https://www.forbes.com/sites/greatspeculations/2019/09/23/pierre-lassonde-says-gold-could-hit-25000-in-30-years/#1ab719763526

Hornberger, J. (2017 September 8) Sanctions Are an Act of War. https://www.fff.org/2017/09/08/sanctions-act-war/

Hribernik, M. and Haynes, S. (2020 January 16) 47 countries witness surge in civil unrest – trend to continue in 2020. https://www.maplecroft.com/insights/analysis/47-countries-witness-surge-in-civil-unrest/

Huang, Y. (2017 September 14) What the West Gets Wrong About China's Economy. https://carnegieendowment.org/2017/09/14/what-west-gets-wrong-about-china-s-economy-pub-73109

Human Rights Watch (2020 March 31) Turkey/Syria: Weaponizing Water in Global Pandemic? https://www.hrw.org/news/2020/03/31/turkey/syria-weaponizing-water-global-pandemic#

Huntington, H.; Huang, Zhuo; Al-Fattah, S.; Gucwa, M.; and Nouri, A. (2012) Oil Markets and Price Movements: A Survey of Determinants. SSRN Electronic Journal. 10.2139/ssrn.2274543.

IEA (2020) Oil Market Report - May 2020. https://www.iea.org/reports/oil-market-report-may-2020

International Monetary Fund. Asia and Pacific Dept. (2018 July 26) People's Republic of China: 2018 Article IV Consultation-Press Release; Staff Report; Staff Statement and Statement by the Executive Director for the People's Republic of China.

https://www.imf.org/en/Publications/CR/Issues/2018/07/25/Peoples-Republic-of-China-2018-Article-IV-Consultation-Press-Release-Staff-Report-Staff-46121

Inozemtsev, V. (2020 March 19) Can Russia win (or survive) the oil price war? Riddle. https://www.ridl.io/en/can-russia-win-or-survive-the-oil-price-war/

Ivanova, I. (2018 October 12) Saudi Arabia is Americas no.1 weapon customer. https://www.cbsnews.com/news/Saudi Arabia-is -the -top-buyer-of-Us-weapons

Jacques, M. When China Rules the World: The End of the Western World and the Birth of a New Global Order.

https://www.goodreads.com/work/quotes/6669984-when-china-rules-the-world-the-end-of-the-western-world-and-the-rise-of

Jarvis, J. (2020 April 29) What happens when you cancel rent, mortgages, and debt? https://www.thedailybell.com/all-articles/news-analysis/what-happens-when-you-cancel-rent-mortgages-and-debt/

Jo, L. (2015 September 15) Husbands A Buyer's Market for Arms Published online: https://doi.org/10.1080/00963402.1990.11459822

John Corrigan, Partner, Strategy, and PwC US (2020) COVID-19 and the oil price collapse. https://www.pwc.com/us/en/industries/energy-utilities-mining/library/oil-price-collapse.html

Johnson, Wilson. Issue Recommendations to Hold China Accountable for COVID-19 Actions (2020 April 26) RSC. https://rsc-johnson.house.gov/news/press-releases/johnson-wilson-issue-recommendations-hold-china-accountable-covid-19-actions

Journal of International Affairs Editorial Board https://www.jstor.org/stable/jinteaffa.69.1.121

Kalish, I. (2020 July 06) Weekly global economic update. https://www2.deloitte.com/us/en/insights/economy/global-economic-outlook/weekly-update.html

Judiciary News (2020 January 28) Bankruptcy Filings Increase Slightly. https://www.uscourts.gov/news/2020/01/28/bankruptcy-filings-increase-slightly

Kemp, M. (2020 May 18) Dump the dollar: Russia has now gotten rid of over 96% of its US debt holdings. https://www.rt.com/business/488928-russia-dumps-us-dollar-debt/

Khadem, N. (2020 March 24) Coronavirus pandemic could see house prices plummet by 20 per cent, economist warns. https://www.abc.net.au/news/2020-03-24/coronavirus-house-prices-to-fall-unemployment-to-double/12082014

Khanna, P. (2019 February 5) https://www.amazon.com/Future-Asian-Parag-Khanna/dp/150119626X

Kheel, R. (2020 June 11) Senate panel approves $740B defense policy bill. https://thehill.com/policy/defense/502271-senate-panel-approves-740b-defense-policy-bill

Kirkman, T. (March 5) Ships Turn into Floating Storage Units for Oil and Gas as Chinese Buyers Back Out. Price Oil. https://community.oilprice.com/topic/10032-ships-turn-into-floating-storage-units-for-oil-and-gas-as-chinese-buyers-back-out/

Kohl WL (1991) After the Oil Price Collapse: OPEC, The United States, And the World Oil Market https://pdfs.semanticscholar.org/4c5e/2867f95322bdc80f91af3fb0b12af2cd9300.pdf

Laishley, R. (2014) Is Africa's land up for grabs? https://www.un.org/africarenewal/magazine/special-edition-agriculture-2014/africa%E2%80%99s-land-grabs

Liudmila, P.; Farkhondeh, J; and Ehsan, R (2017) Oil Price Shocks and Russia's Economic Growth: The Impacts and Policies for Overcoming Them. https://dx.doi.org/10.22059/wsps.2017.62277

Lozada, C. (2005 January) The Economics of World War I. NBER Digest. https://www.nber.org/digest/jan05/w10580.htmlLuther D.(

Maçães, B. (2018 February 14) Eurasia, the supercontinent that will define our century. https://www.weforum.org/agenda/2018/02/how-countries-can-find-their-place-in-the-new-eurasian-century/

Macias, A. (2018 December 12) Led by Saudi Arabia, Middle Eastern countries are the biggest buyers of US military equipment https://www.cnbc.com/2018/12/12/middle-eastern-countries-are-biggest-buyers-of-us-military-equipment.html

Macleod, A. (2020 May 28) Statistics, lies and the reservoir effect. https://www.goldmoney.com/research/goldmoney-insights/statistics-lies-and-the-reservoir-effect

Malo, S. (2019 March 04) US faces fresh water shortages due to climate change, research says. https://www.weforum.org/agenda/2019/03/us-faces-fresh-water-shortages-due-to-climate-change-research-says

Maloney, M. Currency vs. Money. https://goldsilver.com/getting-started-guide/chapter-one/

Mangi, F.; Kay, C.; and Chaudhary, A. (2019 January 26) https://economictimes.indiatimes.com/news/politics-and-nation/water-crisis-brews-between-india-and-pakistan-as-rivers-run-dry/articleshow/67700195.cms?from=mdr

Martenson, C. (2020 May 29) As the world burns. Peak Prosperity. https://www.peakprosperity.com/as-the-world-burns/

Matthews, C. (2020 April 8) Founder of world's largest hedge fund doubles down on 'cash is trash' argument, warning of debt-fueled inflation. https://www.marketwatch.com/story/founder-of-worlds-largest-hedge-fund-doubles-down-on-cash-is-trash-argument-warning-of-debt-fueled-inflation-2020-04-08

Maugeri, L. (2012 June) "Oil: The Next Revolution" Discussion Paper 2012-10, Belfer Center for Science and International Affairs, Harvard Kennedy School. https://www.valueplays.net/wp-content/uploads/Maugeri-Leonardo-harvard.edu-Oil-The-Next-Revolution-6-25-2012.pdf

McCarthy, N. (2020 February 10) U.S. Farm Bankruptcies Reach Eight-Year High [Infographic]. https://www.forbes.com/sites/niallmccarthy/2020/02/10/us-farm-bankruptcies-reach-eight-year-high-infographic/#33fe1a297de0

McDermott, R. (2017 September) Russia's Electronic Warfare Capabilities to 2025 September 2017 Roger N. McDermott Challenging NATO in the Electromagnetic Spectrum. https://icds.ee/wp-content/uploads/2018/ICDS_Report_Russias_Electronic_Warfare_to_2025.pdf

McIntosh, M. (April 20, 2020) How 2020 is Oil Prices Will Challenge Saudi Arabian Economic Diversification.

https://www.internationalaffairshouse.org/how-2020s-oil-prices-will-stall-saudi-arabian-economic-diversification/

McSweeney, R. (2019 August 6) Explainer: 'Desertification' and the role of climate change. https://www.carbonbrief.org/explainer-desertification-and-the-role-of-climate-change

Mende, M. (2019 June) Retail Apocalypse or Golden Opportunity for Retail Frontline Management? Journal of retailing. DOI:10.1016/j.jretai.2019.06.002https://search.proquest.com/openview/36a e6f115a607d3346947fe82c6f30f1/1?pq-origsite=gscholar&cbl=41988

Mezneva, E. (2019 July 19) Central Banks' Gold-Buying Spree Is far From Over, Poll Shows. https://www.bloomberg.com/news/articles/2019-07-19/central-banks-gold-buying-spree-is-far-from-over-poll-shows

Miao, C. (2018 December 18) The US-China Trade War. https://sites.utexas.edu/longhornglobalbiznet/the-us-china-trade-war/

Mirzabaev, A. and Wu, J. Special Report: Special Report on Climate Change and Land

Morath, E. (2020 April 28) Corona virus Relief Often Pays Workers More Than Work. U.S. Economy. https://www.wsj.com/articles/coronavirus-relief-often-pays-workers-more-than-work-11588066200

COVID-19: Healthy environmental impact for public safety and menaces oil market. (2020 June 6) https://www.sciencedirect.com/science/article/pii/S0048969720335749#s0 005

Nabi, G.; Ali, M.; Khan, S.; et al. The crisis of water shortage and pollution in Pakistan: risk to public health, biodiversity, and ecosystem. Environ Sci Pollut Res 26, 10443–10445 (2019)

Naylor, R. and Higgins, M. (2017 May 2) The Political economy of bio-diesel in an era of low oil price. https://doi.org|10.1016|j.rser.2017.04.026

Nicola, M.; Alsafi, Z.; Sohrabi, C.; Kerwan, A; Al-Jabir, A; Iosifidis, C.; Agha, M.; and Agha, R. (2020 April 17) The socio-economic implications of the coronavirus pandemic (COVID-19): A review Int J Surg. 2020 Jun; 78: 185–193. https://dx.doi.org/10.1016%2Fj.ijsu.2020.04.018

Nielson, J. (2004 September 9) China Urges Citizens to Buy Gold and Silver. https://seekingalpha.com/article/159962-china-urges-citizens-to-buy-gold-and-silver

NS Energy (2019 September 13) Hydropower in China and other top generators across Asia. https://www.nsenergybusiness.com/features/hydropower-china-top-generators-asia/

Nugent, C. (2018 November 30) How Doctors Became Cuba's Biggest Export. https://time.com/5467742/cuba-doctors-export-brazil/

O'Byrne, M. (2020 July 12) India Gold Imports Surge To 5 Year High – 220 Tons In May Alone. https://news.goldcore.com/us/gold-blog/india-gold-imports-surge-5-year-high-220-tons-may-alone/

Oil NOW (2020 April 27) Oil price skid on oversupply, storage Concerns.

https://oilnow.gy/featured/oil-prices-skid-on-oversupply-storage-concerns/

Oh, M. (2018 November 2) How energy infrastructure is shaping geopolitics in East Asia. https://www.weforum.org/agenda/2018/11/impact-shaping-energy-infrastructure-asian-geopolitics/

Ortiz, R. J. Agro-Industrialization, Petrodollar Illusions and the Transformation of the Capitalist World Economy in the 1970s: The Latin American Experience https://doi.org/10.1177%2F0896920514540187

Palumbo, D. and da Costa, A. N. (2019 May 10) Trade war: US-China trade battle in charts. BBC NEWS. https://www.bbc.com/news/business-48196495

Pearce, B. (2020 July 1) COVID-19 Air travel turns up but outlook uncertain.iata. https://www.iata.org/en/iata-repository/publications/economic-reports/Air-travel-turns-up-but-outlook-uncertain/

Plumer, B. (2015 May 15) Why Wall Street investors and Chinese firms are buying farmland all over the world.
https://www.vox.com/2014/11/20/7254883/farmland-trade-land-grab

Plushnick, R. Masti (2006 September 10) Raw Sewage Taints Sacred Jordan River. https://www.washingtonpost.com/wp-dyn/content/article/2006/09/10/AR2006091001354.html

Polleit, T. (2020 June 6) Governments Have Crippled the World's Economies. Revolution May Soon Follow.

https://mises.org/wire/governments-have-crippled-worlds-economies-revolution-may-soon-follow

Popova, M. The Banality of Evil: Hannah Arendt on the Normalization of Human Wickedness and Our Only Effective Antidote to It.
https://www.brainpickings.org/2017/02/07/hannah-arendt-the-banality-of-evil/

Pound, J. (2020 May 11) JPMorgan makes the case for gold, said the trade works under a number of scenarios.
https://www.cnbc.com/2020/05/11/jpmorgan-make-the-case-for-gold-said-the-trade-works-under-a-number-of-scenarios.html

Press Tv (2020 June 8) No debt relief for Africa.
https://www.presstv.com/Detail/2020/06/08/626972/No-Debt-Relief-for-Africa

Press Releases (2020 June 11) With New Bill, Ernst Continues Work to Decrease US Dependency on China.
https://www.ernst.senate.gov/public/index.cfm/press-releases?ID=57DFF2E1-5C02-4290-87A7-ACAA25370895

[P.R. Shukla, J. Skea, E. Calvo Buendia, V. Masson-Delmotte, H.- O. Pörtner, D. C. Roberts, P. Zhai, R. Slade, S. Connors, R. van Diemen, M. Ferrat, E. Haughey, S. Luz, S. Neogi, M. Pathak, J. Petzold, J. Portugal Pereira, P. Vyas, E. Huntley, K. Kissick, M. Belkacemi, J. Malley, (eds.)]. In press. (2019)
https://www.ipcc.ch/srccl/chapter/summary-for-policymakers/

Radford, T. (2019 October 14) When will the world's wells run out of water? https://climateandcapitalism.com/2019/10/14/when-will-the-worlds-wells-run-out-of-water/

Radford, T. (2019 October 9) Water stress rises as more wells run dry.

https://climatenewsnetwork.net/water-stress-rises-as-more-wells-run-dry/

Red Gold: China's Stealth Plan to Use Gold for World Domination (2020 February 10) https://katusaresearch.com/red-gold-chinas-stealth-plan-to-use-gold-for-world-domination/

Rex/Max Canada (2020 April 7) Is the Real Estate Market in Canada Going to Crash? https://blog.remax.ca/is-the-real-estate-market-in-canada-going-to-crash/

Reuters, T. (2020 May 26) U.S. imports record amount of gold from Switzerland as virus upends trade. https://www.reuters.com/article/swiss-trade-gold/u-s-imports-record-amount-of-gold-from-switzerland-as-virus-upends-trade-idUSL8N2D8311

Reuters, T. (2020 January 22) Trump threatens big tariffs on car imports from EU at Davos if no trade deal struck. https://www.cbc.ca/news/business/trump-threatens-big-tariffs-car-imports-eu-davos-1.5435764

Rickards, J. (2020 May 22) Is War Next? https://dailyreckoning.com/is-war-next-2/

Robertson, D. (2020 May 28) Robertson: Investing For the End Game.

https://realinvestmentadvice.com/robertson-investing-for-the-end-game/

Robertson, P. (2019 October 2) China's military might is much closer to the US than you probably think. https://theconversation.com/chinas-military-might-is-much-closer-to-the-us-than-you-probably-think-124487

Robinson, J. (2012) followthemoney.com

Romei, V. and Reed, J. (2019 March 26) The Asian century is set to begin. Global Economy. https://www.ft.com/content/520cb6f6-2958-11e9-a5ab-ff8ef2b976c7

Roig Zeballos, J. (2020 May 19) California is offering $500 cash payments to unauthorized immigrants who do not qualify for stimulus checks or unemployment benefits. https://www.businessinsider.com/california-offers-500-cash-payments-to-undocumented-immigrants-2020-5

Rousset, N. (2008 April 8) The Impact of Climate Change, Water Security and the Implications for Agriculture.

http://journals.openedition.org/chinaperspectives/1213; DOI: https://doi.org/10.4000/chinaperspectives.1213

Saefong, M. (2020 April 21) The oil market is running out of storage space and the production cuts loom. https://www.marketwatch.com/story/the-oil-market-is-running-out-of-storage-options-2020-04-21P.

SCHIFFGOLD (2020 April 16) Peter Schiff: This Is a Financial Crisis.

https://schiffgold.com/peters-podcast/peter-schiff-this-is-a-financial-crisis/

Schneider, K.(2018 December 4) https://www.circleofblue.org/2018/world/groundwater-scarcity-pollution-set-india-on-perilous-course/

Sheng, A. and Geng, X. (2018 September 3) China is building 19 'supercity clusters'.

https://www.weforum.org/agenda/2018/09/how-cities-are-saving-china/

Sherfinski, D. (2020 June 1) Gun sales surge 80% in May, says research firm. https://www.washingtontimes.com/news/2020/jun/1/gun-sales-surge-80-may-research-firm/

Singh, A. (2020 April 23) Canada Housing Market Outlook: Tough Times Ahead. https://www.moodysanalytics.com/-/media/article/2020/April-Canada-Housing-Outlook.pdf

Slavo, M. (2020 June 9) ORWELL & HUXLEY'S WARNINGS TO THE WORLD. https://www.shtfplan.com/headline-news/orwell-huxleys-warnings-to-the-world_06092020

Smith, C. H. (2020 May 4) Surviving 2020 #1: Bug-Out Bunkers, Taoism and the Warring States.

https://charleshughsmith.blogspot.com/2020/05/the-art-of-survival-taoism-and-warring.html

Smith, C. H. (2020 May 4) Surviving 2020 #2: 16 Suggestions.

https://charleshughsmith.blogspot.com/2020/05/where-rubber-meets-road.html

Smith, W. A Dictionary of Greek and Roman biography and mythology

http://www.perseus.tufts.edu/hopper/text?doc=Perseus:text:1999.04.0104:entry=cassandra-bio-1

Snow, N. (2010 October 26) If Goods Don't Cross Borders. https://fee.org/resources/if-goods-dont-cross-borders/

Snyder, M. (2020 June 8) As U.S. Cities Crumble, Demand For Rural And Suburban Properties Is Soaring. http://endoftheamericandream.com/archives/as-u-s-cities-crumble-demand-for-rural-and-suburban-properties-is-soaring

Snyder, M. (2020 June 7) Millions On The Brink Of Famine: "We Have Never, Ever Seen What We Have In The Last Six Months". http://theeconomiccollapseblog.com/archives/a-biblical-plague-of-locusts-has-put-millions-on-the-brink-of-famine-we-have-never-ever-seen-what-we-have-in-the-last-six-months

Snyder, M. (2020 May 12) A Taste Of What Is Coming – Food Prices Just Increased By The Most That We Have Seen Since 1974. http://theeconomiccollapseblog.com/archives/a-taste-of-what-is-coming-food-prices-just-increased-by-the-most-that-we-have-seen-since-1974

Snyder, M. (2020 March 3) Here Is Why The U.S. Economy Would Continue To Crash Even If All The Lockdowns Were Lifted Immediately. http://themostimportantnews.com/archives/here-is-why-the-u-s-economy-would-continue-to-crash-even-if-all-the-lockdowns-were-lifted-immediately

Staff, G. (2018 November 29) We broke down what climate change will do, region by region. https://grist.org/article/we-broke-down-what-climate-change-will-do-region-by-region/

Staff, R. (2020 June 9) As many as 25,000 retail stores could close in 2020. https://nypost.com/2020/06/09/up-to-25000-retail-stores-could-close-in-2020-new-data/

Spiro, D. (1999) The Hidden Hand of American Hegemony: Petrodollar Recycling and International Markets. Ithaca; London: Cornell University Press. doi:10.7591/j.ctvv414gb

Steinbock, D. U.S.-China Trade War and Its Global Impacts. https://www.worldscientific.com/doi/pdf/10.1142/S2377740018500318

Stiglitz, J. (2018 July 30) The US is at Risk of Losing a Trade War with China. https://www.project-syndicate.org/commentary/trump-loses-trade-war-with-china-by-joseph-e--stiglitz-2018-07?a_la=english&a_d=5b5f470478b6c72060e4de48&a_m=&a_a=click&a_s=&a_p=%2Fcommentary%2Fchina-trade-war-risks-to-xi-jinping-by-minxin-pei-2018-08&a_li=trump-loses-trade-war-with-china-by-joseph-e--stiglitz-2018-07&a_pa=editorpicks&a_ps=&barrier=accesspaylog

Stock, J. and Watson, M. (2012 July) Disentangling the Channels of the 2007-2009 Recession https://www.nber.org/papers/w18094

Stockman, D. (2020). David Stockman on Inflation, Gold, and Personal Freedom in the Post COVID-19 World. https://internationalman.com/articles/david-stockman-on-inflation-gold-and-personal-freedom-in-the-post-covid-world/

Street, L. (2020 May 29) Safety and expected returns attract German investors to gold. https://www.gold.org/goldhub/gold-focus/2020/05/safety-and-expected-returns-attract-german-investors-gold

Sy, A. (2015 November 5) What do we know about the Chinese land grab in Africa? https://www.brookings.edu/blog/africa-in-focus/2015/11/05/what-do-we-know-about-the-chinese-land-grab-in-africa/

Tate, K. (2020 May 05) What American life will look like after the coronavirus crisis ends. https://thehill.com/opinion/civil-rights/495624-what-american-life-will-look-like-after-the-coronavirus-crisis-ends

T. Lowder, N. Lee, J.E. Leisch. (2020) nrel.gov Covid-19 and the Power Sector in Southeast Asia: Impacts And Opportunities.

https://www.nrel.gov/docs/fy20osti/76963.pdf

Tharoor, I. (2020 February 10) E.U. to Trump: 'We are not foes'.

https://www.washingtonpost.com/world/2020/02/10/eu-trump-we-are-not-foes/

The Associated Press (2020 June 12) Twitter removes 170,000 China-linked accounts spreading disinformation.
https://www.cbc.ca/news/technology/twitter-china-removing-disinformation-1.5610073

The Economist (2020 June 9) NATO sets its sights on China.

https://www.economist.com/international/2020/06/08/nato-sets-its-sights-on-china?utm_campaign=the-economist-today&utm_medium=newsletter&utm_source=salesforce-marketing-cloud&utm_term=2020-06-10&utm_content=article-link-1

The Economist (2020 April 8) An unprecedented plunge in oil demand will turn the industry upside down.
https://www.economist.com/briefing/2020/04/08/an-unprecedented-plunge-in-oil-demand-will-turn-the-industry-upside-down

The Economist (2018 May 9) Climate change will affect developing countries more than rich ones. https://www.economist.com/graphic-detail/2018/05/09/climate-change-will-affect-developing-countries-more-than-rich-ones

The impact of plummeting crude oil prices on company finances (2019) Deloitte Market Point.

The Magazine of International Economic Policy (2014) Will the Dollar Remain the Reserve Currency? International Economy.
http://www.internationaleconomy.com/TIE_F14_ReserveCurrencySymp.pdf

Thompson, D. (n.d.) AMERICA'S MONOPOLY PROBLEM. The Atlantic. https://www.theatlantic.com/magazine/archive/2016/10/americas-monopoly-problem/497549/

Thompson, D. (2020 May 18) We Can Prevent a Great Depression. It'll Take $10 Trillion. https://www.theatlantic.com/ideas/archive/2020/05/we-can-prevent-a-great-depression-itll-take-10-trillion/611749/

Torry, H. and DeBarros, A. (2020 April 08) WSJ Survey: Corona virus to Cause Deep U.S. Contraction, 13% Unemployment. https://www.wsj.com/articles/wsj-survey-coronavirus-to-cause-deep-u-s-contraction-13-unemployment-11586354400?mod=search-results&page=1&pos=1

Turchin, P. (2018 December 3) The 50-year Cycle of Political Violence Strikes Again. http://peterturchin.com/cliodynamica/the-50-year-cycle-of-political-violence-strikes-again/

Turak, N. (2020 June 8) The Saudi-Russia oil price war was a 'very big mistake,' Qatar energy minister says. CNBC. https://www.cnbc.com/2020/06/09/saudi-russia-oil-price-war-was-very-big-mistake-qatar-energy-minister.html

Turkewitz, J. (2020 May 25) Oil-Starved Venezuela Celebrates Arrival of Tankers From Iran. https://www.nytimes.com/2020/05/25/world/americas/Iranian-oil-tankers-venezuela.html

Venard, B. (2019 October 17) The Cold War 2.0 between China and the US is already a virtual reality. https://theconversation.com/the-cold-war-2-0-between-china-and-the-us-is-already-a-virtual-reality-125081

Velkov, D. (2014 July 16) Finding the World's Economic Center of Gravity. https://danielvelkov.blogspot.com/2014/07/finding-worlds-economic-center-of.html

Vikram, Bhalekar (2020 April 30) Novel Corona Virus Pandemic Impact on Indian Economy, E-commerce Education and Employment.

https://ssrn.com/abstract=3580342 or https://dx.doi.org/10.2139/ssrn.3580342

Visualizing the Purchasing Power of the Dollar Over the Last Century. https://howmuch.net/articles/rise-and-fall-dollar

Wade, K. and Jennings, M. (2015 July 26) Climate change and the global economy: regional effects. https://www.schroders.com/en/us/insights/economic-views/climate-change-and-the-global-economy-regional-effects/

Watson, P. J. (2020 January 17) 40% of Countries in the World to Experience Civil Unrest in 2020. https://summit.news/2020/01/17/40-of-countries-in-the-world-to-experience-civil-unrest-in-2020/

Walmart (2020 May 6) Doug McMillon: How the Pandemic Will Change the Retail Industry and the World.

https://corporate.walmart.com/newsroom/2020/05/06/doug-mcmillon-how-the-pandemic-will-change-the-retail-industry-and-the-world

Washington, G. (2011 June 9) The Handling of the Economic Crisis May Lead to Civil Unrest. https://www.zerohedge.com/article/handling-economic-crisis-may-lead-civil-unrest

Water.org (2020) The Water Crisis. https://water.org/our-impact/water-crisis/

Watkins, S. (2020 May 11) Oil Price War Puts Entire Kingdom Of Saudi Arabia At Risk. https://oilprice.com/Geopolitics/Middle-East/Oil-Price-War-Puts-Entire-Kingdom-Of-Saudi-Arabia-At-Risk.html

Wilde, R. (2019 May 27) American Soil Is Increasingly Foreign Owned. https://www.npr.org/2019/05/27/723501793/american-soil-is-increasingly-foreign-owned

Wilson, L. (2020 June 5) U.S. Dollar Will Collapse When This Upcoming Event Happens. https://www.munknee.com/u-s-dollar-will-collapse-upcoming-event-happens/

Whiteman, D. (2020 June 25) These Chains Are Permanently Closing the Most Stores in 2020. Money wise.

https://moneywise.com/a/chains-closing-the-most-stores-in-2020

Whitley, A. (2020 April 25) How Corona virus Will Forever Change Airlines and the Way We Fly.
https://www.bloombergquint.com/business/coronavirus-travel-covid-19-will-change-airlines-and-how-we-fly

Woetzel, J.; Remes, J.; Boland, B.; Lv, K.; Sinha, S.; Strube, G.; Means, J.; Law J., Cadena, A.; and von der Tann, V. (2018 June 5) Smart cities: Digital solutions for a more livable future.
https://www.mckinsey.com/industries/capital-projects-and-infrastructure/our-insights/smart-cities-digital-solutions-for-a-more-livable-future

Wolf, R. (2020 Feb 22) Subprime An Credit Card Delinquencies Spike to Record High, Past Financial-Crisis Peak, as Other Consumers Relish the Good Times. Why? Wolf Street.
https://wolfstreet.com/2020/02/22/subprime-credit-card-delinquencies-spike-to-record-high-past-financial-crisis-peak-as-other-consumers-relish-the-good-times-why/

World Wildlife Fund (2020) Water Scarcity.
https://www.worldwildlife.org/threats/water-scarcity

Wuebbles, D.J.; D.W. Fahey, K.A. Hibbard, D.J. Dokken, B.C. Stewart, and T.K. Maycock (2017) Climate Science Special Report.
https://science2017.globalchange.gov/

Yılmaz, B. (2019 October) The Us-China "Trade War": The War Nobody Can Win. https://eaf.ku.edu.tr/wp-content/uploads/2019/10/erf_wp_1911.pdf

Zeese, K. and Flowers, M. (2020 January 14) The World Must End the US' Illegal Economic War. Sanctions Imposed on 39 Countries.
https://www.globalresearch.ca/world-must-end-us-illegal-economic-war/5700594

Zero Hedge (2019 April) The ultimate Pivot: Saudi betrayal of petrodollar.
oglinks.news.https://www.google.com/amp/s/oglinks.news/opec/news/am
p/the-ulitimate-pivot-saudi-betrayal-of-petrodollar

Zhadannikov, D.; Gamal, R.E.; Lawler, A. (2019 April 5) Saudi Arabia
threatens to ditch dollar oil trade to stop NOPEC.
https://www.reuters.com/article/us-saudi-usa-oil-exclusive/exclusive-saudi-
arabia-threatens-to-ditch-dollar-oil-trades-to-stop-nopec-sources-
idUSKCN1RH008

ABOUT THE AUTHOR

Andranik Aghazarian is a Canadian-born writer, educator, and technical analyst of Armenian heritage. Graduating from Kwantlen Polytechnic University with a BA in Anthropology and an NGO certificate, he spent some time working in the non-profit field doing research. After gaining a Micro-Masters in Leading Educational Innovation and Improvement from Michigan University, and a teaching license, he has since become an educator.

Having lived in several different countries, he especially enjoys life in Mainland China. He has dedicated himself to educating young Chinese students, and inspiring them to leave a legacy through informed action. With an Anthropological background, coupled with experiences in entrepreneurship, business, day trading, and education, Andranik is particularly well-suited to bring together the realms of economics and political analysis to make intelligent predictions of what is to come in this new millennium. Cold War 2.0 is his first full-length novel.